Cisco Access Control Security: AAA Administrative Services

Brandon Carroll

Cisco Press

Cisco Press
800 East 96th Street
Indianapolis, IN 46240 USA

Cisco Access Control Security: AAA Administrative Services

Brandon Carroll

Copyright © 2004 Cisco Systems, Inc.

Published by:
Cisco Press
800 East 96th Street
Indianapolis, IN 46240 USA

Printed in the United States of America   1 2 3 4 5 6 7 8 9 0

First Printing June 2004

Library of Congress Cataloging-in-Publication Number: 2002112745

ISBN: 1-58705-124-9

Warning and Disclaimer

This book is designed to provide information about Access Control Security. Every effort has been made to make this book as complete and as accurate as possible, but no warranty or fitness is implied.

The information is provided on an "as is" basis. The author, Cisco Press, and Cisco Systems, Inc., shall have neither liability nor responsibility to any person or entity with respect to any loss or damages arising from the information contained in this book or from the use of the discs or programs that may accompany it.

The opinions expressed in this book belong to the author and are not necessarily those of Cisco Systems, Inc.

Trademark Acknowledgments

All terms mentioned in this book that are known to be trademarks or service marks have been appropriately capitalized. Cisco Press or Cisco Systems, Inc., cannot attest to the accuracy of this information. Use of a term in this book should not be regarded as affecting the validity of any trademark or service mark.

Corporate and Government Sales

Cisco Press offers excellent discounts on this book when ordered in quantity for bulk purchases or special sales. For more information, please contact:

U.S. Corporate and Government Sales   1-800-382-3419   corpsales@pearsontechgroup.com

For sales outside of the U.S. please contact:

International Sales   international@pearsoned.com

Feedback Information

At Cisco Press, our goal is to create in-depth technical books of the highest quality and value. Each book is crafted with care and precision, undergoing rigorous development that involves the unique expertise of members from the professional technical community.

Readers' feedback is a natural continuation of this process. If you have any comments regarding how we could improve the quality of this book, or otherwise alter it to better suit your needs, you can contact us through e-mail at feedback@ciscopress.com. Please make sure to include the book title and ISBN in your message.

We greatly appreciate your assistance.

Publisher	John Wait
Editor-in-Chief	John Kane
Executive Editor	Brett Bartow
Cisco Representative	Anthony Wolfenden
Cisco Press Program Manager	Nannette M. Noble
Production Manager	Patrick Kanouse
Acquisitions Editor	Brett Bartow
Development Editor	Jill Batistick
Project Editor	San Dee Phillips
Copy Editor	Kevin Kent
Technical Editors	Randy Ivener, Sanjeev Patel, Stevan Pierce, Mark Wilgus
Team Coordinator	Tammi Barnett
Cover Designer	Louisa Adair
Composition	Octal Publishing, Inc.
Indexer	Tim Wright

CISCO SYSTEMS

Corporate Headquarters
Cisco Systems, Inc.
170 West Tasman Drive
San Jose, CA 95134-1706
USA
www.cisco.com
Tel: 408 526-4000
    800 553-NETS (6387)
Fax: 408 526-4100

European Headquarters
Cisco Systems International BV
Haarlerbergpark
Haarlerbergweg 13-19
1101 CH Amsterdam
The Netherlands
www-europe.cisco.com
Tel: 31 0 20 357 1000
Fax: 31 0 20 357 1100

Americas Headquarters
Cisco Systems, Inc.
170 West Tasman Drive
San Jose, CA 95134-1706
USA
www.cisco.com
Tel: 408 526-7660
Fax: 408 527-0883

Asia Pacific Headquarters
Cisco Systems, Inc.
Capital Tower
168 Robinson Road
#22-01 to #29-01
Singapore 068912
www.cisco.com
Tel: +65 6317 7777
Fax: +65 6317 7799

Cisco Systems has more than 200 offices in the following countries and regions. Addresses, phone numbers, and fax numbers are listed on the
Cisco.com Web site at www.cisco.com/go/offices.

Argentina • Australia • Austria • Belgium • Brazil • Bulgaria • Canada • Chile • China PRC • Colombia • Costa Rica • Croatia • Czech Republic
Denmark • Dubai, UAE • Finland • France • Germany • Greece • Hong Kong SAR • Hungary • India • Indonesia • Ireland • Israel • Italy
Japan • Korea • Luxembourg • Malaysia • Mexico • The Netherlands • New Zealand • Norway • Peru • Philippines • Poland • Portugal
Puerto Rico • Romania • Russia • Saudi Arabia • Scotland • Singapore • Slovakia • Slovenia • South Africa • Spain • Sweden
Switzerland • Taiwan • Thailand • Turkey • Ukraine • United Kingdom • United States • Venezuela • Vietnam • Zimbabwe

About the Author

Brandon J. Carroll has been in the networking industry for more than six years. He is a certified Cisco Systems instructor with Ascolta Training Company, where he teaches many of the certified Cisco courses. Prior to joining Ascolta, he was an ADSL specialist with GTE Network Services, as well as a technical lead/trainer, a field engineer, and customer zone technician. He has published proprietary documentation internally to GTE, and has also done in-house course development. Brandon holds CCNA, CCNP, and CSS-1 certifications.

About the Technical Reviewers

Randy Ivener, CCIE No. 10722, is a security specialist with Cisco Systems Advanced Services. He is a CISSP and ASQ CSQE. Randy has spent several years as a network security consultant helping companies understand and secure their networks. He has worked with many security products and technologies including firewalls, VPNs, intrusion detection, and authentication systems. Before becoming immersed in security, he spent time in software development and as a training instructor. Randy graduated from the U.S. Naval Academy and holds a master's degree in business administration.

Sanjeev Patel has been working in the networking industry for 10 years. He started his career in network and systems support. Currently he works in Product Marketing at Cisco Systems as a technical marketing engineer and supports the Cisco CNS Access Registrar family of products.

Stevan Pierce is a network/security consultant currently under contract on the Texas Medicaid & Healthcare Partnership (TMHP). His certifications include CCDP and CCNP along with several third-party certifications.

Mark Wilgus works for Cisco Systems, Inc., where he has served as the lead technical writer for Cisco Secure ACS for the past five major releases. He also develops XML-based writing solutions for Cisco technical documentation. Prior to working for Cisco Systems, Mark worked as a technical writer and software configuration engineer for Eclipsys Corporation, Motorola, and Blood Systems, Inc. He received a master of fine arts degree and a bachelor of arts degree from Arizona State University, where he also taught writing courses for four years.

Dedications

This book is dedicated to my daughter, Victoria,

Who is my motivation,

And,

To my family,

My mom Debbie, my dad Sonny, my brothers Mykel and Jason, my sister Tiffany, and my grandparents Jim and Shirley,

Whose encouragement and support have been my driving force.

Acknowledgments

There are so many people that I regard as my reason for this book. I would not feel right without mentioning them and how much each one of them has inspired me in some way or another.

Ascolta Training Company, for your support along the way, especially Irene Kinoshita, Ted Wagner, William Kivlen, Jack Wood, Kevin Masui, Dennis Ogata, Colby Morita, Ann Mattair, Karl Homa, Chris Smith, Hilson Shen, Fred Cutaran, Randi Rubenstein, John Rauma, and the rest of the gang!

The Verizon Gang, especially Gil Leon for giving a Field Tech the chance to cross over to the data side, Matt Cummings and Virgil Miller for helping me to remember to NEVER erase Flash! I also want to mention Robert Alaniz for helping me out in a pinch, Dana Christensen for always being there, Bruce Cain, Mack Brown, Randy Kwan, Edward Villaflor, Shawn Schneider, Earl Aboytes, Ken Schwartz, Lori Scott, Steve Scott, Paul Scott, and the rest of the gang.

This would not be complete without mentioning Brett Bartow, for putting up with my missed deadlines and millions of questions over the last year. Your support has kept me on track and has made this one of the best experiences in my life. I also want to mention my development editor, Jill Batistick, for being so patient and keeping my spirits up when I began to wear thin, and my technical editors, Mark Wilgus, Randy Ivner, Stevan Pierce, and Sanjeev Patel, for doing such a great job at keeping me straight.

Thank you all so much!

Contents at a Glance

Table of Contents

Icons Used in This Book

You will see a number of icons throughout this book. The following legend gives detail as to what these icons represent.

Router

Multilayer Switch

Switch

Firewalls

ATM Switch

Route/Switch
Processor

Cisco 7500
Series Router

ISDN/Frame
Relay switch

Hub

Bridge

Intrusion Detection
System

Load Balancer

Access
Server

CiscoSecure
Scanner

IP/TV
Broadcast
Server

Cisco
CallManager

Cisco
Directory Server

PC

Laptop

Cisco Works
Workstation

Web
Browser

Web
Server

Network Cloud

Concentrator

Gateway

Fax

File Server

Printer

VPN Concentrator

Phone

Cache or
Content Engine

Multilayer Switch
with Load Balancer

SSL Offloader

Tape Subsystem

Fibre Channel
Switch

DWDM-CWDM

Storage Subsystem

Introduction

This book is focused on providing the skills necessary to successfully configure authentication, authorization, and accounting (AAA) services on Cisco devices using external authentication servers such as Cisco Secure Access Control Server and the Cisco Access Registrar. The goals of this book are as follows:

- Provide a general overview of the AAA architecture

- Provide a general configuration overview of AAA on Cisco routers

- Provide detailed discussion on the TACACS+ and RADIUS protocols

- Provide installation and configuration examples and explanations for the Cisco Secure Access Control Server (ACS)

- Provide installation and configuration examples and explanations for the Cisco CNS Access Registrar (AR)

How This Book Is Organized

This book is separated into three logical parts. The first part is a basic overview of AAA. In this part, you will learn how the AAA architecture is built. You will learn how to configure a Cisco router to support the AAA framework, as well as some command syntax.

The second part is an overview to enterprise AAA management using the ACS. In this part, you will install ACS, configure users, groups, and shared profile components, as well as a number of other configuration options in the ACS HTML interface. You will perform database backup, replication, and RDBMS synchronization. This part will teach you the caveats to watch out for and how to troubleshoot configurations.

In the third and final part, you will learn about service provider AAA management using the AR. In this part, you will learn the role of a service provider in the AAA environment, as well as the architecture that the AR is built upon. You will walk through an install of the AR on a Solaris system, as well as configure a basic site for local user authentication. This book is designed to give a general understanding as to the aspects of Cisco's AAA implementation at any level.

Target Audience

This book is targeted toward the following people:

- Network Security Professionals tasked with the implementation and management using ACS or AR

- Those who are pursuing their CCSP, or Cisco Qualified Specialist, and want to gain more detailed knowledge of AAA

- Non-CCIEs and CCIEs in other disciplines working toward their CCIE Network Security Certifications

Although this book does not provide all the answers to AAA implementation and management, it is intended to bridge the gap between the software configuration of ACS and AR and the configuration of the Cisco router IOS.

Features of this Book

This book contains discussion on the extended features of ACS as well as AR. This book also combines configuration examples with a step-by-step how-to for each item. This book uses a "ground up" approach. You will not configure a device until it has been built from the ground up. This will assist in you installation and implementation process.

As you work through the book, you'll note that shorthand commands are sometimes used in the code examples. In addition, comments within code most often appear on the line that they are describing. This format was used by the author was clarity and conciseness.

Troubleshooting

Many sections of this book include troubleshooting tips and tricks to assist in the common configuration mistakes that are made. This will ease the pain of getting used to yet another product that you have to manage in your secure network environment.

AAA Overview

In this chapter, you learn the following topics:

- Authentication overview
- Authentication example
- Authorization overview
- Authorization example
- Accounting overview
- Accounting example
- Cisco device support

## CHAPTER 1

Authentication, Authorization, and Accounting Overview

Authentication, authorization, and accounting (AAA) is a way to control who is allowed to access your network (authenticate), what they can do while they are there (authorize), and to audit what actions they performed while accessing the network (accounting).

AAA can be used in Internet Protocol Security (IPSec) to provide preshared keys during the Internet Security Association and Key Management Protocol (ISAKMP) process or to provide per-user authentication, known as XAUTH, during ISAKMP. AAA can be used to provide a mechanism for authorizing commands that administrators enter at the command line of a Cisco device. This is called command-line authorization. AAA is also seen in a Virtual Private Dial-Up Networking (VPDN) tunnel set up between two routers.

It is overall a very simple process to configure. In fact, it is easily comparable to day-to-day scenarios such as gaining access to golf clubs or sitting in first class on a commercial airline. In each of these situations, you must provide some type of proof as to your right to enter the golf club or sit in a nice comfortable first-class seat.

In each of the following sections, you see more specific details on the functions of AAA. Throughout the course of this book, you learn how to take the functions of AAA and implement a local solution, providing a username and password that is actually stored on a Cisco device, and a network-wide solution, using an external authentication server such as the Cisco Secure Access Control Server (CSACS) for Windows Server and Cisco Access Registrar for the service provider environment.

TIP

AAA is discussed in a number of Requests For Comments (RFCs). RFC 2903 discusses the general AAA architecture. This is an "experimental" RFC. Since then, AAA has been more clearly defined in other RFCs. Other RFCs include RFC 2924, Accounting Attributes and Record Formats; RFC 2975, Introduction to Accounting Management; RFC 2989, Criteria for Evaluating AAA Protocols for Network Access; and RFC 3127, Authentication, Authorization, and Accounting: Protocol Evaluation. A great deal of information on AAA can be obtained at http://www.ietf.org/html.charters/aaa-charter.html.

Authentication Overview

Just as many types of authentication processes take place in today's world, many types of authentication methods can be performed on a Cisco device. An example of an authentication method might be a state-issued driver license or a boarding pass for a specific airline. When the airline attendants request identification for the use of their services, you are prepared with the proper identification. This is the most basic process of AAA.

Authentication provides a method for identifying users and includes login and password prompting, challenge and response functions, messaging support, and quite possibly encryption, as well. This authentication action takes place prior to the user being allowed access to any of the network resources.

NOTE   Authentication can take place as an individual process or can be combined with authorization and accounting.

When you configure a Cisco device for authentication, you need to complete a few steps. Although these steps are covered in detail in Chapter 3, "Authentication Configuration on Cisco Routers," a high-level overview is provided here for the configuration of Cisco IOS, CAT OS, and PIX OS.

The following steps are performed:

Step 1   Enable the AAA process.

Although AAA is a common protocol that is seen in most enterprise networks, the protocol is not enabled by default.

Step 2   Define the location, protocol, and secret key for the server communication.

Step 3   Define a method list for authentication.[1]

A method list defines the type of authentication to be performed and which sequence to perform it in. It is necessary to apply it to an interface before the authentication methods are used. However, one exception to this rule of application exists. A default list exists, named "default," that is applied to all the interfaces provided a specific list is not configured on the interface already.

Once again, this follows the example of the airlines—as users attempt to access a network service, they are given an authentication prompt. The users can then prove that they are who they say they are. In your network environment, this prompt can be served up in a Telnet application, File Transfer Protocol (FTP) application, or web application. You can also use virtual authentication methods such as virtual Hypertext Transfer Protocol (HTTP) and virtual Telnet. Refer to the Cisco Secure PIX Firewall Advanced book for more information.

If users need access to other resources, one of the previously mentioned methods of access must be performed first or an alternative method such as *virtual Telnet* must be used. This is simply a method of delivering an authentication prompt to the user.

All the methods for authentication on Cisco routers are required to use AAA with the exception of local, line, and enable passwords.

NOTE   By using the term *methods* here, we are talking about authentication methods. These can include but are not limited to line authentication, enable authentication, and login authentication.

Although you can store an enable password on the device itself, this doesn't scale, and the password can be viewed in the configuration file of the device in clear text unless you use the enable secret option. The other options discussed here for authenticating local, line, and enable passwords will be discussed in greater depth in Chapter 3.

Authentication Example

In this example, your user local-admin is attempting to Telnet to a Cisco router. The Cisco router is configured to request authentication from anyone that attempts to access it via Telnet. As the user enters a password, it is sent as clear text to the router. The router then takes that username and password and places it in a packet that is sent to either an AAA server, such as CSACS, or it compares it to a local username and password that are configured.

A more detailed look at the process is as follows:

Step 1   The client establishes connection with the router.

Step 2   The router prompts the user for their username and password.

Step 3   The router authenticates the username and password in the local database. The user is authorized to access the network based on information in the local database.

The process is illustrated in Figure 1-1.

Figure 1-1 *A Simple Authentication Example*

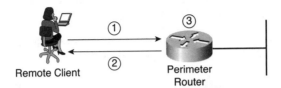

Of course, this is not the best type of authentication to perform because anyone that has access to the network and the path that local-admin is taking from their workstation to the router can see the username and password simply by using some type of "sniffer" software or protocol analyzer. In fact, most protocols don't encrypt the password, while others use weak ciphers and can be susceptible to brute force attacks. More secure methods might include protocols such as the Challenge Handshake Authentication Protocol (CHAP), or even the use of one-time passwords or the use of smart tokens like RSA SecurID or CRYPTOCard. These types of authentication will be discussed Chapter 11, "System Configuration."

Authorization Overview

To take AAA a step further, imagine that you are about to take a vacation. You are going to take a commercial airline to your vacation hot spot. The airplane has a couple of rows in the front that are very nice, leather, wide, and comfortable. You would prefer to sit here instead of the seats that are farther back, because those are stiff, uncomfortable, and do not offer much leg room. Unfortunately, if you purchased a coach class ticket, you cannot sit in the first-class seat in the front of the plane. Similar to this process is the authorization function of AAA. If you have a "coach" authorized ticket, you cannot access "first-class resources." This information is all kept in the airline's computer and can easily be verified by looking your name up in the computer and referencing the seat assignment.

Authorization is a method of providing certain privileges or rights to remote users for services requested. Support for authorization includes IP, Internetwork Packet Exchange (IPX), AppleTalk Remote Access (ARA), and Telnet. Authorization can be configured to the group that a member is a part of or on an individual user basis. User authorization overrides group authorization. Authorization can be configured locally in some cases or kept on a remote AAA server. The remote server might be easier for administration depending on your network environment. Authorization is the second module of the AAA framework.

The following steps are needed for authorization to take place:

Step 1 AAA assembles a set of attributes based on the services that a user is requesting authorization to perform.

Step 2 These attributes are compared against a database that contains the users' actual permissions.

Step 3 After a user is verified to be, or not to be, authorized, the result is returned to the AAA process.

Step 4 After the preceding step sequence, the AAA process is then able to impose the proper restrictions to the user data.

Step 5 If the users' authorizations are located on a remote server, they are usually determined by comparing to Attribute-Value (AV) pairs , which are discussed in Chapter 13, "Exploring TACACS+ Attribute Values."

A method list configures authentication; a method list is also configured to define methods of authorization. It is necessary to authenticate a user before you can determine what that user is authorized to do. Therefore, authorization requires authentication.

Authorization Example

You can clearly see the process of authorization using the same network example from earlier in the chapter.

Figure 1-2 demonstrates a basic authorization process that can take place, in addition to the authentication process that is seen in the previous example. One difference you might note here is that in the authentication example, only a local authentication is discussed. In this authorization example, an AAA server is added, which includes authorizations. More detail on local authentication versus authentication using a server will be discussed in Chapter 3.

Figure 1-2 *Basic Authorization of FTP*

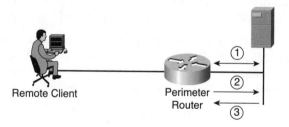

In this situation, the following steps take place:

Step 1 To perform authorization, a session is established with an AAA server.

Step 2 The router requests authorization for the requested service from the AAA server.

Step 3 The AAA server returns a PASS/FAIL for authorization.

Again, the method list that is configured determines what authorization is to be performed. The configuration of a method list is discussed in Chapter 3; however, you might want to note that the configuration of a method list for authorization is the same as the method list configuration for authentication as well as accounting.

Accounting Overview

The final portion of AAA is the accounting module. Accounting can also be explained using an example of the airline industry. As you enter or board the plane, you hand a boarding pass to the agent, and it is scanned through a machine. This accounts for you boarding the plane. As far as the airline is concerned, you were there, and you were on the airplane. AAA accounting is similar. When you access the network, AAA can begin to track any actions you take. Once you authenticate, you were there, as far as the AAA process is concerned.

Accounting in a Cisco environment allows you to track the amount of network resources your users are accessing and the types of services they are using. For example, system administrators might need to bill departments or customers for connection time or resources used on the network (for example, total time connected). AAA accounting allows you to track this activity, as well as suspicious connection attempts into the network.

When you use AAA accounting, the router can send messages either to the AAA server or to a remote SYSLOG server, depending on your configuration. You then have the ability to import the accounting records into a spreadsheet or accounting program for viewing. The CSACS can be used to store these accounting messages, and you can also download these accounting statements in .CSV format or use Open Database Connectivity (ODBC) logging, which is supported in CSACS.

Cisco devices performing accounting can be configured to capture and display accounting data by using the AAA accounting commands including the following: EXEC commands; network services such as SLIP, PPP, and ARAP; and system-level events not associated with users.

These accounting records that are sent by a Cisco device to the accounting server are sent in the form of an AV pair. An AV pair is an attribute and a value. Some of these AV pairs contain information such as username, address, service that is being requested, and the Cisco device that this request is going through, also known as the access server or AAA client.

AAA actually supports six types of accounting:

- Network accounting
- Connection accounting
- EXEC accounting
- System accounting
- Command accounting
- Resource accounting

Network Accounting

Network accounting provides information for all Point-to-Point Protocol (PPP), Serial Line Internet Protocol (SLIP), or Apple Remote Access Protocol (ARAP) sessions, including packet and byte counts.

Connection Accounting

Connection accounting provides information about all outbound connections made from the AAA client, such as Telnet, local-area transport (LAT), TN3270, packet assembler/disassembler (PAD), and rlogin.

EXEC Accounting

EXEC accounting provides information about user EXEC terminal sessions (user shells) on the network access server, including username, date, start and stop times, the access server IP address, and (for dial-in users) the telephone number the call originated from.

System Accounting

System accounting provides information about all system-level events (for example, when the system reboots or when accounting is turned on or off).

Command Accounting

Command accounting provides information about the EXEC shell commands for a specified privilege level that are being executed on a network access server. Each command accounting record includes a list of the commands executed for that privilege level, as well as the date and time each command was executed, and the user who executed it.

Resource Accounting

The Cisco implementation of AAA accounting provides "start" and "stop" record support for calls that have passed user authentication. The additional feature of generating "stop" records for calls that fail to authenticate as part of user authentication is also supported. Such records are necessary for users employing accounting records to manage and monitor their networks.

Accounting Example

Back once again to our sample network, you can now use AAA accounting to perform one of the previously mentioned types of accounting. In this example, you pick up after authentication and authorization have taken place. Here resource accounting performs start stop accounting for FTP on the network. See Figure 1-3.

Figure 1-3 *Basic Accounting of Resources*

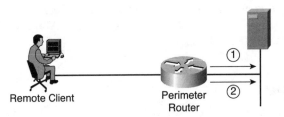

Remote Client Perimeter Router

In this example, the following process is performed. Note that once again authentication must take place.

Step 1 When a user has been authenticated, the AAA accounting process generates a start message to begin the accounting process.

Step 2 When the user finishes, a stop message is recorded ending the accounting process.

Once again, a method list determines what type of accounting is to be performed.

Cisco Device Support for AAA

It is pretty safe to say that most Cisco devices support the AAA framework. In some cases, the support for AAA is not the issue, but rather the support for either Terminal Access Controller Access Control System Plus (TACACS+) or Remote Authentication Dial-In User Service (RADIUS), because these are the protocols that AAA uses to communicate with an AAA server. In some situations, the protocol might be LOCAL, however, and RADIUS or TACACS+ are not needed.

In some cases, the RADIUS protocol is the only type of communication protocol that is used. In other cases, RADIUS can be used for user AAA, and TACACS+ can be used in administrative AAA, as is the case for Cisco VPN 3000 series concentrators. It is best that you determine this prior to the configuration of AAA. The RADIUS and TACACS+ protocols have different ways that they communicate and likewise have different ways that you might need to configure them.

AAA services are often provided by a dedicated AAA server, such as CSACS, a program that performs these functions. The current standards by which network access servers interface with the AAA servers are the RADIUS and TACACS+ protocols. These are supported by the CSACS server software. This server is discussed in greater detail in the following chapters.

An AAA server is simply a server program that handles user requests for access to network resources and provides AAA services. The AAA server typically interacts with network access and gateway servers and with databases and directories containing user information. The current standard by which devices or applications communicate with an AAA server is RADIUS. Most Cisco devices also support the TACACS+ protocol; however, this is a proprietary protocol. Not all devices support it.

Summary

AAA is a framework for authentication, authorization, and accounting in a Cisco environment. To perform these processes, a Cisco device uses a method list, along with other configuration tasks to designate the server and protocol. At this point, you should have a basic understanding of what the AAA framework is, what it provides in your network, and the most basic process of configuration.

Chapter 2, "TACACS+ and RADIUS" will discuss the TACACS+ and RADIUS protocols and how they communicate between the AAA server and the AAA client. In Chapter 3, you will configure AAA on a Cisco router and discuss some of the implications that might come along with these configurations.

End Notes

[1] Leon Katcharian, *Securing Cisco IOS Services (SECUR)*, Cisco Systems, Inc., p. 3-47.

In this chapter, you learn the following topics:

- A brief overview of TACACS+
- A brief overview of RADIUS
- TACACS+ in detail
- RADIUS in detail

TACACS+ and RADIUS

In the authentication arena, an authentication, authorization, and accounting (AAA) client can use multiple protocols to communicate with an AAA server. These are protocols such as TACACS, XTACACS, TACACS+, and RADIUS. This chapter focuses on two of these protocols, Terminal Access Controller Access Control System Plus (TACACS+) and Remote Authentication Dial-In User Service (RADIUS). Specifically, you see the differences between the two, situations that warrant the use of either, and the underlying concepts of each.

When you are done with this chapter, you will find that, while both TACACS+ and RADIUS end up with the same result in general, the underlying architecture is quite different between the two.

A Brief Overview of TACACS+

TACACS+ is a recent protocol providing detailed accounting information and flexible administrative control over authentication and authorization processes. TACACS+ is facilitated through AAA and can be enabled only through AAA commands.

TACACS+ is the result of the evolution of TACACS and extended TACACS (XTACACS). The Cisco IOS supports all three of these protocols. Note the following details:

- TACACS is an older access protocol, incompatible with the newer TACACS+ protocol. It provides password checking and authentication, and notification of user actions for security and accounting purposes. TACACS uses User Datagram Protocol (UDP) as its communication protocol.

- XTACACS is an extension to the older TACACS protocol, supplying additional functionality to TACACS. XTACACS provides information about protocol translator and router use. This information is used in UNIX auditing trails and accounting files. XTACACS is incompatible with TACACS+. XTACACS also uses UDP.

In a situation where TACACS+ is used, a server runs the TACACS+ daemon and uses this to communicate and build packets destined for AAA clients. This TACACS+ is a Cisco proprietary implementation and is described in Internet Draft versions 1.77 and 1.78. TACACS+ uses the TCP protocol to provide reliable delivery of AAA requests. A shared secret key is also used between the AAA client and the AAA server running the TACACS+

protocol. Each portion of AAA is performed separately with TACACS+. Each one of these services, authentication, authorization, or accounting, can be tied to its own database on the AAA server to take advantage of other services available on that server or on the network, depending on the capabilities of the daemon.

A Brief Overview of RADIUS

RADIUS is also a protocol that supports the three portions of AAA. Cisco Systems introduced support for RADIUS in Cisco IOS Software Release 11.1. The RADIUS authentication protocol is documented separately from the accounting protocol; however, the two can be used together.

RADIUS was initially developed by Livingston Enterprises, Inc. RADIUS, covered in RFC 2865, is an open standard, as opposed to the TACACS+ protocol that is implemented by Cisco. RADIUS is an IP-based protocol that uses UDP, a client, and a server. The server returns a result on the information that is requested by a client. The information that the server returns to the client can be located on the RADIUS server or on an external device that the RADIUS server communicates with directly. When this is the case, the requesting client does not have any knowledge of this. Unlike TACACS+, RADIUS performs authentication and authorization at the same time and accounting separately.

TACACS+ in Detail

This section provides information about the architecture of TACACS+. TACACS+ performs reliable communication between the AAA server and AAA client. This communication, as well as the TACACS+ format, is reviewed in the following sections. In addition to this reliable format, TACACS+ performs encryption and authentication of the entire message between the AAA server and AAA client. Finally, we wrap up with the actual operation of the protocol.

TACACS+ Communication

TACACS+ communication between the network access server (NAS) and AAA client is based on the TCP protocol and provides a reliable delivery mechanism to the AAA messaging. TACACS+ uses TCP port 49 and creates a session to facilitate the messaging in an AAA exchange. Many benefits in using TCP for session control in TACACS+ exist. Among these benefits is the fact that TACACS+ uses TCP to provide an acknowledgment of requests that are made by a NAS or an AAA client.

In addition to the acknowledgments provided within TCP, TACACS+ also has the ability, through inherent functionality of the TCP protocol, to adapt to congestion and bandwidth. An example of this functionality is the utilization of TCP windowing. TACACS+ also has the ability to immediately determine when an AAA server is not available by using TCP resets to alert the AAA client of server communication issues. This functionality cannot be provided with the RADIUS protocol because the RADIUS protocol uses UDP for segment delivery.

TACACS+ Format and Header Values

The TACACS+ ID defines a 12-byte header that appears in all TACACS+ packets. This header is always sent in clear text format. The following defines the TACACS+ ID fields, which are also shown in Figure 2-1:

- **Major_version**—This is the major version number of TACACS+. The value appears in the header as TAC_PLUS_MAJOR_VER=0xc.

- **Minor_version**—This field provides revision number for the TACACS+ protocol. It also provides for backward compatibility of the protocol. A default value, as well as a version one, is defined for some commands. These values appear in the TACACS+ header as TAC_PLUS_MINOR_VER_DEFAULT=0x0 and TAC_PLUS_MINOR_VER_ONE=0x1. Should an AAA server running the TACACS+ daemon receive a TACACS+ packet defining a minor version other than one of the ones just listed, it sends an error status back and sets the minor_version to the closest version that is supported.

- **Type**—This distinguishes the packet type. Only certain types are legal. The legal packet types are as follows:
  - TAC_PLUS_AUTHEN=0x01—This is the packet type that signifies authentication.
  - TAC_PLUS_AUTHOR-0x02—This is the packet type that signifies authorization.
  - TAC_PLUS_ACCT=0x03—This is the packet type that signifies accounting.

NOTE   The significance of these possible message types is that TACACS+ has the ability to perform authentication, authorization, and accounting as separate functions. RADIUS does not have this capability.

- **Seq_no**—This determines the sequence number for the current session. TACACS+ has the ability to perform multiple TACACS+ sessions or to use one TACACS+ session per AAA client. The beginning packet of a session is identified by the sequence number 1. All subsequent packets are an increment from that initial number. Because the AAA client sends the first packet to the AAA server running the TACACS+ daemon, it is always the number 1, and all subsequent packets from the AAA client are identified with odd sequence numbers. In addition to this sequencing scheme, the highest sequence number that can be reached is 2^8-1. After this value is reached, the session that is established between the AAA client and the AAA server is reset, and a new session is started. When the session restarts, it begins, once again, with a sequence number of 1.

- **Flags**—In this section, the field can contain various flags. These flags can be TAC_PLUS_UNENCRYPTED_FLAG and TAC_PLUS_SINGLE_CONNECT_FLAG. The TAC_PLUS_UNENCRYPTED_FLAG flag specifies if encryption is being performed on the body of the TACACS+ packet. If this flag is set, meaning that the value is set to 1, encryption is not being performed and likewise, if the value of this flag is set to 0, the packet is, in fact, being encrypted. The ability to disable TACACS+ encryption should be used primarily for debugging purposes. This functionality is nice when you need to see all the information in the body of the packet. Keep in mind that the header is always sent clear text. The TAC_PLUS_SINGLE_CONNECT_FLAG determines whether or not multiplexing multiple TACACS+ sessions over one TCP session is supported. This is determined in the first two TACACS+ messages of a session. When determined, this does not change.

- **Session_id**—This is a random value that designates the current session between the AAA client and the AAA server running the TACACS+ daemon. This value remains the same for the duration of a session.

- **Length**—This field states the total length of the TACACS+ packet, not to include the 12-byte header.

Figure 2-1   *TACACS+ Header Format*

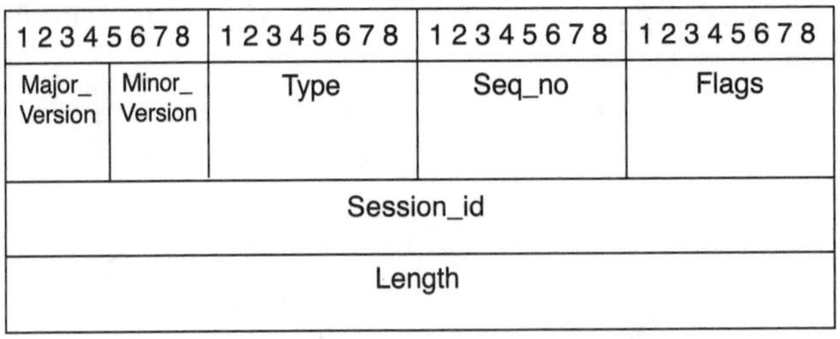

1 2 3 4 5 6 7 8	1 2 3 4 5 6 7 8	1 2 3 4 5 6 7 8	1 2 3 4 5 6 7 8
Major_ Version	Minor_ Version	Type	Seq_no	Flags
Session_id			
Length			

Encrypting TACACS+

One feature that provides more security under TACACS+, as opposed to its alternative RADIUS, is the encryption of the entire packet. This encryption is sent between the AAA client and the AAA server running the TACACS+ daemon. This is not to be confused with encryption of user data. This is not an encryption such as 3DES-IPSec or RSA encryption, but is rather a combination of a hashing algorithm and an XOR function. TACACS+ uses MD5 to hash using a secret key provided on both ends.

The process of TACACS+ encryption is as follows:

Step 1   Information is taken from the packet header, and the preshared key calculates a series of hashes. The first is a hash that is calculated on a concatenation of the session_id, the version, the seq_no, and the pre-shared key value. Each hash that is created has the previous hash in it as well. This is done a number of times that is dependent on the particular implementation of TACACS+.

Step 2   The calculated hash is concatenated and then truncated to the length of the data that is being encrypted. Each hash has the previous hash concatenated to its input values. The result is called the pseudo_pad.

Step 3   The cipher text is produced by doing a bytewise XOR on the pseudo_pad with the data that is being encrypted.

Step 4   The receiving device uses its pre-shared key to calculate the pseudo_pad, and then an XOR of the newly created pseudo_pad results in the original data in clear text.

TACACS+ Operation

Three possible activities can be performed during TACACS+ operation. The first operation performed is authentication. This is done to clearly identify the user. The second operation is authorization and is possible only once a user has been identified. Therefore, you must authenticate prior to authorizing. The third operation is accounting. The accounting process keeps track of actions performed. The three processes are each independent of the other.

TACACS+ and Authentication

When authentication is performed in TACACS+, three distinct packet exchanges take place. The three types of packets are

- **START**—This packet is used initially when the user attempts to connect.
- **REPLY**—Sent by the AAA server during the authentication process.
- **CONTINUE**—Used by the AAA client to return username and password to the AAA server.

In Figure 2-2, a user initiates a connection to an AAA client. The following is the process that occurs during this time:

Step 1   The AAA client receives the connection request from the user.

Step 2   The first packet type, START, is sent to the AAA server that is running the TACACS+ daemon.

This START message contains information about the type of authentication.

Step 3 The TACACS+ server then sends the REPLY packet back to the AAA client. At this point, the server requests the username.

Step 4 The AAA client sends a CONTINUE packet to the TACACS+ server with the username provided by the user.

Step 5 The TACACS+ server then sends the REPLY packet back to the AAA client to ask the client to get the password.

Step 6 The AAA client sends a CONTINUE packet to the TACACS+ server with the password provided by the user.

Step 7 The TACACS+ server then sends the REPLY packet back to the AAA client to indicate a pass/fail of authentication. The possible returned values can be

— **ACCEPT**—The user is authenticated and service can begin. If the NAS is configured to require authorization, authorization begins at this time.

— **REJECT**—The user has failed to authenticate. The user can be denied further access or is prompted to retry the login sequence depending on the TACACS+ daemon.

— **ERROR**—An error occurred at some time during authentication. This can be either at the daemon or in the network connection between the daemon and the NAS. If an ERROR response is received, the NAS typically tries to use an alternative method for authenticating the user.

— **CONTINUE**—The user is prompted for additional authentication information.

NOTE START and CONTINUE packets are always sent by the AAA client, and REPLY packets are always sent by the TACACS+ server.

TACACS+ and Authorization

In the previous section, you saw the authentication process in TACACS+. This section discusses the authorization process.

To facilitate authorization in TACACS+, two message types are used. The first message is an authorization REQUEST, and the second is the authorization RESPONSE. The REQUEST sources from the AAA client, and the RESPONSE sources from the AAA server.

Figure 2-2   *TACACS+ Messaging*

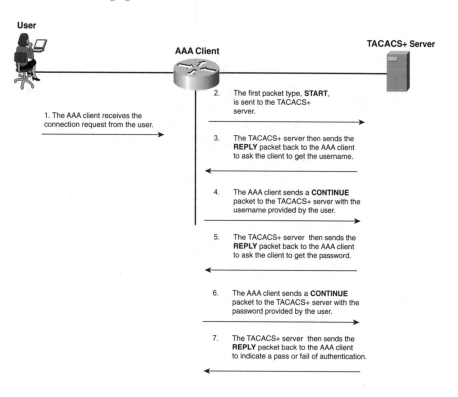

Figure 2-3 shows a basic authorization attempt.

Figure 2-3   *Simple TACACS+ Authorization*

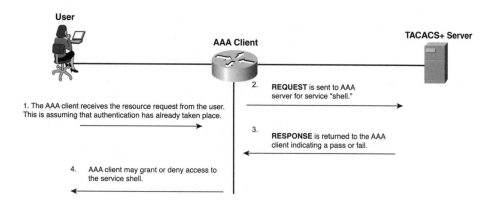

The RESPONSE message (in Step 3 in Figure 2-3) contains one of the following replies:

- A FAIL response from the server indicates that the services requested for authorization are not granted.

- If the server responds with a PASS_ADD, the request is authorized, and the information returned in the RESPONSE is used in addition to the requested information. If no additional arguments are returned by the AAA server in the RESPONSE, the request is authorized.

- In some cases, a PASS_REPL might be returned to the AAA client. In this case, the server is choosing to ignore the REQUEST and is replacing it with the information returned in the RESPONSE.

- If the status is set to FOLLOW, this indicates that the AAA server that is sending the RESPONSE wants to have the authorization take place on another server, and this server information is listed in the RESPONSE packet. The AAA client has the option of using this server or simply can treat it as a FAIL.

- If the status returned is ERROR, this indicates an error on the AAA server. This is commonly a preshared key mismatch; however, it can be a number of issues and further troubleshooting needs to take place.

In authorization, Attribute-Value (AV) determine authorized services. Table 2-1 provides the AV pairs that are currently supported on Cisco IOS up to version 12.2 for authentication and authorization.

Table 2-1 *Cisco IOS Supported AV Pairs for Accounting and Authorization[1]*

Attribute	Description	11.0	11.1	11.2	11.3	12.0	12.1	12.2
acl=x	ASCII number representing a connection access list. Used only when service=shell.	yes	yes	yes	yes	yes	yes	yes
addr=x	A network address. Used with service=slip, service=ppp, and protocol=ip. Contains the IP address that the remote host should use when connecting via Serial Line Internet Protocol (SLIP) or PPP/IP. For example, addr=10.2.3.4.	yes	yes	yes	yes	yes	yes	yes

Table 2-1   *Cisco IOS Supported AV Pairs for Accounting and Authorization[1] (Continued)*

Attribute	Description	11.0	11.1	11.2	11.3	12.0	12.1	12.2
addr-pool=x	Specifies the name of a local pool from which to get the address of the remote host. Used with service=ppp and protocol=ip. Note that addr-pool works in conjunction with local pooling. It specifies the name of a local pool (which must be preconfigured on the network access server). Use the **ip-local pool** command to declare local pools. For example: **ip address-pool local** **ip local pool boo 10.0.0.1 10.0.0.10** **ip local pool moo 10.0.0.1 10.0.0.20** You can then use TACACS+ to return addr-pool=boo or addr-pool=moo to indicate the address pool from which you want to get this remote node's address.	yes	yes	yes	yes	yes	yes	yes
autocmd=x	Specifies an autocommand to be executed at EXEC startup (for example, autocmd=telnet example.com). Used only with service=shell.	yes	yes	yes	yes	yes	yes	yes
callback-dialstring	Sets the telephone number for a callback (for example, callback-dialstring=408-555-1212). Value is NULL or a dial-string. A NULL value indicates that the service might choose to get the dial string through other means. Used with service=arap, service=slip, service=ppp, service=shell. Not valid for ISDN.	no	yes	yes	yes	yes	yes	yes

continues

Table 2-1 *Cisco IOS Supported AV Pairs for Accounting and Authorization[1] (Continued)*

Attribute	Description	11.0	11.1	11.2	11.3	12.0	12.1	12.2
callback-line	The number of a TTY line to use for callback (for example, callback-line=4). Used with service=arap, service=slip, service=ppp, service=shell. Not valid for ISDN.	no	yes	yes	yes	yes	yes	yes
callback-rotary	The number of a rotary group (between 0 and 100 inclusive) to use for callback (for example, callback-rotary=34). Used with service=arap, service=slip, service=ppp, service=shell. Not valid for ISDN.	no	yes	yes	yes	yes	yes	yes
cmd-arg=x	An argument to a shell (EXEC) command. This indicates an argument for the shell command that is to be run. Multiple cmd-arg attributes can be specified, and they are order dependent. Note: This TACACS+ AV pair cannot be used with RADIUS attribute 26.	yes	yes	yes	yes	yes	yes	yes
cmd=x	A shell (EXEC) command. This indicates the command name for a shell command that is to be run. This attribute must be specified if service equals "shell." A NULL value indicates that the shell itself is being referred to. Note: This TACACS+ AV pair cannot be used with RADIUS attribute 26.	yes	yes	yes	yes	yes	yes	yes
data-service	Used with the service=outbound and protocol=ip.	no	no	no	no	no	yes	yes
dial-number	Defines the number to dial. Used with the service=outbound and protocol=ip.	no	no	no	no	no	yes	yes

Table 2-1   *Cisco IOS Supported AV Pairs for Accounting and Authorization[1] (Continued)*

Attribute	Description	11.0	11.1	11.2	11.3	12.0	12.1	12.2
dns-servers=	Identifies a DNS server (primary or secondary) that can be requested by Microsoft Point-to-Point Protocol (PPP) clients from the network access server during IP Control Protocol (IPCP) negotiation. To be used with service=ppp and protocol=ip. The IP address identifying each DNS server is entered in dotted decimal format.	no	no	no	yes	yes	yes	yes
force-56	Determines whether the network access server uses only the 56 K portion of a channel, even when all 64 K appears to be available. To turn on this attribute, use the "true" value (force-56=true). Any other value is treated as false. Used with the service=outbound and protocol=ip.	no	no	no	no	no	yes	yes
gw-password	Specifies the password for the home gateway during the Layer 2 Forwarding (L2F) tunnel authentication. Used with service=ppp and protocol=vpdn.	no	no	yes	yes	yes	yes	yes
idletime=x	Sets a value, in minutes, after which an idle session is terminated. A value of zero indicates no timeout.	no	yes	yes	yes	yes	yes	yes
inacl#<n>	ASCII access list identifier for an input access list to be installed and applied to an interface for the duration of the current connection. Used with service=ppp and protocol=ip, and service=ppp and protocol =ipx. Per-user access lists do not currently work with ISDN interfaces.	no	no	no	yes	yes	yes	yes

continues

Table 2-1 *Cisco IOS Supported AV Pairs for Accounting and Authorization[1] (Continued)*

Attribute	Description	11.0	11.1	11.2	11.3	12.0	12.1	12.2
inacl=x	ASCII identifier for an interface input access list. Used with service=ppp and protocol=ip. Per-user access lists do not currently work with ISDN interfaces.	yes	yes	yes	yes	yes	yes	yes
interface-config#<n>	Specifies user-specific AAA interface configuration information with Virtual Profiles. The information that follows the equal sign (=) can be any Cisco IOS interface configuration command. Multiple instances of the attributes are allowed, but each instance must have a unique number. Used with service=ppp and protocol=lcp. Note: This attribute replaces the "interface-config=" attribute.	no	no	no	yes	yes	yes	yes
ip-addresses	Space-separated list of possible IP addresses that can be used for the endpoint of a tunnel. Used with service=ppp and protocol=vpdn.	no	no	yes	yes	yes	yes	yes
l2tp-busy-disconnect	If a vpdn-group on an L2TP network server (LNS) uses a virtual template that is configured to be precloned, this attribute controls the disposition of a new L2TP session that finds no pre-cloned interface to which to connect. If the attribute is true (the default), the session is disconnected by the LNS. Otherwise, a new interface is cloned from the virtual template. Used with service=ppp and protocol=vpdn.	no	no	no	no	no	yes	yes
l2tp-cm-local-window-size	Specifies the maximum receive window size for L2TP control messages. This value is advertised to the peer during tunnel establishment. Used with service=ppp and protocol=vpdn.	no	no	no	no	no	yes	yes

Table 2-1 *Cisco IOS Supported AV Pairs for Accounting and Authorization[1] (Continued)*

Attribute	Description	11.0	11.1	11.2	11.3	12.0	12.1	12.2
l2tp-drop-out-of-order	Respects sequence numbers on data packets by dropping those that are received out of order. This does not ensure that sequence numbers are sent on data packets, just how to handle them if they are received. Used with service=ppp and protocol=vpdn.	no	no	no	no	no	yes	yes
l2tp-hello-interval	Specifies the number of seconds for the hello keepalive interval. Hello packets are sent when no data has been sent on a tunnel for the number of seconds configured here. Used with service=ppp and protocol=vpdn.	no	no	no	no	no	yes	yes
l2tp-hidden-avp	When enabled, sensitive Attribute Value Pairs (AVPs) in L2TP control messages are scrambled or hidden. Used with service=ppp and protocol=vpdn.	no	no	no	no	no	yes	yes
l2tp-nosession-timeout	Specifies the number of seconds that a tunnel stays active with no sessions before timing out and shutting down. Used with service=ppp and protocol=vpdn.	no	no	no	no	no	yes	yes
l2tp-tos-reflect	Copies the IP type of service (ToS) field from the IP header of each payload packet to the IP header of the tunnel packet for packets entering the tunnel at the LNS. Used with service=ppp and protocol=vpdn.	no	no	no	no	no	yes	yes
l2tp-tunnel-authen	If this attribute is set, it performs L2TP tunnel authentication. Used with service=ppp and protocol=vpdn.	no	no	no	no	no	yes	yes

continues

Table 2-1   *Cisco IOS Supported AV Pairs for Accounting and Authorization[1] (Continued)*

Attribute	Description	11.0	11.1	11.2	11.3	12.0	12.1	12.2
l2tp-tunnel-password	Shared secret used for L2TP tunnel authentication and AVP hiding. Used with service=ppp and protocol=vpdn.	no	no	no	no	no	yes	yes
l2tp-udp-checksum	This is an authorization attribute and defines whether L2TP should perform UDP checksums for data packets. Valid values are "yes" and "no." The default is no. Used with service=ppp and protocol=vpdn.	no	no	no	no	no	yes	yes
link-compression=	Defines whether to turn on or turn off "stac" compression over a PPP link. Used with service=ppp. Link compression is defined as a numeric value as follows: 0: None 1: Stac 2: Stac-Draft-9 3: MS-Stac	no	no	no	yes	yes	yes	yes
load-threshold=<*n*>	Sets the load threshold for the caller at which additional links are either added to or deleted from the multilink bundle. If the load goes above the specified value, additional links are added. If the load goes below the specified value, links are deleted. Used with service=ppp and protocol=multilink. The range for <*n*> is from **1** to **255**.	no	no	no	yes	yes	yes	yes
map-class	Allows the user profile to reference information configured in a map class of the same name on the network access server that dials out. Used with the service=outbound and protocol=ip.	no	no	no	no	no	yes	yes

Table 2-1   *Cisco IOS Supported AV Pairs for Accounting and Authorization[1] (Continued)*

Attribute	Description	11.0	11.1	11.2	11.3	12.0	12.1	12.2
max-links=*<n>*	Restricts the number of links that a user can have in a multilink bundle. Used with service=ppp and protocol=multilink. The range for *<n>* is from **1** to **255**.	no	no	no	yes	yes	yes	yes
min-links	Sets the minimum number of links for Multilink PPP (MLP). Used with service=ppp, protocol=multilink, and protocol=vpdn.	no	no	no	no	no	yes	yes
nas-password	Specifies the password for the NAS during the L2F tunnel authentication. Used with service=ppp and protocol=vpdn.	no	no	yes	yes	yes	yes	yes
nocallback-verify	Indicates that no callback verification is required. The only valid value for this parameter is 1 (for example, nocallback-verify=1). Used with service=arap, service=slip, service=ppp, service=shell. There is no authentication on callback. Not valid for ISDN.	no	yes	yes	yes	yes	yes	yes
noescape=*x*	Prevents user from using an escape character. Used with service=shell. Can be either true or false (for example, noescape=true).	yes	yes	yes	yes	yes	yes	yes
nohangup=*x*	Used with service=shell. Specifies the nohangup option, which means that after an EXEC shell is terminated, the user is presented with another login (username) prompt. Can be either **true** or **false** (for example, nohangup=false).	yes	yes	yes	yes	yes	yes	yes

continues

Table 2-1   *Cisco IOS Supported AV Pairs for Accounting and Authorization[1] (Continued)*

Attribute	Description	11.0	11.1	11.2	11.3	12.0	12.1	12.2
old-prompts	Allows providers to make the prompts in TACACS+ appear identical to those of earlier systems (TACACS and extended TACACS). This allows administrators to upgrade from TACACS or XTACACS to TACACS+ transparently to users.	yes	yes	yes	yes	yes	yes	yes
outacl#<n>	ASCII access list identifier for an interface output access list to be installed and applied to an interface for the duration of the current condition. Used with service=ppp, protocol=ip, service service=ppp, and protocol=ipx. Per-user access lists do not currently work with ISDN interfaces.	no	no	no	yes	yes	yes	yes
outacl=x	ASCII identifier for an interface output access list. Used with service=ppp, protocol=ip, service service=ppp, and protocol=ipx. Contains an IP output access list for SLIP or PPP/IP (for example, outacl=4). The access list itself must be preconfigured on the router. Per-user access lists do not currently work with ISDN interfaces.	yes (PPP/IP only)	yes	yes	yes	yes	yes	yes
pool-def#<n>	Defines IP address pools on the NAS. Used with service=ppp and protocol=ip.	no	no	no	yes	yes	yes	yes
pool-timeout=	Defines (in conjunction with pool-def) IP address pools on the NAS. During IPCP address negotiation, if an IP pool name is specified for a user (see the addr-pool attribute), a check is made to see if the named pool is defined on the NAS. If it is, the pool is consulted for an IP address. Used with service=ppp and protocol=ip.	no	no	yes	yes	yes	yes	yes

Table 2-1   *Cisco IOS Supported AV Pairs for Accounting and Authorization[1] (Continued)*

Attribute	Description	11.0	11.1	11.2	11.3	12.0	12.1	12.2
port-type	Indicates the type of physical port the NAS is using to authenticate the user. Physical ports are indicated by a numeric value as follows: 0: Asynchronous 1: Synchronous 2: ISDN-Synchronous 3: ISDN-Asynchronous (V.120) 4: ISDN-Asynchronous (V.110) 5: Virtual Used with service=any and protocol=aaa.	no	no	no	no	no	yes	yes
ppp-vj-slot-compression	Instructs the Cisco router not to use slot compression when sending VJ-compressed packets over a PPP link.	no	no	no	yes	yes	yes	yes
priv-lvl=x	Privilege level to be assigned for the EXEC. Used with service=shell. Privilege levels range from 0 to 15, with 15 being the highest.	yes	yes	yes	yes	yes	yes	yes
protocol=x	A protocol that is a subset of a service. An example would be any PPP Network Control Protocol (NCP.) Currently known values are **lcp**, **ip**, **ipx**, **atalk**, **vines**, **lat**, **xremote**, **tn3270**, **telnet**, **rlogin**, **pad**, **vpdn**, **osicp**, **deccp**, **ccp**, **cdp**, **bridging**, **xns**, **nbf**, **bap**, **multilink**, and **unknown**.	yes	yes	yes	yes	yes	yes	yes

continues

Table 2-1 *Cisco IOS Supported AV Pairs for Accounting and Authorization[1] (Continued)*

Attribute	Description	11.0	11.1	11.2	11.3	12.0	12.1	12.2
proxyacl#<n>	Allows users to configure the downloadable user profiles (dynamic access control lists [ACLs]) by using the authentication proxy feature so that users can have the configured authorization to permit traffic going through the configured interfaces. Used with service=shell and protocol=exec.	no	no	no	no	no	yes	yes
route	Specifies a route to be applied to an interface. Used with service=slip, service=ppp, and protocol=ip. During network authorization, the route attribute can be used to specify a per-user static route, to be installed by TACACS+ as follows: route="*dst_address mask [gateway]*" This indicates a temporary static route that is to be applied. The *dst_address*, *mask*, and *gateway* are expected to be in the usual dotted decimal notation, with the same meanings as in the familiar **ip route** configuration command on a NAS. If *gateway* is omitted, the peer's address is the gateway. The route is expunged when the connection terminates.	no	yes	yes	yes	yes	yes	yes
route#<n>	Like the route AV pair, this specifies a route to be applied to an interface, but these routes are numbered, allowing multiple routes to be applied. Used with service=ppp, protocol=ip, service=ppp, and protocol=ipx.	no	no	no	yes	yes	yes	yes

Table 2-1   *Cisco IOS Supported AV Pairs for Accounting and Authorization[1] (Continued)*

Attribute	Description	11.0	11.1	11.2	11.3	12.0	12.1	12.2
routing=*x*	Specifies whether routing information is to be propagated to and accepted from this interface. Used with service=slip, service=ppp, and protocol=ip. Equivalent in function to the /routing flag in SLIP and PPP commands. Can either be **true** or **false** (for example, routing=true).	yes	yes	yes	yes	yes	yes	yes
rte-fltr-in#<*n*>	Specifies an input access list definition to be installed and applied to routing updates on the current interface for the duration of the current connection. Used with service=ppp, protocol=ip, service=ppp, and protocol=ipx.	no	no	no	yes	yes	yes	yes
rte-fltr-out#<*n*>	Specifies an output access list definition to be installed and applied to routing updates on the current interface for the duration of the current connection. Used with service=ppp, protocol=ip, service=ppp, and protocol=ipx.	no	no	no	yes	yes	yes	yes
sap#<*n*>	Specifies static Service Advertising Protocol (SAP) entries to be installed for the duration of a connection. Used with service=ppp and protocol=ipx.	no	no	no	yes	yes	yes	yes
sap-fltr-in#<*n*>	Specifies an input SAP filter access list definition to be installed and applied on the current interface for the duration of the current connection. Used with service=ppp and protocol=ipx.	no	no	no	yes	yes	yes	yes

continues

Table 2-1 *Cisco IOS Supported AV Pairs for Accounting and Authorization[1] (Continued)*

Attribute	Description	11.0	11.1	11.2	11.3	12.0	12.1	12.2
sap-fltr-out#<n>	Specifies an output SAP filter access list definition to be installed and applied on the current interface for the duration of the current connection. Used with service=ppp and protocol=ipx.	no	no	no	yes	yes	yes	yes
send-auth	Defines the protocol to use (Password Authentication Protocol [PAP] or Challenge Handshake Authentication Protocol [CHAP]) for username-password authentication following Caller Line Identification (CLID) authentication. Used with service=any and protocol=aaa.	no	no	no	no	no	yes	yes
send-secret	Specifies the password that the NAS needs to respond to a CHAP/PAP request from the remote end of a connection on an outgoing call. Used with service=ppp and protocol=ip.	no	no	no	no	no	yes	yes
service=x	The primary service. Specifying a service attribute indicates that this is a request for authorization or accounting of that service. Current values are **slip**, **ppp**, **arap**, **shell**, **tty-daemon**, **connection**, and **system**. This attribute must always be included.	yes	yes	yes	yes	yes	yes	yes
source-ip=x	Used as the source IP address of all Virtual Private Dial-Up Networking (VPDN) packets generated as part of a VPDN tunnel. This is equivalent to the Cisco **vpdn outgoing** global configuration command.	no	no	yes	yes	yes	yes	yes

Table 2-1   *Cisco IOS Supported AV Pairs for Accounting and Authorization[1] (Continued)*

Attribute	Description	11.0	11.1	11.2	11.3	12.0	12.1	12.2
spi	Carries the authentication information needed by the home agent to authenticate a mobile node during registration. The information is in the same syntax as the **ip mobile secure host <addr>** configuration command. Basically, it contains the rest of the configuration command that follows that string, verbatim. It provides the security parameter index (SPI), key, authentication algorithm, authentication mode, and replay protection timestamp range. Used with service=mobileip and protocol=ip.	no	no	no	no	no	yes	yes
timeout=*x*	The number of minutes before an EXEC or AppleTalk Remote Access (ARA) session disconnects (for example, timeout=60). A value of zero indicates no timeout. Used with service=arap.	yes	yes	yes	yes	yes	yes	yes
tunnel-id	Specifies the username that authenticates the tunnel over which the individual user message identifier (MID) is projected. This is analogous to the *remote name* in the **vpdn outgoing** command. Used with service=ppp and protocol=vpdn.	no	no	yes	yes	yes	yes	yes
wins-servers=	Identifies a Windows NT server that can be requested by Microsoft PPP clients from the network access server during IP Control Protocol (IPCP) negotiation. To be used with service=ppp and protocol=ip. The IP address identifying each Windows NT server is entered in dotted decimal format.	no	no	no	yes	yes	yes	yes
zonelist=*x*	A numeric zonelist value. Used with service=arap. Specifies an AppleTalk zonelist for ARA (for example, zonelist=5).	yes	yes	yes	yes	yes	yes	yes

TACACS+ Accounting

The functionality of accounting in TACACS+ is similar to that of authorization. Accounting takes place by sending a record to the AAA server. Each of these records includes an AV pair for accounting. Three types of records can be sent to the AAA server. They are as follows:

- The **Start record** indicates when a service begins and contains the information that was included in the authorization process, as well as specific information to the account.

- A **Stop record** indicates when a service is about to stop or is terminated and also includes information that was included in the authorization process, as well as specific information to the account.

- A **Continue record** is also called a **Watchdog.** This is sent when a service is still in progress and allows the AAA client to provide updated information to the AAA server. As seen in the previous records, this also includes information that was included in the authorization process, as well as specific information to the account.

NOTE   A record can be sent as both a Start record and a Continue record. This indicates that the Continue record is a duplicate of the Start record.

Accounting also uses the two message types that authorization uses, a REQUEST and a RESPONSE. The AAA server has the capability to send the following in a RESPONSE:

- SUCCESS indicates that the server received the record that was sent by the AAA client.

- An ERROR indicates that the server failed to commit the record to its database.

- A FOLLOW is similar to that of a FOLLOW in authorization. This indicates that the server wishes the AAA client to send the record to another AAA server, and the AAA server information is included in the RESPONSE.

Figure 2-4 shows a basic example of the accounting process between the AAA client and the AAA server.

Figure 2-4   *Basic Accounting*

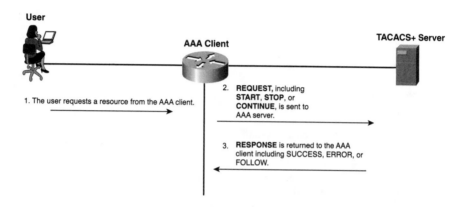

In Table 2-2, the TACAS+ accounting AV pairs that are supported in IOS versions up to 12.2 are shown.

Table 2-2   *TACACS+ Accounting AV Pairs[2]*

Attribute	Description	11.0	11.1	11.2	11.3	12.0	12.1	12.2
Abort-Cause	If the fax session aborts, it indicates the system component that signaled the abort. Examples of system components that could trigger an abort are Fax Application Process (FAP), TIFF (the TIFF reader or the TIFF writer), fax-mail client, fax-mail server, Enhanced Simple Mail Transport (ESMTP) client, or ESMTP server.	no	no	no	no	no	yes	yes
bytes_in	The number of input bytes transferred during this connection.	yes	yes	yes	yes	yes	yes	yes
bytes_out	The number of output bytes transferred during this connection.	yes	yes	yes	yes	yes	yes	yes

continues

Table 2-2 *TACACS+ Accounting AV Pairs[2] (Continued)*

Attribute	Description	11.0	11.1	11.2	11.3	12.0	12.1	12.2
Call-Type	Describes the type of fax activity: fax receive or fax send.	no	no	no	no	no	yes	yes
cmd	The command the user executed.	yes	yes	yes	yes	yes	yes	yes
data-rate	This AV pair has been renamed. See nas-rx-speed.							
disc-cause	Specifies the reason a connection was taken off line. The disc-cause attribute is sent in accounting-stop records. This attribute also causes Stop records to be generated without first generating Start records if disconnection occurs before authentication is performed for a list of disc-cause values and their meanings.	no	no	no	yes	yes	yes	yes
disc-cause-ext	Extends the disc-cause attribute to support vendor-specific reasons why a connection was taken off line.	no	no	no	yes	yes	yes	yes
elapsed_time	The elapsed time in seconds for the action. Useful when the device does not keep real time.	yes	yes	yes	yes	yes	yes	yes
Email-Server-Address	Indicates the IP address of the e-mail server handling the on-ramp fax-mail message.	no	no	no	no	no	yes	yes
Email-Server-Ack-Flag	Indicates that the on-ramp gateway has received a positive acknowledgment from the e-mail server accepting the fax-mail message.	no	no	no	no	no	yes	yes
event	Information included in the accounting packet that describes a state change in the router. Events described are accounting starting and accounting stopping.	yes	yes	yes	yes	yes	yes	yes
Fax-Account-Id-Origin	Indicates the account ID origin as defined by the system administrator for the **mmoip aaa receive-id** or the **mmoip aaa send-id** command.	no	no	no	no	no	yes	yes
Fax-Auth-Status	Indicates whether or not authentication for this fax session was successful. Possible values for this field are success, failed, bypassed, or unknown.	no	no	no	no	no	yes	yes

Table 2-2 *TACACS+ Accounting AV Pairs[2] (Continued)*

Attribute	Description	11.0	11.1	11.2	11.3	12.0	12.1	12.2
Fax-Connect-Speed	Indicates the modem speed at which this fax-mail was initially transmitted or received. Possible values are 1200, 4800, 9600, and 14,400.	no	no	no	no	no	yes	yes
Fax-Coverpage-Flag	Indicates whether or not a cover page was generated by the off-ramp gateway for this fax session. True indicates that a cover page was generated; false means that a cover page was not generated.	no	no	no	no	no	yes	yes
Fax-Dsn-Address	Indicates the address to which delivery status notifications (DSNs) are to be sent.	no	no	no	no	no	yes	yes
Fax-Dsn-Flag	Indicates whether or not DSN has been enabled. True indicates that DSN has been enabled; false means that DSN has not been enabled.	no	no	no	no	no	yes	yes
Fax-Mdn-Address	Indicates the address to which MDNs are to be sent.	no	no	no	no	no	yes	yes
Fax-Mdn-Flag	Indicates whether or not message delivery notification (MDN) has been enabled. True indicates that MDN has been enabled; false means that MDN has not been enabled.	no	no	no	no	no	yes	yes
Fax-Modem-Time	Indicates the amount of time in seconds the modem sent fax data (x) and the amount of time in seconds of the total fax session (y), which includes both fax-mail and Public Switched Telephone Network (PSTN) time, in the form x/y. For example, 10/15 means that the transfer time took 10 seconds, and the total fax session took 15 seconds.	no	no	no	no	no	yes	yes
Fax-Msg-Id=	Indicates a unique fax message identification number assigned by store and forward fax.	no	no	no	no	no	yes	yes

continues

Table 2-2 *TACACS+ Accounting AV Pairs[2] (Continued)*

Attribute	Description	11.0	11.1	11.2	11.3	12.0	12.1	12.2
Fax-Pages	Indicates the number of pages transmitted or received during this fax session. This page count includes cover pages.	no	no	no	no	no	yes	yes
Fax-Process-Abort-Flag	Indicates that the fax session was aborted or successful. True means that the session was aborted; false means that the session was successful.	no	no	no	no	no	yes	yes
Fax-Recipient-Count	Indicates the number of recipients for this fax transmission. Until e-mail servers support Session mode, the number should be 1.	no	no	no	no	no	yes	yes
Gateway-Id	Indicates the name of the gateway that processed the fax session. The name appears in the following format: *hostname.domain-name.*	no	no	no	no	no	yes	yes
mlp-links-max	Gives the count of links that are known to have been in a given multilink session at the time the accounting record is generated.	no	no	no	yes	yes	yes	yes
mlp-sess-id	Reports the identification number of the multilink bundle when the session closes. This attribute applies to sessions that are part of a multilink bundle. This attribute is sent in authentication-response packets.	no	no	no	yes	yes	yes	yes
nas-rx-speed	Specifies the average number of bits per second over the course of the connection's lifetime. This attribute is sent in accounting-stop records.	no	no	no	yes	yes	yes	yes
nas-tx-speed	Reports the transmit speed negotiated by the two modems.	no	no	no	yes	yes	yes	yes
paks_in	The number of input packets transferred during this connection.	yes	yes	yes	yes	yes	yes	yes
paks_out	The number of output packets transferred during this connection.	yes	yes	yes	yes	yes	yes	yes
port	The port the user was logged in to.	yes	yes	yes	yes	yes	yes	yes

Table 2-2   *TACACS+ Accounting AV Pairs[2] (Continued)*

Attribute	Description	11.0	11.1	11.2	11.3	12.0	12.1	12.2
Port-Used	Indicates the slot/port number of the Cisco AS5300 used to either transmit or receive this fax-mail.	no	no	no	no	no	yes	yes
pre-bytes-in	Records the number of input bytes before authentication. This attribute is sent in accounting-stop records.	no	no	no	yes	yes	yes	yes
pre-bytes-out	Records the number of output bytes before authentication. This attribute is sent in accounting-stop records.	no	no	no	yes	yes	yes	yes
pre-paks-in	Records the number of input packets before authentication. This attribute is sent in accounting-stop records.	no	no	no	yes	yes	yes	yes
pre-paks-out	Records the number of output packets before authentication. The pre-paks-out attribute is sent in accounting-stop records.	no	no	no	yes	yes	yes	yes
pre-session-time	Specifies the length of time, in seconds, from when a call first connects to when it completes authentication.	no	no	no	yes	yes	yes	yes
priv_level	The privilege level associated with the action.	yes	yes	yes	yes	yes	yes	yes
protocol	The protocol associated with the action.	yes	yes	yes	yes	yes	yes	yes
reason	Information included in the accounting packet that describes the event that caused a system change. Events described are system reload, system shutdown, or accounting reconfiguration (being turned on or off).	yes	yes	yes	yes	yes	yes	yes
service	The service the user used.	yes	yes	yes	yes	yes	yes	yes
start_time	The time the action started (in seconds since the epoch, 12:00 a.m. January 1, 1970). The clock must be configured to receive this information.	yes	yes	yes	yes	yes	yes	yes
stop_time	The time the action stopped (in seconds since the epoch). The clock must be configured to receive this information.	yes	yes	yes	yes	yes	yes	yes

continues

Table 2-2 *TACACS+ Accounting AV Pairs[2] (Continued)*

Attribute	Description	11.0	11.1	11.2	11.3	12.0	12.1	12.2
task_id	Start and Stop records for the same event must have matching (unique) task_id numbers.	yes	yes	yes	yes	yes	yes	yes
timezone	The time zone abbreviation for all timestamps included in this packet.	yes	yes	yes	yes	yes	yes	yes
xmit-rate	This AV pair has been renamed. See nas-tx-speed.							

RADIUS in Detail

RADUIS is an Internet Engineering Task Force (IETF) standard that is used for AAA. It is also a client/server model. This means the AAA client sends user information to the AAA server, in this case via the RADIUS protocol, and the RADIUS server responds with all the information that is needed for the AAA client to provide connectivity and service to the end user. The AAA client acts in response to the reply it receives from the RADIUS server.

For network authentication, a shared secret key authenticates messages between the AAA/ RADIUS server and the AAA client. The shared secret key is never actually sent across the wire so the integrity of the key is maintained.

When RADIUS authenticates users, numerous authentication methods can be used. RADIUS supports authentication via Point-to-Point Protocol Challenge Handshake Authentication Protocol (PPP CHAP) and PPP Password Authentication Protocol (PAP), as well as others.

In addition to these features, RADIUS is an extensible protocol that allows vendors the ability to add new attribute values without creating a problem for existing attributes values.

A major difference between TACACS+ and RADIUS is that RADIUS does not separate authentication and authorization. RADIUS also provides for better accounting. In this section, you see the operation and functionality of RADIUS.

NOTE   Note that in June 1996, draft 5 of the RADIUS protocol specification was submitted to the Internet Engineering Task Force (IETF). The RADIUS specification (RFC 2058) and RADIUS accounting standard (RFC 2059) are now proposed standard protocols. The text of the IETF proposed standards can be found at the following URLs:

http://www.ietf.org/rfc/rfc2058.txt?number=2058

http://www.ietf.org/rfc/rfc2059.txt?number=2059

RADIUS operates under the UDP protocol. RADIUS uses ports 1645 and 1812 for authentication and 1646 and 1813 for accounting. The ports 1812 and 1813 are seen in newer RADIUS implementations. The use of RADIUS port 1645 in early implementations conflicts with the "datametrics" service. Therefore, the officially assigned port is 1812.

Generally, the RADIUS protocol is considered to be a connectionless service. Issues related to server availability, retransmission, and timeouts are handled by the RADIUS-enabled devices rather than the transmission protocol. This functionality differs from TACACS+, where the reliability in the protocol is dependent on the TCP protocol.

RADIUS Operation

The following is the process used in a RADIUS managed login:

Step 1   A user login generates a query (Access-Request) from the AAA client to the RADIUS server.

Step 2   A corresponding response (Access-Accept or Access-Reject) is returned by the server.

The Access-Request packet contains the username, encrypted password, IP address of the AAA client, and port. The format of the request also provides information on the type of session that the user wants to initiate.

The format of the RADIUS packet is seen in Figure 2-5.

Figure 2-5   *RADIUS Packet Format*

Code	Identifier	Length
Request Authenticator		
Attributes		

Each RADIUS packet contains the following information:

- **Code**—The code field is one octet; it identifies one of the following types of RADIUS packets:
    — Access-Request (1)
    — Access-Accept (2)
    — Access-Reject (3)
    — Accounting-Request (4)
    — Accounting-Response (5)

— Access-Challenge (11)

— Status-Server (12)

— Status-Client (13)

— Reserved (255)

NOTE Status-Server and Status-Client are experimental.

- **Identifier**—The identifier field is one octet; it helps the RADIUS server match requests and responses and detect duplicate requests.
- **Length**—The length field is two octets; it specifies the length of the entire packet.
- **Request Authenticator**—The authenticator field is 16 octets. The most significant octet is transmitted first; it authenticates the reply from the RADIUS server. Two types of authenticators are as follows:
  - **Request-Authenticator**—Available in Access-Request and Accounting-Request packets
  - **Response-Authenticator**—Available in Access-Accept, Access-Reject, Access-Challenge, and Accounting-Response packets

The attributes that are seen in Figure 2-5 are RADIUS AV pairs. These specific attributes and corresponding values are discussed in Appendix A, "RADIUS Attribute Tables."

RADIUS Encryption

Encryption in RADIUS differs from that of TACACS+ because RADIUS encrypts only the password and the rest is sent in clear text.

The process of encrypting the password in RADIUS is as follows:

Step 1 A RADIUS packet includes an Authenticator field, as seen in Figure 2-5. This is a field that contains a 16-octet random number called the Request Authenticator.

Step 2 The Request Authenticator is combined with the pre-shared key value and runs through an MD5 hash algorithm. This derives a 16-octet hash. For this example, this is called HASH_A. Therefore, HASH_A is equal to the MD5 request authentication plus pre-shared key.

Step 3 The user-provided password is padded in the message with a null value so that it reaches a 16-octet value.

Step 4   HASH_A is then XORed with the padded password from Step 3, and that generates the cipher text that is transmitted to the AAA server running RADIUS.

Step 5   The AAA server calculates HASH_A on its own and XORs it with the received cipher text to get the padded user-provided password back to clear text.

RADIUS Authentication and Authorization

When an AAA server running RADIUS receives the Access-Request from the AAA client, it searches a database for the username listed. If the username does not exist in the database, either a default profile is loaded, or the RADIUS server immediately sends an Access-Reject message. This Access-Reject message can be accompanied by an optional text message, which could indicate the reason for the refusal.

If the username is found and the password is correct, the RADIUS server returns an Access-Accept response, including a list of Attribute-Value pairs that describe the parameters to be used for this session. Typical parameters include service type (shell or framed), protocol type, IP address to assign the user (static or dynamic), access list to apply, or a static route to install in the AAA client's routing table. The configuration information in the RADIUS server defines what is installed on the AAA client.

Optionally, the AAA server can send an Access-Challenge request to the AAA client to request a new password.

Figure 2-6 demonstrates a RADIUS exchange between an AAA client and AAA server.

Figure 2-6   *A RADIUS Exchange*

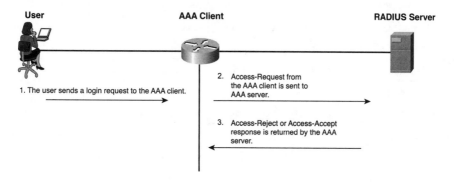

Authorization within RADIUS is done in conjunction with authentication. As a server returns an Access-Accept message, it also includes the list of AV pairs that the user is authorized for. Table 2-3 lists the RADIUS AV pairs (nonproprietary) supported in Cisco IOS up to version 12.2. These AV pairs are discussed in further detail in Appendix A.

Table 2-3   *RADIUS AV Pairs (Nonproprietary)*

Number	IETF Attribute	11.1	11.2	11.3	11.3 AA	11.3T	12.0	12.1	12.2
1	User-Name	yes	yes	yes	yes	yes	yes	yes	yes
2	User-Password	yes	yes	yes	yes	yes	yes	yes	yes
3	CHAP-Password	yes	yes	yes	yes	yes	yes	yes	yes
4	NAS-IP Address	yes	yes	yes	yes	yes	yes	yes	yes
5	NAS-Port	yes	yes	yes	yes	yes	yes	yes	yes
6	Service-Type	yes	yes	yes	yes	yes	yes	yes	yes
7	Framed-Protocol	yes	yes	yes	yes	yes	yes	yes	yes
8	Framed-IP-Address	yes	yes	yes	yes	yes	yes	yes	yes
9	Framed-IP-Netmask	yes	yes	yes	yes	yes	yes	yes	yes
10	Framed-Routing	yes	yes	yes	yes	yes	yes	yes	yes
11	Filter-Id	yes	yes	yes	yes	yes	yes	yes	yes
12	Framed-MTU	yes	yes	yes	yes	yes	yes	yes	yes
13	Framed-Compression	yes	yes	yes	yes	yes	yes	yes	yes
14	Login-IP-Host	yes	yes	yes	yes	yes	yes	yes	yes
15	Login-Service	yes	yes	yes	yes	yes	yes	yes	yes
16	Login-TCP-Port	yes	yes	yes	yes	yes	yes	yes	yes
18	Reply-Message	yes	yes	yes	yes	yes	yes	yes	yes
19	Callback-Number	no	no	no	no	no	no	yes	yes
20	Callback-ID	no	no	no	no	no	no	no	no
22	Framed-Route	yes	yes	yes	yes	yes	yes	yes	yes
23	Framed-IPX-Network	no	no	no	no	no	no	no	no
24	State	yes	yes	yes	yes	yes	yes	yes	yes
25	Class	yes	yes	yes	yes	yes	yes	yes	yes
26	Vendor-Specific	yes	yes	yes	yes	yes	yes	yes	yes
27	Session-Timeout	yes	yes	yes	yes	yes	yes	yes	yes
28	Idle-Timeout	yes	yes	yes	yes	yes	yes	yes	yes
29	Termination-Action	no	no	no	no	no	no	no	no

Table 2-3   *RADIUS AV Pairs (Nonproprietary) (Continued)*

Number	IETF Attribute	11.1	11.2	11.3	11.3 AA	11.3T	12.0	12.1	12.2
30	Called-Station-Id	yes	yes	yes	yes	yes	yes	yes	yes
31	Calling-Station-Id	yes	yes	yes	yes	yes	yes	yes	yes
32	NAS-Identifier	no	no	no	no	no	no	no	yes
33	Proxy-State	no	no	no	no	no	no	no	no
34	Login-LAT-Service	yes	yes	yes	yes	yes	yes	yes	yes
35	Login-LAT-Node	no	no	no	no	no	no	no	yes
36	Login-LAT-Group	no	no	no	no	no	no	no	no
37	Framed-AppleTalk-Link	no	no	no	no	no	no	no	no
38	Framed-AppleTalk-Network	no	no	no	no	no	no	no	no
39	Framed-AppleTalk-Zone	no	no	no	no	no	no	no	no
40	Acct-Status-Type	yes	yes	yes	yes	yes	yes	yes	yes
41	Acct-Delay-Time	yes	yes	yes	yes	yes	yes	yes	yes
42	Acct-Input-Octets	yes	yes	yes	yes	yes	yes	yes	yes
43	Acct-Output-Octets	yes	yes	yes	yes	yes	yes	yes	yes
44	Acct-Session-Id	yes	yes	yes	yes	yes	yes	yes	yes
45	Acct-Authentic	yes	yes	yes	yes	yes	yes	yes	yes
46	Acct-Session-Time	yes	yes	yes	yes	yes	yes	yes	yes
47	Acct-Input-Packets	yes	yes	yes	yes	yes	yes	yes	yes
48	Acct-Output-Packets	yes	yes	yes	yes	yes	yes	yes	yes
49	Acct-Terminate-Cause	no	no	no	yes	yes	yes	yes	yes
50	Acct-Multi-Session-Id	no	yes	yes	yes	yes	yes	yes	yes
51	Acct-Link-Count	no	yes	yes	yes	yes	yes	yes	yes
52	Acct-Input-Gigawords	no	no	no	no	no	no	no	no
53	Acct-Output-Gigawords	no	no	no	no	no	no	no	no
55	Event-Timestamp	no	no	no	no	no	no	no	yes
60	CHAP-Challenge	yes	yes	yes	yes	yes	yes	yes	yes
61	NAS-Port-Type	yes	yes	yes	yes	yes	yes	yes	yes
62	Port-Limit	yes	yes	yes	yes	yes	yes	yes	yes
63	Login-LAT-Port	no	no	no	no	no	no	no	no

continues

Table 2-3   *RADIUS AV Pairs (Nonproprietary) (Continued)*

Number	IETF Attribute	11.1	11.2	11.3	11.3 AA	11.3T	12.0	12.1	12.2
64	Tunnel-Type	no	no	no	no	no	no	yes	yes
65	Tunnel-Medium-Type	no	no	no	no	no	no	yes	yes
66	Tunnel-Client-Endpoint	no	no	no	no	no	no	yes	yes
67	Tunnel-Server-Endpoint	no	no	no	no	no	no	yes	yes
68	Acct-Tunnel-Connection-ID	no	no	no	no	no	no	yes	yes
69	Tunnel-Password	no	no	no	no	no	no	yes	yes
70	ARAP-Password	no	no	no	no	no	no	no	no
71	ARAP-Features	no	no	no	no	no	no	no	no
72	ARAP-Zone-Access	no	no	no	no	no	no	no	no
73	ARAP-Security	no	no	no	no	no	no	no	no
74	ARAP-Security-Data	no	no	no	no	no	no	no	no
75	Password-Retry	no	no	no	no	no	no	no	no
76	Prompt	no	no	no	no	no	no	yes	yes
77	Connect-Info	no	no	no	no	no	no	no	yes
78	Configuration-Token	no	no	no	no	no	no	no	no
79	EAP-Message	no	no	no	no	no	no	no	no
80	Message-Authenticator	no	no	no	no	no	no	no	no
81	Tunnel-Private-Group-ID	no	no	no	no	no	no	no	no
82	Tunnel-Assignment-ID	no	no	no	no	no	no	yes	yes
83	Tunnel-Preference	no	no	no	no	no	no	no	yes
84	ARAP-Challenge-Response	no	no	no	no	no	no	no	no
85	Acct-Interim-Interval	no	no	no	no	no	no	yes	yes
86	Acct-Tunnel-Packets-Lost	no	no	no	no	no	no	no	no
87	NAS-Port-ID	no	no	no	no	no	no	no	no
88	Framed-Pool	no	no	no	no	no	no	no	no
90	Tunnel-Client-Auth-ID	no	no	no	no	no	no	no	yes
91	Tunnel-Server-Auth-ID	no	no	no	no	no	no	no	yes
200	IETF-Token-Immediate	no	no	no	no	no	no	no	no

RADIUS Accounting

RADIUS accounting is performed by sending messages at the start and the stop of a session. These messages include information about the session. Information that might be included includes time, packets, bytes, and so on. These messages are sent using UDP port 1813. The accounting process for RADIUS is seen in RFC 2866. The messages that are sent between the AAA server and the AAA client are Accounting-Request and Accounting-Response. The basic process of RADIUS accounting is seen in Figure 2-7.

Figure 2-7   *RADIUS Accounting*

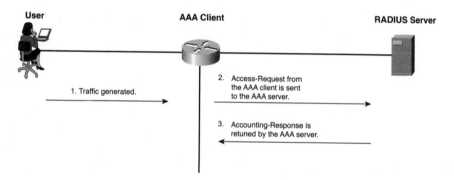

During this process, the accounting information is also sent via AV pairs. The RADIUS AV pairs supported in Cisco IOS up to version 12.2 are also included in Table 2-3.

Summary

TACACS+ is a proprietary protocol implemented by Cisco Systems to facilitate the AAA model in Cisco devices. It is one of a number of choices available for AAA communication between an AAA client and AAA server. TACACS+ is TCP based and separates each function of authentication, authorization, and accounting.

RADIUS is an IETF-standardized protocol that is also implemented in Cisco devices to facilitate the AAA model communications between an AAA server and AAA client. RADIUS uses UDP as its transport protocol and relies on the protocol itself to resend and recover from lost or missing data. RADIUS does not separate authentication and authorization; however, it does separate accounting. RADIUS typically provides more complete accounting capabilities than TACACS+.

As you continue implementing a secure network using AAA, you are often faced with the decision of which protocol to use. In some situations, you have no option. As you proceed though this book, keep in mind the functions of these protocols as you implement them in chapters to come.

End Notes

[1] Cisco Systems, *Securing Cisco IOS Security Configuration Guide*, Cisco Systems, Inc., p. SC-501.

[2] Cisco Systems, *Securing Cisco IOS Security Configuration Guide*, Cisco Systems, Inc., p. SC-510.

In this chapter, you learn the following topics:

- Local authentication
- Authentication configurations using Cisco Secure ACS for Windows Server and Cisco Secure ACS Solution Engine
- Debugging authentication
- Authentication command references

## CHAPTER 3

Authentication Configuration on Cisco Routers

Authentication, authorization, and accounting (AAA) is an integral component in today's networks. AAA is configurable on most Cisco products and can play an important role in securing and managing Cisco networks.

This chapter provides a configuration overview to the authentication component of AAA, as well as configuration examples of some of the authentication methods discussed. In addition, it includes a discussion of command references for Cisco IOS Release 12.0 through 12.3 to help you to locate the right commands to use on your network devices.

NOTE   As you read this chapter, note that Cisco products support different methods for performing AAA authentication. These methods include the following:

- **Local Authentication**—No external user database is used in the authentication, and all user passwords are stored on the router.

- **Cisco Secure ACS for Windows Server**—An external server is used along with the TACACS+ or RADIUS protocol to communicate between the user database and the Cisco router for authentication.

- **Cisco Secure ACS Solution Engine**—This is similar to the previous bullet point; however, the Solution Engine is a dedicated appliance.

Local Authentication

Local authentication is a configuration that is available on Cisco products in which the AAA service is contained on the device itself. In this situation, a username and password are created and contained on the device. While this is a simple configuration, it is not very scalable. This configuration is common in smaller networks.

To configure a Cisco router for local authentication, you must perform the following tasks:

Step 1 Secure access to privileged exec and configuration modes for the vty, asynchronous, auxiliary, and TTY ports. Although this is not actually part of the AAA process, this must be enabled prior to enabling AAA.

Step 2 Enable AAA on the router.

Step 3 Configure AAA on the router.

Step 4 Secure access to privileged exec and configuration modes for the vty, asynchronous, auxiliary, and TTY ports.

The focus of this chapter is on AAA authentication; therefore, you need to understand how to secure access to each of the following points of access:

- EXEC (both user and privileged mode)
- vty ports
- asynchronous lines
- auxiliary ports
- TTY ports

In this chapter, you learn how to configure the EXEC mode as well as the vty, auxiliary, and TTY ports for authentication.

Enabling AAA on the Router

AAA is a framework or model for security and authentication. To enable the AAA process on a Cisco router, you must enable the AAA model. This creates a configuration location within the configuration for AAA.

When you enable AAA, it forces the Cisco router to override every other authentication method configured. This might cause you to lose connectivity to the management session that you are using to configure AAA. This might force you into an unwanted password recovery procedure.

To enable AAA, enter the following command in global configuration mode of a Cisco router:

```
router(config)#aaa new-model
```

You can disable AAA functionality with a single command. To disable AAA, use the following command in global configuration mode:

```
router(config)#no aaa new-model
```

Method Lists

From this point, you use a method list to configure what method to use AAA in. A method list is a list that defines the point of authentication and the method to be used. Figure 3-1 displays two different modes: character mode and packet mode. If you access the command-line interface, you are using character mode. If you access the network as a user through a PPP link, for example, you are using packet mode. Figure 3-1 shows the AAA command elements that are used in each of these modes.

Figure 3-1   *Packet and Character Modes*

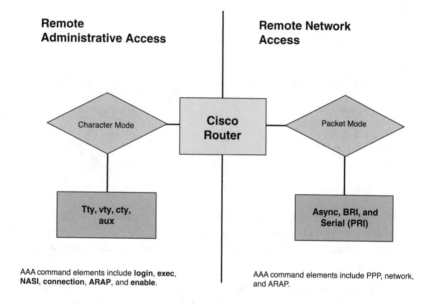

To begin authentication configuration, you define a method list that protects administrative access to the console port of a Cisco router. The console port of a Cisco router is distinguished as **Line Console 0.** Example 3-1 shows a basic starting configuration. In this configuration, note that an enable password and enable secret password are configured. Additionally, a username and password have been created.

Example 3-1   *Basic Configuration*

```
!
version 12.2
<text omitted>
!
hostname router
```

continues

Example 3-1 *Basic Configuration (Continued)*

```
!
enable secret san-fran
enable password cisco
!
username admin password cisco
!
!
interface Ethernet0/0
 description ******* INSIDE
ip address 10.0.1.2 255.255.255.0
!
interface Ethernet1/0
 description ******* OUTSIDE
ip address 172.30.1.2 255.255.255.0
!
line con 0
 transport input none
login
password pa55w0rd
line aux 0
line vty 0 4
 password cisco
 login
!
```

At this point in the configuration, AAA has not been enabled. Line Console 0 is configured to authenticate using the password **pa55w0rd.** After the AAA process is enabled, the username and password of **admin/cisco** are used, and the password configured on the line is overridden.

To enable AAA, enter the **aaa new-model** command in global configuration mode. After AAA has been enabled, configure a method list to define what mode or command element and what method of authentication are to be performed.

The syntax for a method list created on a Cisco router is shown here in a generic form:

```
router(config)# aaa authentication service {default | list-name} method1 [method2]
```

The *service* option can be one of the following:

- **ARAP**—Performs authentication for AppleTalk Remote Access.
- **Enable**—Performs authentication of users attempting to access privileged level on the device.
- **Login**—Performs authentication of users accessing the console of the device. This is done prior to the Enable authentication.

- **NASI**—This is for authentication of NetWare Asynchronous Serviced Interface (NASI) clients connecting through the access server.

- **PPP**—This is for authentication on serial interfaces using the PPP protocol.

In the configuration shown in the code before the preceding bulleted list, it is the console port that is going to be secured. For this method, use the **Login** service. You also specify **Login** for Telnet through the vty ports, as well as access the aux port.

The second option to be determined is the name of the list. This binds the list to an interface or line. This list must be configured; however, you do have the option to choose the **default** option. This option is applied to all lines on which you do not specify a more specific list name. For example, Figure 3-2 shows the console port, five vty ports (line vty 0 4), and auxiliary ports. A generic method list named **TEST1** is created along with the **default** list. If this **TEST1** list is applied to Line Console 0, all other lines are automatically assigned the method list. Note that in Figure 3-2, a specific method list is not applied to any other line.

Figure 3-2 *Application of Method Lists*

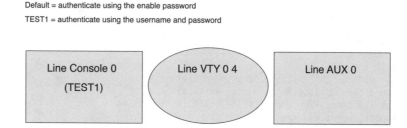

Finally, you must select the method of authentication. The method can be TACACS+, RADIUS, or local. You can also configure multiple methods. In this fashion, you give yourself a backup. It is always a good idea to use local authentication as a second method in the event that the AAA server becomes unavailable on the network; however, you can use another RADIUS or TACACS+ server.

The completed configuration includes the following method lists:

```
aaa authentication login default enable
aaa authentication login TEST1 local
```

The first list, **default**, specifies that the enable password is used for authentication. The second list specifies that the username and password that have been configured are to be used. At this point, the enable password is used everywhere because the more specific list has not been specified on any line. To make the vty ports authenticate using the username of admin and password cisco, you need to apply the **TEST1** method list to line vty 0 4. To do so, use the **login authentication** configuration command.

The following statement applies the **TEST1** method of authentication to line vty 0 4:

```
line vty 0 4
login authentication TEST1
```

To further configure the authentication on this device, another method list has been created for the service **login.** This method list is named **is-in**, and the method of authentication used is the local username and password. This is applied to line con 0.

The additional command statements are as follows:

```
router(config)#aaa authentication login is-in local
router(config)#line con 0
router(config-line)#login authentication is-in
```

The final configuration resembles the configuration in Example 3-2. Note that although a login statement and a password are still applied to line vty 0 4, as well as line con 0, the login authentication statement in AAA overrides this password.

Example 3-2 *Finished AAA Authentication Configuration*

```
!
version 12.2
!
hostname router
!
aaa new-model
!
!
aaa authentication login default enable
aaa authentication login admins-in local
aaa authentication login is-in local
enable secret san-fran
enable password cisco
!
username admin password cisco

interface Ethernet0/0
 description ******* INSIDE
 ip address 10.0.1.2 255.255.255.0
!
interface Ethernet1/0
 description ******* OUTSIDE
 ip address 172.30.1.2 255.255.255.0
!
!
!
line con 0
password pa55w0rd
login authentication is-in
!
line aux 0
```

Example 3-2 *Finished AAA Authentication Configuration (Continued)*

```
!
line vty 0 4
 password cisco
 login authentication admins-in
!
end
```

To recap this configuration, AAA has been enabled, and a username and password have been created locally to this router. For users attempting to access the command-line interface via Telnet or console 0, they are authenticated using the **admins-in** method list or the **is-in** method list, which specifies the local username and password. When authenticated, the user attempts to access privileged EXEC mode by typing the command **enable.** Now, the method list **default** prompts for yet another password, requiring the admin to enter the line password. All other points of access take the **default** method list, which specifies the use of the **enable** password for authentication.

Authentication Configurations Using Cisco Secure ACS for Windows Server and Cisco Secure ACS Solution Engine

Other configurations and implementations of authentication might differ from the preceding example. The example is not intended to provide a complete solution and guide to configuring authentication. Rather, it is to assist in the understanding of how AAA is enabled on a Cisco router, how a method list is designed and implemented, and how you can read an AAA configuration.

For additional information on configuring AAA on Cisco routers, including examples of authorization and accounting, see the Cisco IOS Security Configuration Guide, Release 12.2 at Cisco.com. More information on the commands and configuration of commands in Cisco IOS Software Release 12.0 are available in the "Authentication Command References" section of this chapter.

Debugging Authentication

Certain debug commands can be enabled on a Cisco router to assist in the troubleshooting of authentication issues. Example 3-3 is the output from the debug text when an administrator accesses the console of the Cisco router with the configuration seen in this chapter. The command that enables the debug is as follows:

```
debug aaa authentication
```

To disable this debug, use the "no" form of the command:

```
no debug aaa authentication
```

You can also use the all-encompassing **undebug all** statement; the output is shown in Example 3-3.

Example 3-3 *Debug Output for Login: Debug AAA Authentication*

```
User Access Verification

Username: admin

7w4d: AAA: parse name=tty0 idb type=-1 tty=-1
7w4d: AAA: name=tty0 flags=0x11 type=4 shelf=0 slot=0 adapter=0 port=0 channel=0
7w4d: AAA/MEMORY: create_user (0x346934) user='NULL' ruser='NULL' ds0=0 port='tty0'
   rem_addr='async' authen_type=ASCII service=LOGIN priv=1 initial_task_id='0'
7w4d: AAA/AUTHEN/START (1108173303): port='tty0' list='is-in' action=LOGIN
   service=LOGIN
7w4d: AAA/AUTHEN/START (1108173303): found list is-in
7w4d: AAA/AUTHEN/START (1108173303): Method=LOCAL
7w4d: AAA/AUTHEN (1108173303): status = GETUSER
Password:
7w4d: AAA/AUTHEN/CONT (1108173303): continue_login (user='(undef)')
7w4d: AAA/AUTHEN (1108173303): status = GETUSER
7w4d: AAA/AUTHEN/CONT (1108173303): Method=LOCAL
7w4d: AAA/AUTHEN (1108173303): status = GETPASS

router>
7w4d: AAA/AUTHEN/CONT (1108173303): continue_login (user='admin')
7w4d: AAA/AUTHEN (1108173303): status = GETPASS
7w4d: AAA/AUTHEN/CONT (1108173303): Method=LOCAL
7w4d: AAA/AUTHEN (1108173303): status = PASS
```

From this point, the user attempts to access privileged EXEC mode and again is authenticated. In Example 3-4, you can see that the user admin is known after the login authentication; however, the enable authentication method is using the default list.

Example 3-4 *Debug Output for Enable: Debug AAA Authentication*

```
router>en
Password:
7w4d: AAA/MEMORY: dup_user (0x199254) user='admin' ruser='NULL' port='tty0'
rem_addr='async' authen_type=ASCII service=ENABLE priv=15 source='AAA dup enable'
7w4d: AAA/AUTHEN/START (332554494): port='tty0' list='' action=LOGIN service=ENABLE
7w4d: AAA/AUTHEN/START (332554494): using "default" list
7w4d: AAA/AUTHEN/START (332554494): Method=ENABLE
7w4d: AAA/AUTHEN (332554494): status = GETPASS
```

Example 3-4 *Debug Output for Enable: Debug AAA Authentication (Continued)*

```
r1#
7w4d: AAA/AUTHEN/CONT (332554494): continue_login (user='(undef)')
7w4d: AAA/AUTHEN (332554494): status = GETPASS
7w4d: AAA/AUTHEN/CONT (332554494): Method=ENABLE
7w4d: AAA/AUTHEN (332554494): status = PASS
```

These are examples of successful authentication attempts.

Authentication Command References

For the most current authentication command references, refer to the Cisco IOS documentation. Since the writing of this book, Cisco IOS Release 12.3 has been released. Rather than providing a command reference, for your convenience the following URLs are provided for the 12.0 and higher AAA command references.

- **Cisco IOS Release 12.0**—http://www.cisco.com/univercd/cc/td/doc/product/ software/ios120/12cgcr/secur_r/srprt1/index.htm

- **Cisco IOS Release 12.1**—http://www.cisco.com/univercd/cc/td/doc/product/ software/ios121/121cgcr/secur_r/srprt1/index.htm

- **Cisco IOS Release 12.2**—http://www.cisco.com/univercd/cc/td/doc/product/ software/ios122/122cgcr/fsecur_r/faaacr/srfathen.htm

- **Cisco IOS Release 12.3**—http://www.cisco.com/univercd/cc/td/doc/product/ software/ios123/123cgcr/secur_r/sec_01g.htm#1011518

Summary

It is the prospect of this chapter to enable you as a security administrator to be able to deploy AAA authentication with a basic understanding of the configuration of authentication. In the subsequent chapters, you will see the capabilities of adding more functionality to your AAA configuration by adding an AAA server such as Cisco Secure Access Control Server (CSACS), Cisco Secure Solution Engine, or Cisco Access Registrar. Also in these chapters, you will see authorization and accounting added to the AAA configuration.

Enterprise AAA and Cisco Secure Access Control Server

In this chapter, you learn the following topics:

- Cisco Secure Access Control Server software and versions
- The Cisco Secure Solution Engine

## CHAPTER 4

Enterprise Authentication Servers

Numerous enterprise level authentication servers are on the market today. Popular among these are Funk's Steel-Belted RADIUS server, Livingston Enterprises' RADIUS Authentication Billing Manager, and Merit Networks' RADIUS servers. While these are reputable companies with popular products, they lack the ability to combine both the TACACS+ and RADIUS protocols into a single box solution. Fortunately, the Cisco Secure ACS for Windows Server (ACS) is a one-stop solution for authentication, authorization, and accounting (AAA) via both TACACS+ and RADIUS. This product is the focus of this chapter.

Cisco Secure Access Control Server Software and Versions

ACS provides a highly scalable, centralized user access control framework. Versions of ACS number from version 2.0 through 3.2, which is the most current version. With each release of ACS, more support has been added for multiple vendors' AAA implementations, as well as external database support. ACS has a browser driven interface that makes configuration a simple task in a centrally located database.

ACS provides for the authentication of Cisco routers, switches, firewalls, and wireless access points. In addition to the Cisco products that ACS supports, ACS also performs authentication for Ascend, Juniper, Nortel, iPass, and other devices that support Internet Engineering Task Force (IETF) implementations of RADIUS.

Cisco Secure Access Control Servers began with what was called Easy ACS version 1.0. Since that time the ACS product line has undergone numerous facelifts and functionality enhancements to create a product that is able to grasp the leading edge in authentication, authorization, and accounting technologies.

In the following sections, you find information about specific versions of the ACS product line.

Cisco Secure ACS for Windows Server Version 2.0

The versions of ACS discussed in this chapter begin with 2.0. ACS 2.0 for Windows NT supported the following features:

- Simultaneous TACACS+ and RADIUS support for a flexible solution
- HTML/Java graphical user interface (GUI) that simplifies and distributes configuration for user profiles, group profiles, and ACS configuration
- Help and online documentation included for quick problem solving
- Group administration of users for maximum flexibility and to facilitate enforcement and changes of security policies
- Virtual private network (VPN) support available at the origination and termination of VPN (L2F) tunnels
- Import mechanism to rapidly import a large number of users
- Hash-indexed flat file database support for high-speed transaction processing
- Windows NT database support to leverage and consolidate Windows NT username and password management
- Windows NT single login
- Runs on Windows NT standalone, PDC, and BDC servers
- Password support that includes Challenge Handshake Authentication Protocol (CHAP), Password Authentication Protocol (PAP), and AppleTalk Remote Access (ARA)
- Token card server support for Security Dynamics and Axent
- Token caching for ISDN terminal adapters of Security Dynamics tokens
- Time-of-day and day-of-week access restrictions
- User restrictions based on remote address calling line identification (CLID)
- Disabling an account on a specific date
- Disabling an account after N failed attempts
- Viewing logged-in user list
- Windows NT Performance Monitor support for real-time statistic viewing
- Accounting and audit information stored in CSV format for convenient import into billing applications
- Simple upgrade from Cisco Secure Easy ACS v1.0

Cisco Secure ACS for Windows Server Version 2.1

The next version of ACS made available was version 2.1. The following enhancements were made:

- User/group assignment was now handled correctly by CSutil. This was a problem in the earlier release of ACS.

- Open DataBase Connectivity (ODBC) threads = 1 (previously was a .reg patch). Set the Access Database engine to single thread mode.

- Corrected grammar in the New-Pin mode prompt. This was also an issue in the earlier release.

- Remote Administration was added.

- Supplementary User ID fields were added.

- Password support that includes Challenge Handshake Authentication Protocol (CHAP), Password Authentication Protocol (PAP), and AppleTalk Remote Access Password (ARAP) was added.

- Support for SafeWord and CRYPTOCard Token Servers was added.

- The User and Group MAX sessions configuration options were added.

- Configurable character string stripping was added.

- Authentication forwarding was added.

- Configurable graphical user interface (GUI) was added.

- RDBMS synchronization was added.

- Database replication was added.

- System/database backup was added.

- Dialed number identification service (DNIS) support was added.

- This version was also Year 2000 compliant.

Cisco Secure ACS for Windows Server Version 2.3

When version 2.3 was deployed, the following new features were added:

- Password aging was added to control user password security.

- IP pools were added to provide for IP address assignment based on an address pool.

- User Changeable Passwords were implemented through a new module that would allow users to browse to a URL and change their password.

- Support for the Microsoft Commercial Internet System Lightweight Directory Access Protocol (MCIS LDAP).

- Support for Open DataBase Connectivity (ODBC)–compliant databases.

- Support for Microsoft's version of the Challenge Handshake Authentication Protocol (MS-CHAP).

- Per-user Advanced Terminal Access Controller Access Control System Plus (TACACS+) and/or Remote Authentication Dial-In User Service (RADIUS) attributes.

- Multilevel administration.

- CSMonitor service was added to keep an eye on the services that were crucial to the functions of ACS.

- ACS Backup and Restore functionality was built in to provide for the backup and restoration of ACS.

- The ability to import password files from a UNIX-based device was added.

- Network Device Groups (NDGs) were added to break AAA clients into groups to ease the management of multiple AAA clients.

- Logging and reporting enhancements were added to this version.

- The ability to upgrade from all previous versions of Cisco Secure ACS for Windows NT was added.

- Support for the null password requirement of Voice over IP (VoIP) was also added to this version.

Cisco Secure ACS for Windows Server Version 2.4 and 2.5

Later, a version 2.4 and 2.5 were released. In an effort to provide support for Windows 2000, release 2.5 was the first version that could be run on a Windows 2000 server.

Cisco Secure ACS for Windows Server Version 2.6

Version 2.6 is a Windows NT/2000 release that included added support for the following:

- A wider range of token servers, such as Security Dynamics, Inc.; ACE/Server version 4.1 and ACE/Client version 1.1 for Windows 2000; CRYPTOAdmin version 5.0 (build 27); Axent Defender versions 4.0.3 and 4.1.0; and Secure Computing SafeWord version 5.1.1.

- Support for Novell 4.6 for Windows NT and Novell client 4.7 for Windows 2000.

- Windows 2000 Service Pack 1 is required and 128-bit encryption with Microsoft Dial-Up Networking was added.

The last revision of the 2.6 version was 2.6.4. This is still widely used in today's enterprise networks.

Cisco Secure ACS for Windows Server Version 3.0

The next version in the ACS product line was version 3.0. ACS version 3.0 was designed for Windows NT/2000. ACS version 3.0 introduced some new functions. These functions are included in the following list:

- 802.1x support was added.
- Extensible Authentication Protocol-Message Digest 5 (EAP-MD5) support was added.
- Extensible Authentication Protocol-Transport Layer Security (EAP-TLS) support was added.
- Command authorization sets were added.
- Microsoft Challenge Authentication Handshake Protocol (MS-CHAP) version 2 support was added.

These were considered to be the major features that were added. Other minor features were added to ACS that deem mentioning. These include the following:

- Per-user access control lists
- Shared Network Access Restriction (NAR)
- Wildcards in the NAR
- Multiple devices per AAA client configuration
- Multiple Lightweight Directory Access Protocol (LDAP) lookups and LDAP failover
- User-defined RADIUS vendor-specific attributes

Many of these features are configured throughout the course of this book.

Cisco Secure ACS for Windows Server Version 3.1

The next version available was ACS version 3.1. ACS version 3.1 added the following features:

- **Protected Extensible Authentication Protocol-Generic Token Cards (PEAP-GTC) support**—PEAP provides stronger security, greater extensibility, and support for one-time token authentication and password aging. The goal of our PEAP implementation is to replace Lightweight Extensible Authentication Protocol (LEAP) client/server user authentication services with the standards-based, non-proprietary PEAP protocol for wireless user authentication. PEAP provides enhanced security and richer extensibility of end user databases than can be provided with LEAP.

- **Secure Sockets Layer (SSL) support for administrative access**—Administrative access to the Cisco Secure ACS HTML interface can be secured with SSL. This security enhancement provides both certificate-based server authentication and encrypted tunnel support so that administrative access is encrypted with SSL.

- **CHPASS improvements**—Cisco Secure ACS allows you to control whether network administrators can change passwords during Telnet sessions hosted by TACACS+ AAA clients.

- **Improved IP Pool addressing**—Cisco Secure ACS uses the IETF RADIUS class attribute as an additional index for user sessions. This reduces the possibility of allocating an IP address that is already in use but incorrectly reported to Cisco Secure ACS as released.

- **Network device search**—You can search for a configured network device based on the device name, IP address, type (AAA client or AAA server), and network device group. This feature is particularly useful if you are managing several network devices.

- **Improved Public Key Infrastructure (PKI) support**—During EAP-TLS authentication, Cisco Secure ACS can perform binary comparison of the certificate received from an end user client to user certificates stored in LDAP directories.

- **EAP proxy enhancements**—Cisco Secure ACS supports LEAP and EAP-TLS proxy to other RADIUS or external databases using EAP over standard RADIUS. Previous versions of Cisco Secure ACS relied on LEAP proxy using MS-CHAP over RADIUS proxy, making it more difficult to scale over an extended range of external user databases.

- **Cisco Management Center application support**—Cisco Secure ACS provides a consolidated administrative TACACS+ control framework for many Cisco security management tools, such as CiscoWorks VPN/Security Management Solution (VMS) and CiscoWorks Management Centers.

ACS version 3.1 also addressed a highly requested feature of being able to access the management interface from outside a firewall. In version 3.1, a function that uses the domain name and translates the IP address in the packet was added.

In addition to these additions and changes, Cisco also changed the way that ACS supports token servers. In previous versions of ACS, token server support was based on proprietary interfaces. In ACS version 3.1.1, all except for the RSA SecurID are supported using RADIUS.

NOTE   CRYPTOCard OTP interface was included in version 3.0; however, it uses RADIUS rather than the CRYPTOCard proprietary protocol interface. In 3.1.1, the CRYPTOCard proprietary protocol interface was added.

Cisco also made enhancements to the database replication functionality so that each ACS requires a handshake from the primary ACS using the secret key for the primary device.

Other changes made included the use of 128-bit encryption to communicate with ACS. This affected remote logging as well as the User Changeable Password (UCP) module. You would need to upgrade to the UCP module provided with ACS version 3.1.

Cisco Secure ACS for Windows Server Version 3.2

The next version of ACS was version 3.2. This is the most current version of ACS. The features and functions added to ACS version 3.2 are seen in the following list:

- In ACS version 3.2, provisions were made for the support of PEAP with EAP-MS-CHAPv2. EAP-MS-CHAP is implemented according to the RFC. EAP-MS-CHAPv2 protocol is implemented as an internal EAP type, but only inside PEAP, as well as extensive EAP-TLS support.

- Version 3.1 supported PEAP-GTC; however, MS-PEAP has many differences. ACS version 3.2 supports EAP-MS-CHAP inside PEAP. In addition to this support, provisions for PEAP version negotiations have been added.

- ACS version 3.2 also includes EAP negotiation for the second EAP type. EAP-GTC and EAP-MS-CHAPv2 are supported simultaneously inside PEAP. If both internal EAP types are configured, ACS starts with EAP-MS-CHAPv2.

- Additional Aironet support has been included in ACS version 3.2 to include extended client support and PEAP support to users created in the ACS internal database.

Other changes to ACS version 3.2 are seen in the following list:

- LDAP multithreading
- Machine authentication support
- EAP mixed configurations
- Accounting support for Aironet
- Downloadable access control; lists for virtual private network (VPN) users

For more information regarding the functional specifications of ACS, see the release notes accessible through http://www.cisco.com/go/acs.

Cisco Secure Solution Engine

An appliance version of Cisco Secure ACS exists. The Cisco Secure Solution Engine is a rack mountable, dedicated platform that provides nearly the same functionality as the Windows versions of Cisco Secure ACS. The Cisco Secure Solution Engine version 3.2 is a hardened operating system that is built on the Windows 2000 kernel; however, you do not have the ability to connect a mouse and keyboard to it. Only the services that are necessary for the Solution Engine to function are enabled, and you do not have access to the file system. In addition to the kernel being locked down, the ports that are open are also restricted to those that are required by the Solution Engine to perform its required task.

Certain features are a little different with the appliance as opposed to the software versions of Cisco Secure ACS. These include the following:

- **Authentication**—Authentication against Windows domain requires an agent to be running on the domain controller. A new ancillary software called a *remote agent* is used for this. Authentication against ODBC source is not supported.

- **Remote logging**—Accounting information is logged to a remote Windows or Solaris server.

- **User database synchronization**—User DB synchronization with ODBC source is not supported. Instead, the administrator can configure the Cisco Secure ACS appliance to synchronize its user DB with a CSV file on an FTP server.

- **ODBC logging**—ODBC logging is not supported. You should use remote logging instead.

- **Backup/restore**—Backup/restore is performed to the remote FTP server.

- **Diagnostics**—A package of gathered diagnostics is sent to the FTP server.

The Cisco Secure Solution Engine is a rack mountable 1U box with an Intel ISP 1100 motherboard, 3.06 GHz Pentium 4 processor with 1 GB memory, and two 10/100 Ethernet interfaces. The Solution Engine also has a 40 GB Integrated Drive Electronics (IDE) hard drive, a floppy drive, and a CD-ROM. A serial interface is also present. The parallel port, video, keyboard, and mouse controllers are not used.

Summary

The Cisco Secure product line has undergone massive improvements and renovations since the initial release dates. With each new version, more and more functionality and capabilities are being built in to provide a high-powered solution to enterprise customers for use in authentication, authorization, and accounting services.

In upcoming chapters of this book, you are given the opportunity to install and deploy an ACS, become familiar with the interface, and explore the multitude of configuration options within its GUI interface.

In this chapter, you learn the following topics:

- What is ACS?
- How to obtain ACS
- Requirements to run ACS
- Installing ACS
- Reinstalling ACS
- Positioning ACS

## CHAPTER 5

Deploying Cisco Secure Access Control Server for Windows Server

Welcome to Cisco Secure Access Control Server, authentication, authorization, and accounting management. In today's networks, it's not good enough to simply install a network; you must secure it as well. As you progress through this book, you learn how to deploy and manage a Cisco Secure Access Control Server (CSACS). You also examine some working examples that can be used as a guideline in your day-to-day management of ACS.

In this chapter, you prepare for and deploy an ACS device in your network. You learn where to obtain the ACS software, the required resources, and the process of installing ACS on a server in your network.

What Is ACS?

ACS is a very powerful tool that enables network security administrators to centrally manage authentication, authorization, and accounting (AAA) on a wide range of Cisco platforms. ACS allows network access devices to act as an AAA client to the server. ACS has many benefits and features, which include some of the following:

- **Automatic service monitoring**—Automatic service monitoring watches the process that runs ACS and alerts the administrator as well as restarts these critical services.

- **Lightweight Directory Access Protocol (LDAP) support**—LDAP support includes user's certificate authority (CA) certificates that are stored in remote LDAP directories when using Active Directory, using the Windows external user database feature. The LDAP external user database feature support is limited to PAP, ASCII, and OTP protocols.

- **Time-of-day and day-of-week restrictions**—Time of day and day of week restrictions allow you, the administrator, to determine when users are permitted to access certain resources on the network.

- **Virtual private network (VPN) authentication and wireless support**—With VPN and wireless support you can terminate VPN connections and authenticate users to ACS and employ Lightweight Extensible Authentication Protocol (LEAP) authentication using the RADIUS protocol with wireless access points.

- **External database synchronization**—Support for external database synchronization allows you to use an existing authentication database rather than spend valuable time creating a new one in ACS. Users found in an external database can be created in the CiscoSecure Database; however, they are not deleted when the users are removed from the external database. Although this is not a true external database synchronization, it can be looked at as an initial external database synchronization.

As you begin to deploy ACS, keep in mind that there is not a "one solution fits all" answer to the deployment of ACS. The deployment of your ACS is dependent on the size of your network as well as the location of the server in relationship to the locations of the clients requesting authentication. Keep in mind that no two networks are exactly the same, and you must take this approach when it comes to your deployment.

How to Obtain ACS

ACS is available as a trial download to registered users on the Cisco website at http://www.cisco.com/go/acs. You should see your local Cisco representative if you are interested in purchasing ACS for use in your network.

Requirements to Run ACS Version 3.2

There are many software requirements for running ACS. The first is that a supported browser must be installed on the system from which you are going to manage ACS. ACS was tested with Microsoft Internet Explorer 5.0, 5.5, and 6.0.

NOTE   I personally use Microsoft Internet Explorer 6.0 with no known issues.

ACS has also been tested with Netscape Communicator 6.2. It is important to understand that regardless of which browser you choose, you must have both Java and JavaScript enabled.

The second software requirement is an English-language version of Windows 2000 Server, with Service Pack 1 or 2 installed. Also, note that Microsoft Windows 2000 Advanced Server or Windows 2000 Datacenter Server are not supported in ACS version 3.2.

NOTE   There is no discussion of the UNIX version of ACS in this book as it has been deemed end of life by Cisco. Additionally, CiscoSecure for UNIX is a completely different product that shares only the commonality of being an AAA server and is therefore out of the scope of this book.

The following hardware requirements are the minimum for running Cisco Secure ACS version 3.2:

- Pentium III processor, 550 MHz or faster is recommended as the minimum.
- 250 MB of free disk space.
- 256 MB of RAM.
- A minimum graphics resolution of 256 colors at 800×600 lines is also recommended.

Now, with the preceding requirements met, you are ready to install ACS.

Installing ACS

If this is your first time installing ACS, you want to follow the next set of instructions as well as provide some information during the install. If you are reinstalling ACS, you need to combine the installation steps in this section with the information in the section titled "Reinstalling ACS and Using an Existing ACS Database."

For a new install, you want to have some basic information prepared as well as be logged in to the device to run the install program of ACS with Administrator rights. You need to know the IP address and name of at least one device that acts as a client to ACS. We call this a network access server (NAS).

You also need to know what protocol the NAS uses to communicate with ACS. The available protocols are Terminal Access Controller Access Control System Plus (TACACS+) or Remote Authentication Dial-In User Service (RADIUS). TACACS+ uses TCP port 49, and RADIUS uses UDP ports 1812 and 1645 for authentication and 1813 and 1646 for accounting. RADIUS ports 1812 and 1813 are the registered RADIUS ports and are specified in newer RADIUS implementations. TACACS+ can encrypt the entire body of the message. RADIUS encrypts only the password portion of the data. TACACS+ was developed by Cisco Systems and is an enhancement of the protocol TACACS, which used UDP.

You should also plan on having a shared secret key. This needs to be the same both on the NAS and the ACS. The shared secret key is used when passing messages between the ACS device and the AAA client. This encrypts the entire packet if you choose to use TACACS+ and the password in the packet if using RADIUS. This does not, however, encrypt communication between the user's device and the AAA client.

The last piece of information to have prepared is the Windows server address. This allows you to use a Windows database for authentication as well as the ACS database.

After you gather the necessary information, you can proceed with the install of the server software, as follows:

Step 1 Begin by inserting the ACS CD into the CD-ROM drive, and as long as you have auto-run enabled, your installation of ACS begins. If you are using the trial download of ACS, you extract the ZIP file to a folder, browse to that folder, and double-click the **setup.exe** icon. If you have not met the service pack requirements, you receive a message; however, you can still proceed with the install. You can install the required service packs at a later time. ACS might not work properly until you do so.

Step 2　The first step of the actual installation process is to read and agree to the software agreement.

Step 3　After you have accepted, you see the Welcome screen. By choosing the **Next** button, you are prompted with the Before You Begin screen. This is where you confirm the minimum requirements to install ACS have been fulfilled. This includes information for the first AAA client that you install. You need information such as the protocol to use for communication, the AAA client name, IP address, and the TACACS+ or RADIUS secret key. This screen does not add this information; rather it verifies that you have the information ready. This is seen in Figure 5-1. Choose the **Explain** button for detailed requirements.

Figure 5-1　*Confirming the Minimum Requirements*

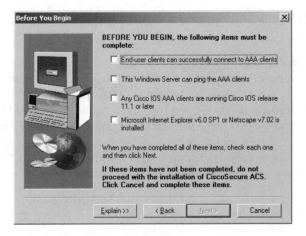

Step 4　After choosing **Next**, you are prompted to choose the destination directory for ACS to install to. Select **Browse** if you want to change the default location. If you select a location that does not exist, the setup program creates the directory for you. When you are finished, select the **Next** button.

Step 5　You now see the Authentication Database Configuration dialog box. You have the option to check only the ACS database or to check a Windows 2000/NT database. The CiscoSecure Database can handle around

100,000 users and has a higher level of performance than choosing to check a Windows 2000/NT database. The performance increase comes from the amount of time saved by checking a local database to ACS as opposed to authenticating and communicating with an external database for authentication.

If you decide to also authenticate users to a Windows Security Access Manager (SAM) or Active Directory user database and have selected the Also check the Windows 2000/NT database option, you are also able to refer to the Grant dial-in permission to user setting in the Windows Database option. Users are not allowed to authenticate if this is not selected in the Windows 2000/NT database.

Step 6   Select the databases to check, and choose the **Next** button.

Step 7   Your next window is for active service monitoring. In this window, you can choose to send e-mail notifications and specify the mail server to use for this. ACS active service monitoring gives you the ability to ensure that the services ACS needs to run are always available, and when an issue occurs, the e-mail function allows you to respond. When you select **Next**, you are taken to a Cisco Secure ACS Network Access Server Details page, as seen in Figure 5-2.

Figure 5-2   *Cisco Secure ACS Network Access Server Details*

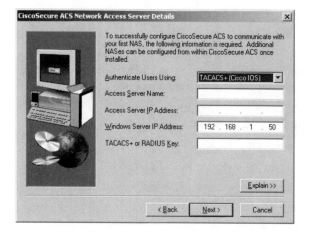

Step 8   In the Cisco Secure ACS Network Access Server Details page, input the information that you prepared before beginning the installation. If you choose any protocol other than TACACS+ (Cisco IOS) or RADIUS (Cisco IOS/PIX), your install begins immediately. If you do choose

TACACS+ (Cisco IOS) or RADIUS (Cisco IOS/PIX), you are given the opportunity to configure the Cisco IOS Software. The install program gives you a list of the required AAA commands, and a button that Telnets to the NAS for you to enter these commands. You can also select the **Print** button to print the minimum Cisco IOS configuration to your default printer.

Step 9   You're not finished yet! You must now choose which advanced options to make visible in your server. You can enable these at a later time; however, I prefer to enable them all at the time of install. These options affect what is visible in the HTML interface. The ones you should select depend on your network and how you plan to use ACS. Your final window starts the ACS services.

ACS runs seven services in total. Those services are

- **CSAdmin**—This provides the HTML interface to administer ACS. The ACS web server listens on port 2002. To access the ACS server in a web browser, type http://127.0.0.1:2002 You are then redirected to another port.

- **CSAuth**—This provides authentication and authorization service. Its role is to permit or deny users authentication or authorization requests. It can retrieve this information from the internal database or an external server. It pulls the authentication and authorization information and store it in the internal database of ACS. It is also responsible for processing unknown user requests.

- **CSDBSync**—This service provides the synchronization between the ACS database and a third-party database.

- **CSLog**—The CSLog service captures all logging information from the TACACS+ or RADIUS packet and CSAuth and then places it in a comma-separated value (CSV) file. More logging information is covered in Chapter 12, "Reports and Logging for Windows Server."

- **CSMon**—CSMon performs four separate activities:
  - Monitoring the ACS.
  - Recording and reporting of all exceptions to a log file.
  - Notification to the administrator of all potential issues with the ACS.
  - Response to these issues by automatically attempting to reconcile these problems. This is an application-specific utility.

- **CSTacacs**—This service speaks between CSAuth and TACACS+ NAS devices. It is capable of running simultaneously with the CSRadius service.

- **CSRadius**—This service speaks between CSAuth and RADIUS NAS devices. It is capable of running simultaneously with the CSTacacs service.

You can now access your ACS:

Step 1   If you selected the checkbox option to launch ACS, you're ready to go. If not, there should be a link on your desktop named ACS admin.

Step 2   You can access ACS by selecting the ACS admin link or opening your web browser and opening http://127.0.0.1:2002. At this time you must configure ACS from the device that it is installed on. Later, you configure a local username and password for administrative access.

Reinstalling ACS and Using an Existing ACS Database

Reinstalling ACS is just as easy as installing ACS for the first time. To reinstall ACS, you must go through the normal install as discussed in the previous section; however, after you select the directory for ACS to be installed to (Step 3), you receive a window that informs you that ACS has detected an existing database. It is here that you can choose to use that database. Figure 5-3 shows an example of this window.

Figure 5-3   *ACS Has Detected an Existing Database*

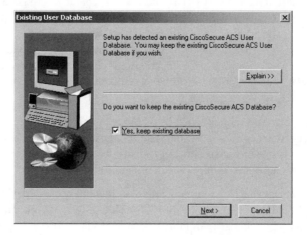

The remainder of the process continues as discussed in the preceding step sequence.

Positioning ACS in Your Network

Positioning ACS in your network is an integral part of the deployment process. This chapter provides only general guidelines for positioning your ACS. Each network has individual traits that influence the determination of where to place your server. Nonetheless, the following sections explore some common network topologies such as dialup access and VPN, as well as possibilities for placement of ACS.

Dialup Access

Dialup access is a key technology that uses the services of ACS for the authentication and authorization of remote users.

In my previous employment, I was in a situation where I would use a notebook computer and dial in to a remote access server (RAS) from the field, to upload and download my job assignments. When I would dial in, a username and password were required to determine who I was and what area, jobs, and network rights I was supposed to receive. This is the perfect place to deploy an ACS device. The size of the company that I worked for was big enough that we could have deployed ACS in multiple locations.

Deployment in large networks works best when separated into geographic locations. You could then use a proxy distribution table for access to the corporate network when you dial in from the road and need access to the network where you have a different ACS device authenticating you. You could also use replication of all ACS devices so that they all have the same database information. You can also deploy multiple servers for redundancy in a large network and perform replication to maintain database synchronization.

In a larger dialup network, the ACS devices can be used to service multiple NAS devices. For smaller business models, a single ACS device might be better suited for all users with a secondary ACS device as a backup. You could use database replication in both situations. In the larger company, database replication can be used to ensure that all ACS devices have the same user accounts, groups, and configurations.

Figure 5-4 is an example of the possible placement of an ACS device in a small dialup network. Note that the ACS is on the dial-in side of the network, protected behind a Cisco Private Internet Exchange (PIX) Firewall. As we add more AAA functionality to ACS, we can incorporate the Cisco PIX Firewall as a NAS device to ACS. For now, we are using only the dialup NAS. In this situation, users dial in to the NAS, and the NAS acts as a client to ACS to verify that the user is authorized to establish a connection into the network.

Figure 5-4   *ACS in a Small Dialup Network*

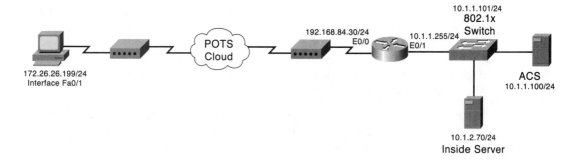

Virtual Private Networks

Virtual private networks (VPNs) are the evolution of the dialup network. VPNs use the Internet to access the corporate network. Because a connection into a service provider is not as secure as a private dialup, network users must make use of today's encryption technologies such as Internet Protocol Security (IPSec).

In an IPSec environment, a user makes a connection into the VPN-enabled NAS that requests authentication information from the ACS device. A common VPN topology is shown in Figure 5-5. This example uses a Cisco Internetwork Operating System (IOS) router as a VPN-enabled NAS, but can be replaced by a PIX Firewall or a VPN concentrator. One catch to using a VPN concentrator is that with the 3000 series concentrators, users must authenticate using the RADIUS protocol. IOS devices require version 12.2(8)T.

Figure 5-5   *VPN Topology*

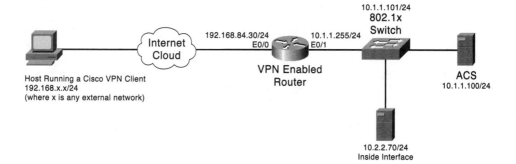

Another common issue to watch out for is access list filtering. Access list filtering is a method of interrogating packets that pass through a router or a PIX Firewall to make a determination as to whether it is permitted traffic, or if it should be denied. The filtering is based on source or destination IP addresses, source or destination ports, and protocol. Often times in a VPN environment, the VPN-enabled device is behind an edge router. If this edge router is filtering traffic coming into your network with access listing, you might need to modify the access list rules to permit UDP port 500, the Encapsulating Security Payload (ESP), and Authentication Header (AH).

Figure 5-6 shows a configuration on a Cisco IOS edge router device that is permitting the IPSec protocols with access list 110. The VPN concentrator is located at the IP address 172.168.4.5. This access list would be applied to interface f0/0. Examine Example 5-1.

Figure 5-6   *Cisco IOS Edge Router*

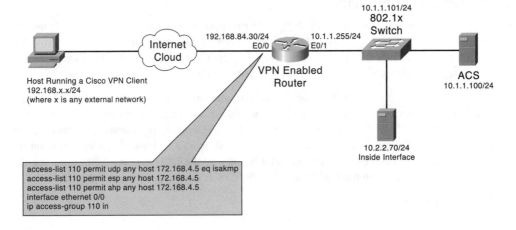

Example 5-1   *Permitting the IPSec Protocols*

```
edge-router#show run | include access-list
!
access-list 110 permit udp any host 172.168.4.5 eq isakmp
access-list 110 permit esp any host 172.168.4.5
access-list 110 permit ahp any host 172.168.4.5
!
edge-router#
```

Wireless Deployment

When deploying ACS into a wireless network, you must determine whether users need to roam from one wireless access point to another. If the answer is yes, the task ahead has just become a bit more difficult, yet not impossible. You might want to consider breaking up your ACS deployment into geographic locations where common users can be grouped. By placing the users into groups defined by geographic locations, you can spread the load placed on each ACS. Keep in mind that your deployment in a wireless local-area network (WLAN) with one access point will be very different than a WLAN with multiple access points and numerous locations that require roaming. Figure 5-7 shows a simple WLAN deployment.

Figure 5-7 *Simple WLAN Deployment*

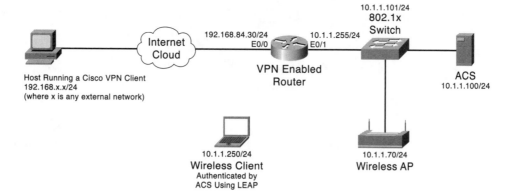

Other Deployments

Up to this point, you have seen AAA implemented for the most part on a user basis. A user accesses network resources and is authenticated to ACS. In some other deployments, you might see switchport authentication on a switchport using EAP-TLS or EAP-MD5. EAP-TLS is the Extensible Authentication Protocol-Transport Layer Security. EAP-TLS uses digital certificates instead of usernames and passwords to fulfill a mutual challenge. When a client authenticates, they receive a certificate as a response from the server.

The client also has a certificate that is in return sent to the challenging device. The two devices can determine authentication based on the value of the certificates that are exchanged. Extensible Authentication Protocol-Message Digest 5 is commonly used in Microsoft Windows XP; however, Windows XP has support for PEAP, EAP-MSCHAP v2, and Smart Card. This is another method where a challenge takes place. EAP-MD5 is not as secure as LEAP or EAP-TLS and is not recommended. You can see these property configuration options in Figure 5-8.

Figure 5-8   *Windows XP Local-Area Connection Properties*

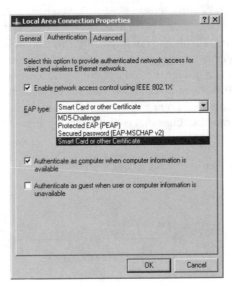

This type of authentication can be used in some Cisco switches to authenticate users at the switchport. Note that this configuration is discussed in Chapter 7, "Configuring User Accounts."

ACS is also commonly deployed to authenticate, authorize, and account for network administrators that access a company's network devices and are issuing commands to that device that might affect network connectivity. By using ACS to authenticate these administrators, you can manage the type of commands that unseasoned administrators can use, keep a paper trail of their activity, and use this as a tool for bringing new employees into the network without jeopardizing network availability to users. For more information on deploying ACS, refer to the following documentation on the Cisco website at http://www.cisco.com/en/US/products/sw/secursw/ps2086/prod_configuration_examples_list.html.

Summary

At this point, you should have ACS installed and are now prepared to take the grand tour of the ACS HTML interface. You should also be familiar with some of the most common topologies where ACS is used and able to deploy ACS in those environments. You now look at the HTML interface of ACS in the next chapter.

In this chapter, you learn the following topics:

- Navigating the HTML interface
- Starting point for configuring your server
- Locating configuration items
- Preparing to add users

## CHAPTER 6

Getting Familiar with CSACS

If you recall during the installation process of Access Control Server (ACS), you were given the opportunity to enable advanced configuration options by enabling a check box. As I look back to my first install and navigation of ACS, this spot is where I thought to myself, "I'll get to it later."

As it turns out, I should have gotten to it sooner because by enabling those check boxes, more configuration items are visible in the HTML interface. For example, when I attempted to configure some authorization parameters, the options were not visible, and I spent a good hour or better trying to figure out what I did.

In this chapter, you familiarize yourself with the interface of ACS and apply some basic configuration to make your job as an administrator a little bit easier.

NOTE I assume throughout the course of this chapter that you have followed the install of ACS according to the laboratory example in Chapter 5, "Deploying Cisco Secure Access Control Server for Windows Server." If you are using a Cisco Secure Solution Engine, you might have some slight differences. All in all, the HTML interface of the Cisco Secure Solution Engine and the software version of ACS for Windows Server should be close to identical.

Navigating the HTML Interface

If this is your first time using ACS, it is important to take the time to learn how to navigate the interface.

Note that the main web page of ACS is divided into frames. You access different menu items on the left-hand side of the page, perform configuration in the middle, and have access to some help on the right-hand side.

Because you use the menu a great deal in you configurations, the next sections look at each menu item and what types of configuration can be performed at each level.

User Setup

When you select the User Setup menu item, your middle frame changes to the "select" screen. Here, you can do a few things. You can add a new user, search for an existing user, find users alphabetically or numerically, or simply list all users at one time. User Setup is seen in Figure 6-1.

Figure 6-1 *User Setup*

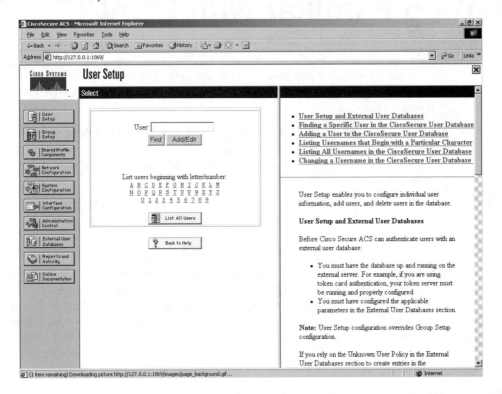

To begin your configuration, add a username. To do so, follow these steps:

Step 1 Enter a username; for our example, use **aaauser** and select the **Add/Edit** button.

Step 2 Now, you can edit user attributes. Moving from top to bottom, you can disable a user account, enter supplementary information, and configure the user's passwords. Figure 6-2 displays the option for authenticating against a Windows NT/2000 database or the Cisco Secure Database.

Step 3 Enter the password **cisco** for this user. Optionally, you could select the
option to use the Windows database. The default is to check the Cisco
Secure database.

Here, you can also distinguish which group the user is a member of. By
not specifying a group, the user is placed in the default group (group 0).
You can have the same attributes to configure in the group setup as you
have in the individual user setup; however, user configurations override
that of the group of which they are a member.

Within User Setup, you can also configure callback settings, IP address
assignment, and account disable properties. Some of the more advanced
user attributes and configurations are discussed in Chapter 7, "Configuring User Accounts."

Step 4 Click **Submit** to create your first AAA user in ACS. Because you have
not selected a group, this user is placed in the default (group 0) group.

Figure 6-2 *Authentication Location Options*

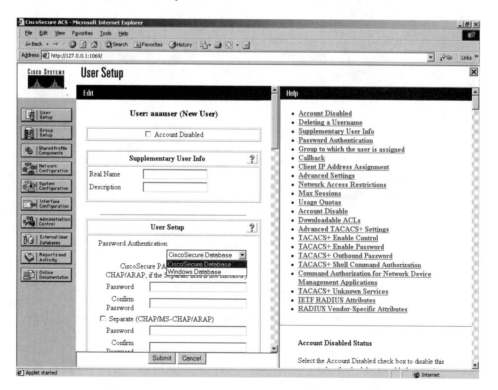

NOTE   By selecting the **List All Users** button after creating your user, you should see a single user entry on the right-hand side of the ACS interface. This ensures that the entry has been successfully created.

Group Setup

To begin your configuration, recap what you have configured thus far. You have a user called **aaauser** who has a password of *cisco* and is placed in the default group. This user is authenticated to the Cisco Secure database only. To examine the group that this user is in, follow these steps:

Step 1   Select the Group Setup menu item. You are given three options there. Figure 6-3 shows these options.

The options are Users in Group, Edit Settings, and Rename Group. Users in Group lists all of the users that are assigned to the group that is visible in the drop-down menu. A total of 500 groups numbered 0 through 499 exist.

Step 2   To view the group settings that your first AAA user is a member of (by default), simply select the **0:Default Group** and then select **Edit Settings**. This selection changes the main window, and you are now in the Group Configuration section. This is seen in Figure 6-4.

You can note a few highlights while you are here. First of all, take a look at *jump to* at the top of the screen. This feature is a real time saver. Try it out a few times by jumping to the IP address assignment section and then back to access restrictions. Notice that in the group configuration you have the ability to configure time-of-day access restrictions. This is not available at the user level. You can also configure Callback, IP Assignment, and TACACS+ settings. Under TACACS+ Settings you can configure shell command authorizations, apply privilege levels, set auto-commands, and so on. These types of configurations are discussed in Chapter 8, "Configuring User Groups," and Chapter 10, "Configuring Shared Profile Components."

NOTE   Some of the fields might not be visible in either the Group Setup or User Setup. As you become more familiar with ACS, you will be able to enable or disable certain fields at either the group level or the user level. This capability is explained in detail in Chapter 7 and Chapter 8, so do not worry if some of the items discussed in this chapter are not visible in you ACS device.

When you make group changes, you are required to submit and restart the ACS services. Your changes do not take place until you have done so. If you are making multiple changes to a group, it is best to submit without restart after each change until you have completed all changes, and then restart the ACS services.

Figure 6-3   *Group Setup*

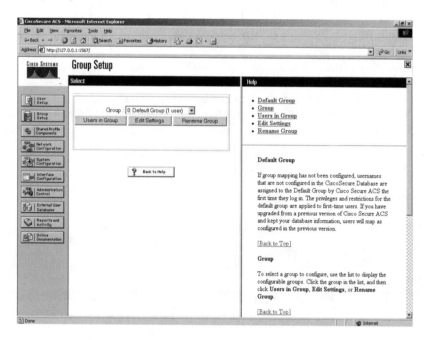

Figure 6-4   *Configuring the Default Group*

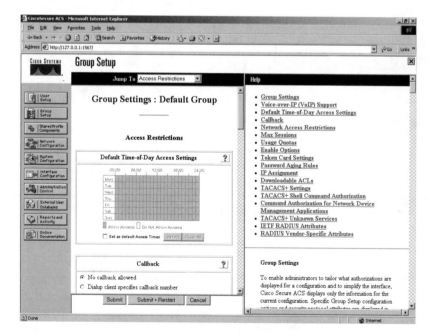

Shared Profile Components

Shared Profile Components allows you to specify Shell Command Authorization Sets and PIX Shell Command Authorization Sets. By creating these command authorization sets, you can control the commands a user can execute on a device by applying the command authorization set to the user profile in the TACACS+ settings, or at the group level. Figure 6-5 displays the Shared Profiles Components configuration menu. By default, you can select Shell Command Authorization Sets and PIX Shell Command Authorization Sets. Optionally, you can configure Downloadable ACLs or Management Center Authorization Sets. For these options to be visible, you must select them in the Interface Configuration page.

Another benefit to the Shared Profile Components configuration page is the ability to configure Shared Network Access Restrictions.

Figure 6-5 *Shared Profile Components*

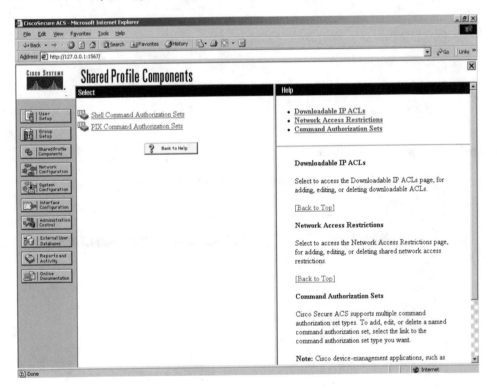

By selecting one of these links, for example, Shell Command Authorization Sets, you are taken to the configuration page for this shared profile component. This configuration is discussed in Chapter 10. You can see what this configuration page looks like in Figure 6-6. As you can tell, at this point, none are defined.

Figure 6-6 *Shell Command Authorization Sets*

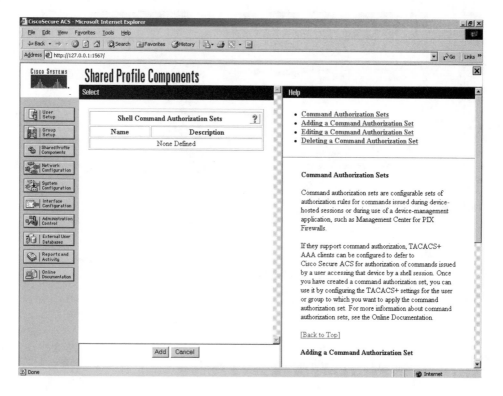

Network Configuration

The Network Configuration section is where you add, delete, or modify settings for AAA clients. At least one entry in this section should be placed there during install of ACS. You can see this in Figure 6-7. The AAA client is the device you added during the install. The AAA server is the Windows server, or rather the ACS server itself, that is entered here during the server installation.

Figure 6-7 *Network Configuration*

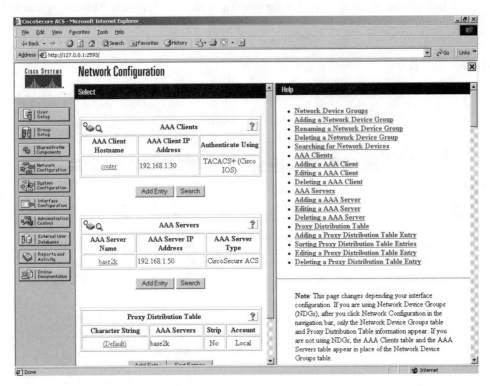

By selecting that entry, note that you can control the IP address of the device, key, and authentication method. You can also see a total of four check boxes in Figure 6-8. They are as follows:

- **Single Connect TACACS+ AAA Client (Record stop in accounting on failure)**— Single Connect TACACS+ AAA Client allows a single TCP connection between this AAA client and ACS. The normal operation is to establish a separate TCP connection for each request. For example, if you are using TACACS+, and you have a user that connects to the AAA client, when authentication occurs, a TCP connection is established. When another user connects, another session is established and so on. This eliminates those multiple TCP sessions. However, this is not recommended unless the connection between the TACACS+ AAA client and ACS is extremely reliable. If you decide to use this option, and the connection between the ACS and TACACS+ AAA client goes down, ACS never receives accounting stop packets for all users accessing the network through that AAA client. This causes them to remain in the logged in users list until it's purged. The logged in users list is covered in Chapter 12, "Reports and Logging for Windows Server."

- **Log Update/Watchdog Packets from this AAA Client**—The Log Update/ Watchdog Packets from this AAA Client allows accounting packets that are sent by the AAA client to be logged by ACS, specifically the logging of update or watchdog packets. It does not control overall logging of accounting packets. Watchdog packets are a means of creating better session length granularity to safeguard against the possibility of a device going down and thus never sending accounting stop packets for the users accessing the network via that device. Customers who have high priority on maintaining session length data might find this more useful than others.

- **Log RADIUS Tunneling Packets from this AAA Client**—The Log RADIUS Tunneling Packets from this AAA Client option allows RADIUS tunneling packets from the AAA client to be logged by ACS.

- **Replace RADIUS Port Info with Username from this AAA Client**—This enables the use of a username rather than port numbers for session state tracking. This option is useful when the AAA client cannot provide unique port values. For example, if you use the Cisco Secure ACS IP Pools server and the AAA client does not provide a unique port for each user, Cisco Secure ACS assumes that a reused port number indicates that the previous user session has ended, and Cisco Secure ACS can reassign the IP address previously assigned to the session with the non-unique port number. By default, this check box is not selected.

When you make changes to an AAA client, you must submit and restart the ACS services, similar to group changes. If you want to delete an AAA client, you are also required to submit and restart the service for changes to take effect.

System Configuration

Under System Configuration, you find many sub-configuration links beginning with Service Control. These sub-configuration links can be seen in Figure 6-9. This is where you can stop and start the ACS services. You can also do so in the Service Control of Windows 2000. By stopping the ACS service inside of ACS, you do not stop the ACS web server. If you want to stop the ACS web server, you need to do so in the Service Control of Windows. This web service is called CSAdmin.

The next System Configuration feature that you can manipulate is Logging. In this feature is where you can configure the local logging configuration, such as failed attempts and TACACS+ and RADIUS Accounting. You also configure Open DataBase Connectivity (ODBC) and remote logging here, as well as other ACSs.

Date Format control is straightforward. This is where you can change the format of the date displayed on reports. After you change the format, you must log out of the server to actually see the changes take place.

Figure 6-8 *AAA Client Setup for ACS*

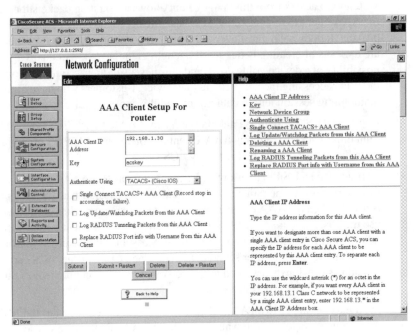

Figure 6-9 *System Configuration*

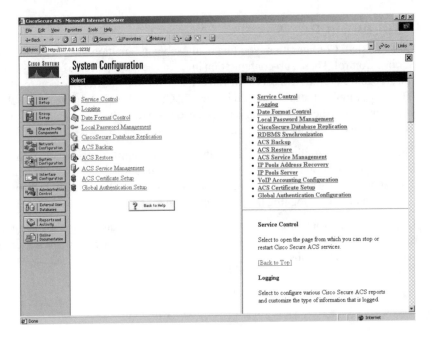

You can log out of ACS, short of closing the browser, in a few ways. One way is by clicking the Cisco Systems logo in the top left corner of the web browser screen and then selecting the Log off button. Another method is by clicking on the X in the top right portion of the window.

The next option is Local Password Management. From here you can set password length, as well as password options. You can also configure options for Remote Password Change and logging of password changes.

As for ACS Backup, you can schedule backups to be done manually or at specific times. You can specify a location for the backup files to be stored as well as manage the files. When ACS is backed up, it creates a file with the extension of .dmp. This file is now present when you enter the ACS Restore link. Here you have the ability to select from numerous backup files, as well as determine if you want to restore the Users and Groups, System Configuration, or both.

ACS Service Management enables the administrator to determine how often to test the availability of ACS authentication services. This is the CSMon service configuration. This allows ACS to test itself and take action when its test is unsuccessful. The available actions, should no authentications be recorded, are as follows:

- Restart all
- Restart RADIUS/TACACS
- Reboot
- Take no action

If the reboot option is selected, this causes the server that is running ACS to reboot. You also have the ability to add custom actions to this list.

You can also decide that you want to log attempts to log in to disabled accounts. Do this by selecting the check box labeled Generate event when an attempt is made to log in to a disabled account.

This is also where you can configure e-mail notifications and NT Event Log setup.

The ACS Certificate Setup is where you configure the ACS device with digital certificates. You use this when you configure the ACS to use https for administrative sessions.

Global Authentication Setup is where you can allow protocols such as PEAP, EAP-TLS, EAP-MD5, and MS-CHAP.

Interface Configuration

Moving on to the Interface Configuration menu item, as seen in Figure 6-10, you find a selection from the following sub-configuration links, depending on whether you have selected TACACS+ or a form of RADIUS when you entered your AAA client:

- User Data Configuration
- TACACS+ (Cisco IOS)
- RADIUS (Microsoft)
- RADIUS (Ascend)
- RADIUS (IETF)
- RADIUS (IOS/PIX)
- Advanced Options

NOTE   If you do not see RADIUS options here, you need to add an AAA client that uses the RADIUS protocol. Interface Configuration is directly affected by Network Configuration.

The User Data Configuration link enables you to customize the fields that appear in the user setup and configuration. Here you can add fields such as phone number, work location, supervisor name, or any other pertinent information.

The TACACS+ (Cisco IOS) link enables the administrator to configure TACACS+ settings as well as add new TACACS+ services. You can also configure advanced options that affect what you see in your interface. It is important you understand how this works. Depending on the current configuration of your server, if you go to the TACACS+ link, you might or might not see two columns. If you do see two columns, you are able to configure user-level settings as well as group level. Figure 6-11 displays what you see before enabling per-user TACACS+/RADIUS attributes.

In Figure 6-12, you can see the change to the TACACS+ (Cisco IOS) settings page after going through the following steps:

Step 1 Select the **Interface Configuration** button on the left side menu.

Step 2 Select **Advanced Options**.

Step 3 Select **Per-user TACACS+/RADIUS Attributes**.

Step 4 Select **Submit**.

Step 5 Select **TACACS+ (Cisco IOS)**.

Figure 6-10 *Interface Configuration*

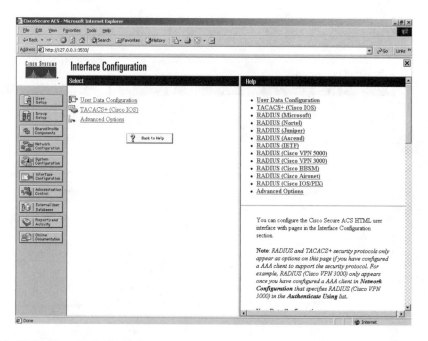

Figure 6-11 *TACACS+ (Cisco IOS) Before User Attributes*

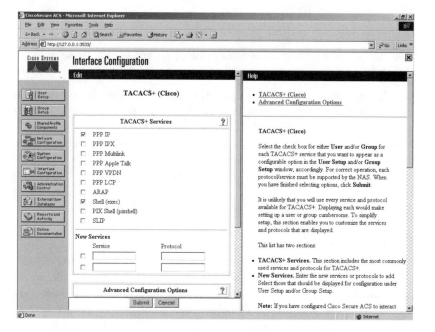

Figure 6-12 *TACACS+ (Cisco IOS) After User Attributes*

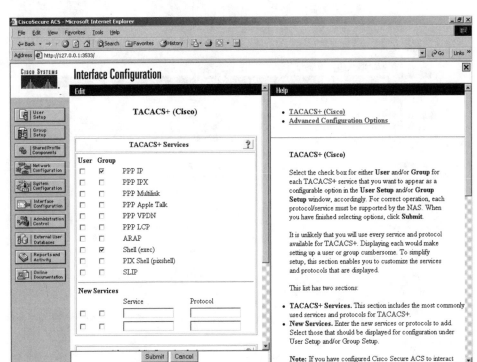

You should now have two columns available, User and Group. By selecting these options at the user level or group level, you enable these configuration options within each menu.

Here is where the user-to-group relationship comes into play. If an option is selected to appear in both the user and group configurations, and the user-level configuration is different than the group level, the user-level configuration takes precedence. Most of the features are available in both user and group configurations with a few exceptions. At the user level, you can configure passwords, expiration, and static IP addresses. At the group level, you can configure password aging as well as time-of-day restrictions for different categories.

Administration Control

The Administration Control section is where you configure all aspects of ACS for administrative access. Here you have the ability to add administrators and configure Access Policy. Information such as IP addresses that are allowed to access ACS, IP addresses that are not allowed to access ACS, and HTTP port allocation can be configured here.

Recall that ACS uses port 2002 as the listening port, but after connection to that port is made, you are redirected to a random port number. When ACS is positioned behind a firewall, this random port assignment becomes a security issue. You have the ability to specify a range of ports used so that you can configure access restrictions within your firewall to match, as seen in Figure 6-13. This is especially helpful when using a PIX Firewall.

NOTE   The Secure Socket Layer Setup option was not available in version 3.0.

Figure 6-13 *HTTP Port Allocation*

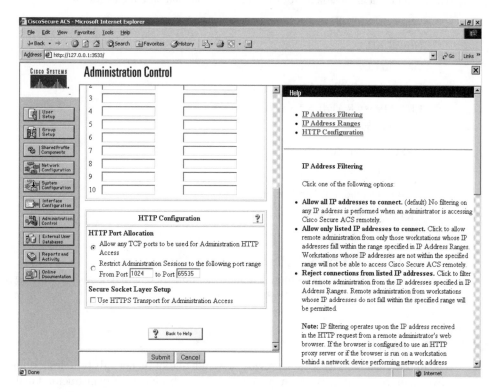

Session Policy enables you to alter the timeout, allow automatic local logins, and respond to invalid IP addresses. You can also choose to lock administrator access after a certain number of tries.

NOTE   Audit Policy enables you to configure File Management and Directory Management options.

External User Database

In this section, you see where to configure an unknown user policy. This same topic is covered in extensive detail in Chapter 11, "System Configuration." You also configure database group mappings to external user databases as well as perform the actual database configuration. Further, you are given a list of compatible databases, and you can choose which one you will configure to be used with ACS.

The servers that are available for use as an external database are as follows:

- Windows NT/2000
- Novell NDS
- Generic LDAP
- External ODBC Database
- LEAP Proxy RADIUS Server
- RADIUS Token Server
- VASCO Token Server
- ActivCard Token Server
- PassGo Defender Token Server
- CRYPTOCard Token Server
- SafeWord Token Server
- RSA SecurID Token Server

Each version of ACS includes more and more support for external databases while greatly improving the functionality of the ACS database.

Reports and Activity

The Reports and Activity section provides a wealth of tools in not only troubleshooting, but also monitoring your network. In the time that I have been a security instructor, I make it a point to teach students that if you are going to log it, you better look at it. So many times I have been in networks running Intrusion Detection Systems, SYSLOG, and other types of monitoring, yet nobody takes the time to look through the logs.

Within ACS, you have the ability as an administrator to monitor your network security on a number of levels. The available logs that ACS keeps for you follow:

- **TACACS+ Accounting**—All the Accounting reports include information such as time/date, username, type of connection, amount of time logged in, and bytes transferred. The information that is included in these reports is configurable by the administrator in the System Configuration section under Logging. This is looked at in more detail in Chapter 12. These reports can be found at Program Files\CiscoSecure ACS v3.x\Logs\TACACS+Accounting.

- **TACACS+ Administration**—The TACACS+ Administration reports include all of the command requests from AAA clients such as routers or firewalls where command authorization is configured. These reports can be found on the hard disk of ACS at Program Files\CiscoSecure ACS v3.x\Logs\TACACS+Administration.

- **RADIUS Accounting**—See the first bullet item in this list. These reports can be found in Program Files\CiscoSecure ACS v3.x\Logs\RADIUSAccounting.

- **VoIP Accounting**—See the first bullet item in this list. These reports can be found in Program Files\CiscoSecure ACS v3.x\Logs\VoIP Accounting.

- **Passed Authentications**—Passed Authentications is straightforward. The information gained within these report assists with user administration as well as in troubleshooting users that are failing authentication. These reports can be found in Program Files\CiscoSecure ACS v3.x\Logs\Passed Authentications.

- **Failed Attempts**—Similar to Passed Authentications, this report assists with user administration as well as in troubleshooting users that are failing authentication. These reports can be found in Program Files\CiscoSecure ACS v3.x\Logs\Failed Attempts.

- **Logged-in Users**—Again this report assists with user administration as well as in troubleshooting users that are failing authentication; however, the Logged-in Users file is rather unique. Most of the logging files in ACS create a comma-separated value (CSV) file and store them for each period, usually one day, on the hard drive of the server. The Logged-in Users file is not saved as a CSV file. As users log in, they are maintained in this file, organized by the name of the AAA client. You can purge the entries if they appear to be hung entries.

- **Disabled Accounts**—This report enables you to view accounts that have been disabled.

- **ACS Backup and Restore**—The ACS Backup and Restore report is available only if the option in Interface Configuration is enabled. This log maintains a history of the dates and times that ACS was backed up and/or restored. These reports can be found in Program Files\CiscoSecure ACS v3.x\Logs\Backup and Restore.

- **Remote Database Management Source (RDBMS) Synchronization**—The RDBMS Synchronization is also available only when the option is configured in the Interface Configuration Advanced Options. You don't enable the report; you enable RDBMS Synchronization. This allows ACS to keep report information on RDBMS Synchronization. This logs the time and reason for RDBMS Synchronization. This is discussed in more depth in Chapter 11. These reports can be found in Program Files\CiscoSecure ACS v3.x\Logs\DbSync.

- **Database Replication**—Database Replication is yet another report that must be enabled in interface configuration. This report logs the time that the ACS database was replicated to the backup server. This configuration is discussed in Chapter 11. These reports can be found in Program Files\CiscoSecure ACS v3.x\Logs\DBReplicate.

- **Administration Audit**—Administration Audit logs all of the activity in ACS that is performed by administrators. This keeps track of who logged in, what users and groups they made changes to, and what time they logged out. These reports can be found in Program Files\CiscoSecure ACS v3.x\Logs\AdminAudit.

- **User Password Changes**—This report tracks changes to users' passwords performed through the User Changeable Password Module. These reports can be found in Program Files\CiscoSecure ACS v3.x\CSAuth\PasswordLogs.

- **ACS Service Monitoring**—The last report is the ACS Service Monitoring report. This report keeps track of all the events that ACS has had within the services it monitors. An example of a service that might be monitored is CSAdmin or CSTacacs. By default, CSMon is enabled. This is, however, configurable. To configure this, you must go to System Configuration and then ACS Service Management. Here, you can choose to monitor the login process, generate events when someone tries to log in to disabled accounts, and so on. These reports can be found in Program Files\CiscoSecure ACSv3.x\Logs\ServiceMonitoring.

The Reports and Activity interface is seen in Figure 6-14.

As far as viewing these reports goes, you can view them in the ACS interface or from the hard drive of the ACS server. The logs are stored as CSV files.

You can view the reports in spreadsheet programs like Microsoft Excel. For even more functionality, you can import these into third-party software such as Crystal Reports. These reports are discussed in more detail in Chapter 12. If you do not have access to the hard drive of the ACS server, you are given the ability to download the logs from the ACS interface.

Figure 6-14 *Reports and Activity*

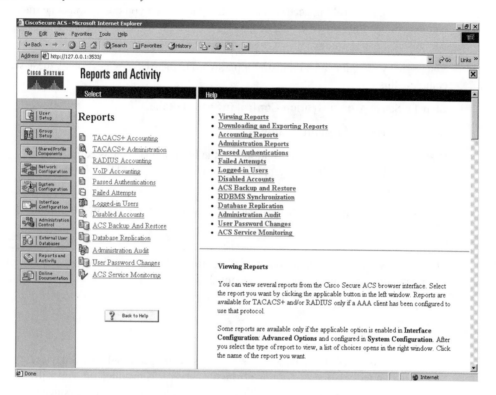

Online Documentation

The online documentation of ACS is there to help you out if you get stuck. If you have followed along on an ACS server up to this point, you have probably noticed that in different configuration menus you find some brief help on the right-hand side of your screen in the browser window. The online help is more detailed configuration information. You can access the PDF form if you have the CD-ROM, or it is available in the ZIP file that you downloaded from the Cisco website.

Starting Point for Configuring Your Server

Often, it is difficult to find a starting point for configuring your ACS. It might seem logical for you to begin in many places.

In this step sequence, you begin your configuration of ACS by applying administrator passwords and controlling access to the ACS device. Then you configure some interface parameters that influence the look of the HTML interface. This makes it easier to administer.

You begin by assigning an administrator password to the ACS device. Follow these steps to complete this task:

Step 1   Select **Administration Control** from the left menu bar.

Step 2   Select **Add Administrator**.

Step 3   Enter the required information into the input fields such as admin name and password. In the example in Figure 6-15, the user ADMIN is entered. The password used is *cisco*.

Step 4   If this is the first entry for an administrator, select the **Grant All** option.

NOTE   This allows your administrator to have full administrative access. Later, as you add more administrators, you can specify what groups they can modify.

Step 5   Select **Submit**.

You now see that your administrator has been added to the ACS device. If you access the ACS device from the server it is installed on, you will, by default, not need to authenticate. This is against some security policies, so change that. Follow the steps below to force ACS to authenticate administrators even when they access ACS from the server itself.

Step 6   Select **Session Policy**.

Step 7   Deselect Allow automatic local login.

Step 8   Select **Submit**.

Step 9   To test your work, click the **X** in the top right-hand corner of the screen. Then, you can log back in to the ACS device. If you see Username and Password fields, you were successful.

Now, plan for the possibility that ACS might be behind a firewall and that perhaps you want to administer it from outside the network. Go back to the Administration Control section and control the ports that are redirected when ACS is accessed.

Step 10   Select **Access Policy**.

Step 11   Scroll to the HTTP Configuration.

Step 12 Select the radio button that indicates you want to **Restrict Administration Sessions** to the following port range.

Step 13 Add a port range, such as 65501 to 65535.

Step 14 Select **Submit**.

Figure 6-15 *Adding an Administrator to ACS*

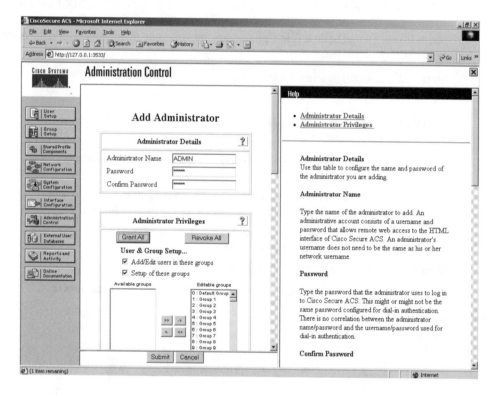

This now restricts the port ranges that ACS redirects your browser to and does so to the range that you specified.

In Figure 6-16, you see an example of a network similar to that described in the preceding step sequence. A PIX Firewall, an ACS server, and a separate workstation are used to demonstrate the login and management actions based on the preceding steps. You are going to run into an issue here. When you access ACS using an IP address, all links to ACS configuration pages use the IP address. When you access the ACS from outside a firewall and you are performing Network Address Translation (NAT), you initially access ACS using a NAT address, but when you are redirected to one of the previously restricted ports, ACS returns the private (nontranslated) IP address. This causes you to lose management connectivity.

By accessing ACS using a domain name, or the hostname, all links to configuration pages return the domain name or hostname instead of the private (nontranslated) IP address. This sustains your management connection.

Figure 6-16 also shows the topology using a PIX Firewall. The ACS is on the inside network, and a workstation from the 192.168.84.0/24 network is going to access ACS for management. Before you can access the ACS device, you need to allow access through the PIX Firewall to ACS. Follow these steps to configure the access list on PIX Firewall to allow access to the ACS. It is assumed that you already have a firewall configuration in place. If you attempt to do this in a production network, you might need to add these steps to an existing access list:

Step 1 Enter Configuration mode on the PIX.

```
Pixfirewall#config t
```

Step 2 Create an access list that enables administrators on any network to access the administrative port of ACS.

```
Pixfirewall(config)#access-list ACS-in permit TCP any host
192.168.84.10 eq 2002
```

Step 3 Add another access list statement that allows the administrator to access ports 65501 and higher on the firewall after the ACS redirects.

```
Pixfirewall(config)#access-list ACS-in permit TCP any host
192.168.84.10 range 65501 65635
```

Step 4 Apply the access list to the outside interface of the PIX Firewall.

```
Pixfirewall(config)#access-group ACS-in in interface outside
```

Figure 6-16 *Simple PIX Firewall Network*

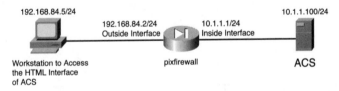

Now you are at the point where you must access the ACS device via Domain Name System (DNS). This causes ACS to return a DNS resolved name to the workstation. If you access the ACS via IP address, it returns the private IP address (RFC 1918), and you can no longer access the device after you sent your login credentials. Figure 6-17 shows the login prompt as seen from the remote workstation when accessing ACS by DNS name.

Figure 6-17 *Login with DNS Name Resolution*

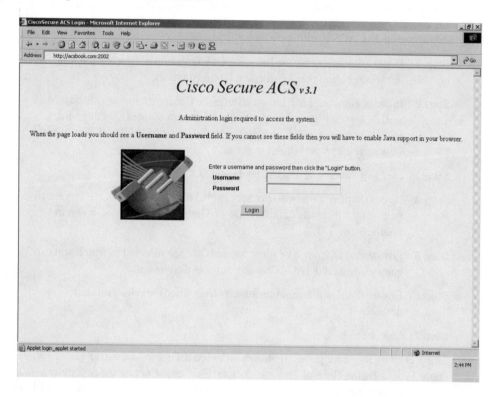

Now that you are logged in, note that your URL has been redirected to a different port and that it matches the HTTP port range that you specified earlier. You also want to note that ACS returned a DNS name and not the private (nontranslated) IP address upon redirection.

Configuring Your Interface

You have modified the authentication policy and configured session policy. You now are almost ready to make ACS work for you. Now you configure the interface to make it easier to manage, which is the goal in the coming sections. To do this, you need to disable some of the advanced options. Don't worry; when the time comes, you will enable them again.

TACACS+ Settings

To ease your configuration and help make things a little easier while you are learning, you need to disable some of the advanced TACACS+ features. You disable any advanced configurations at this point, and as you increase the functionality of ACS by adding more for it to do, you bring these configuration parameters back. Follow these steps to turn off the advanced TACACS+ settings:

Step 1   Begin with accessing the Interface Configuration section by clicking the left menu button titled **Interface Configuration**.

Step 2   In the beginning of this chapter, Interface Configuration was discussed as well as how selecting an option makes certain options visible in the HTML interface. Here, simply select the link **TACACS+ (Cisco IOS)**. This refreshes your screen to the edit page.

Step 3   Deselect Advanced TACACS+ Features.

Step 4   Select **Display Time-of-Day** access grid for every TACACS+ service so you can override the default Time-of-Day settings. This is shown in Figure 6-18.

Step 5   Ensure that Display a window for each service selected in which you can enter customized TACACS+ attributes is deselected.

Step 6   Ensure that Display enable default (Undefined) service configuration is deselected.

Step 7   Select **Submit**.

The preceding steps are going to allow you to see a Time-of-Day grid where you have the control to configure Time-of-Day parameters. This might not be the first thing you always want to do; however, it is very noticeable when made visible, and that is the goal here.

To check your work, follow these steps:

Step 1   Click **Group Setup**.

Step 2   Select **Edit Settings**.

Step 3   You should be able to see the Time-of-Day grids.

Figure 6-18 *Configuring Time-of-Day Settings*

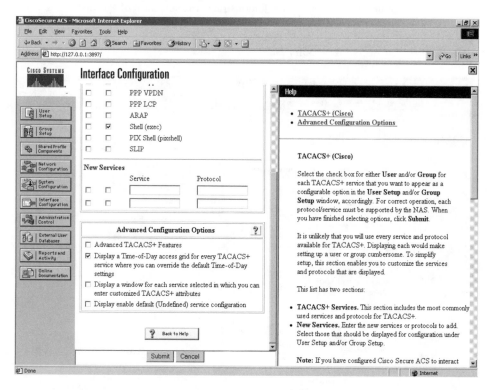

Advanced Options

Another way to clear out some of the clutter when you are learning is to disable the Advanced Configuration options. You might want to configure these settings, but for now, turn all of them off except for the Per-user TACACS/RADIUS Attributes. To do so, follow these simple steps:

Step 1 Select **Interface Configuration**.

Step 2 Select **Advanced Options**.

Step 3 Ensure sure that everything except Per-user TACACS+/RADIUS Attributes is deselected. This enables you to do some individual user configurations without crowding the interface with all the available options.

Step 4   After you complete these steps, verify that your configuration matches
Figure 6-19. Figure 6-19 demonstrates the selection of Per-user
TACACS+/RADIUS Attributes.

Figure 6-19   *Per-User TACACS+/RADIUS Attributes*

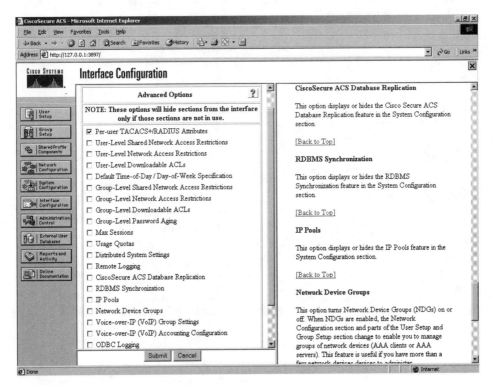

Preparing to Add Users

You are almost ready to add users to the ACS database. Before you do so, customize the
interface a little more so that you can keep some more detailed information that might help
you in keeping track of users. In the ACS user configuration, you have the ability, by
default, to include Supplementary User Info, as shown in Figure 6-20. This includes a real
name and description.

Figure 6-20 *Supplementary User Info*

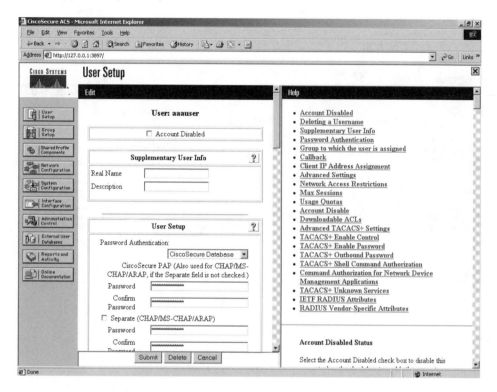

To add additional fields for more information to be added, follow these steps:

Step 1   Access the **Interface Configuration** menu.

Step 2   Select **User Data Configuration**. Place a check mark in the box titled **Display for number 3 and 4** to indicate that you want these fields to be displayed.

Step 3   Edit or input the relevant headings for each field you plan to use in addition to the two defaults. In Figure 6-21, Phone Extension and Cubicle Location was used.

Step 4   Select **Submit**.

Figure 6-21 *User Data Configuration*

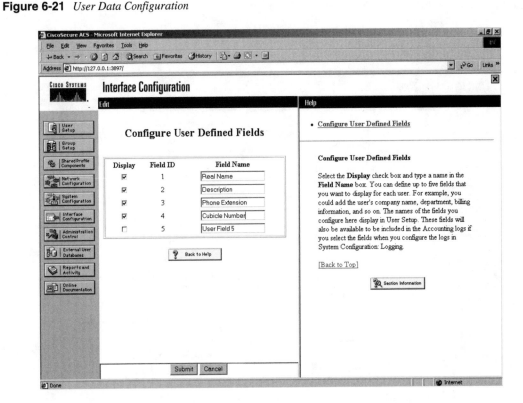

You can check your work by following these steps:

Step 1 Select **User Setup**.

Step 2 Enter **aaauser** in the field provided.

Step 3 Select **Add/Edit**.

Step 4 You should now see the two new Supplementary User Info fields that you created. See Figure 6-22.

Figure 6-22 *Supplementary User Info (After Edits)*

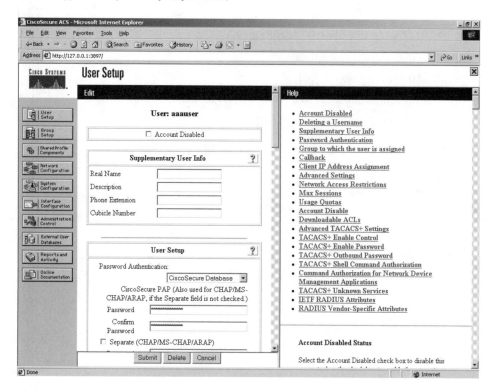

Summary

At this point, you should be familiar with the interface of ACS and prepared to add a user to the database. Remember that the look and feel of your interface are dependent on what features you have made available in the Interface Configuration section. As you progress with your configuration of ACS, you will add more features and make more configuration options visible in the interface. This is merely a starting point.

In this chapter, you learn the following topics:

- Adding users to the database
- User Changeable Passwords
- Authenticating users to a Windows NT/2000 database
- Advanced configurations

## CHAPTER 7

Configuring User Accounts

Access Control Server (ACS) has the capability to authenticate users against numerous databases. From token servers to Active Directory servers, ACS provides the flexibility of integration into an existing environment, or the power to use its own database for user authentication. Cisco Secure can keep a record of all users locally, regardless of whether you configured the user there.

Note that the user database might exist on a Windows 2000 server. ACS checks the Windows server for user credentials and adds the user locally to ACS. The user entry that is learned from the Windows 2000 database is still authenticated against the Windows database. Adding the username to ACS is done because all users are authorized against the ACS database when authorization is present.

In this chapter, you add a user to your ACS database. The user profile that you configure in ACS allows you to configure several parameters that were discussed in Chapter 2, "TACACS+ and RADIUS." In this chapter, you actually perform the task of configuring a user and adding some advanced parameters.

Adding Users to the Database

To add local users to the ACS database, use the following step sequence. This adds a user to the ACS database. It also adds that user to the default group.

When you add a user to a group, the settings within that group are inherited by the user members of that group. As discussed previously in the book, you can configure user specific settings that can override the group settings. User's settings *always* override the group settings.

Step 1 Select the **User Setup** button from the left frame menu.

Step 2 In the form field, enter the new username and select **Add/Edit**. For our examples, we use *aaauser* as the username and *cisco* as the password.

Step 3 Enter the password that is to be assigned to this user in the field labeled "CiscoSecure PAP" (this is also used for CHAP/MS-CHAP/ARAP, if the Separate field is not checked).

Step 4 Confirm the password by entering it again in the field below.

Step 5 Select **Submit**.

In this example, the password authentication database in the drop-down list is the CiscoSecure database. This does not use a Windows database or other external user database. Rather, this entry is contained in the ACS database. Also, the "Separate (CHAP/MS-CHAP/ARAP)" option is not selected. In this situation, the same password would be used for PAP, CHAP, MS-CHAP, and ARAP authentications.

Authenticating a User

The preceding step sequence has now added a single user to the ACS database. The defaults are to use the local database to authenticate and to add the user to the default group. For example purposes, you can use a PIX Firewall to authenticate a user when that user makes an outbound connection to an Internet web page or any TCP connection. Figure 7-1 shows this topology.

Figure 7-1 *PIX Firewall AAA Topology*

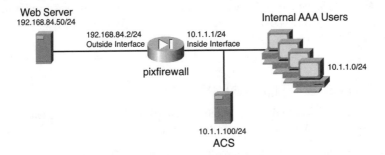

The way that PIX Firewalls work for AAA is a little tricky to understand. While you can perform AAA to any type of traffic, you can deliver an authentication prompt to a user only via Telnet, HTTP, or FTP. Therefore, if you want to authenticate a user that makes a connection to a device outside of the firewall and the protocol in use is NOT Telnet, HTTP, or FTP, the user must authenticate first with one of those three protocols. After users open a Telnet and authenticate, they can then use other protocols. Of course, this is assuming that other protocol traffic is permitted through the PIX Firewall. Example 7-1 demonstrates a basic PIX Firewall configuration with AAA authentication taking place.

Example 7-1 *PIX Firewall Configuration with AAA*

```
timeout uauth 3:00:00 absolute uauth 0:30:00 inactivity
aaa-server TACACS+ protocol tacacs+
aaa-server RADIUS protocol radius
aaa-server LOCAL protocol local
aaa-server MYTACACS protocol tacacs+
aaa-server MYTACACS (inside) host 10.1.1.50 secretkey timeout 10
aaa authentication match AAA inside MYTACACS  ←This tells the PIX to authenticate
all outbound TCP connections.
aaa authentication telnet console MYTACACS  ←This tells the PIX to authenticate
administrators that telnet to the PIX Firewall.  This is not the recommended method
of management for a firewall, rather you should use ssh.  This is here for example
purposes.
aaa authorization match AAA insode MYTACACS  ←This tells the PIX to authorize all
TCP traffic making connections from the inside interface.
aaa accounting match AAA inside MYTACACS  ←This tells the PIX to perform accounting
for all TCP traffic originating on the inside interface.
```

The most important part of this configuration is defining the ACS device as the server for authentication. This is done by entering the **aaa-server** command. When you use the **aaa-server** command, you define the protocol that the AAA client will use to communicate, in this case the PIX Firewall, with the options of **TACACS+** or **RADIUS**. In Figure 7-1, we use the TACACS+ protocol.

Another key element of the AAA configuration is the secret key that is defined. In this example, we use *secretkey* as the secret key. The key note of this key is that it must match the *secretkey* that is defined on the ACS device. Figure 7-2 demonstrates the configuration of the PIX Firewall as an AAA client in the ACS device.

Adding a New AAA Client

To add a new AAA client, follow these steps:

Step 1   Select **Network Configuration**.

Step 2   Select **Add Entry**.

Step 3   Enter the information for the new AAA client. For our example, we use the following information:

  — Name: pixfirewall

  — AAA Client IP Address: 192.168.1.1

  — Key: secretkey

  — Authenticate Using: TACACS+ (Cisco IOS)

  — All other options deselected

Step 4   Select **Submit + Restart**.

Figure 7-2   *Editing the AAA Client in ACS*

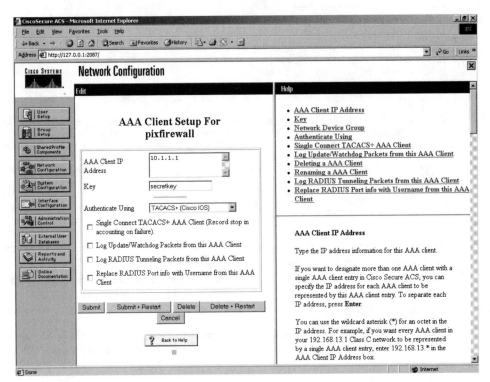

This sequence adds a new AAA client to the ACS database. Figure 7-1 also illustrates the parameters that you need to include when you enter an AAA client. These parameters include the IP address of the AAA client, secret key, and AAA client name. To edit an existing entry, simply select the name of the entry you want to edit.

For the configured parameters to take effect, you must submit and restart. Also, you can see in Figure 7-3 that after you select the option to submit and restart, the page refreshes to Network Configuration.

Figure 7-3   *Network Configuration*

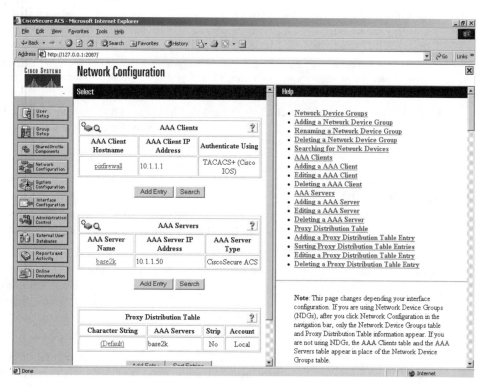

User Changeable Passwords

One issue that you face when storing the user information and passwords in the local database is the strength of the user passwords. The longer the user has the same password, the weaker it becomes. Because of this vulnerability with keeping the same password for a long time, you want to provide the user with a way to change his or her password on a regular basis. This can be done with ACS by installing a User Changeable Password (UCP) module. This module is available on the ACS CD if you have purchased the full product, or in the folder that you extracted ACS to if you are using a trial download.

Note the following specific information regarding the UCP web page:

> The UCP web page requires users to login. The password required is the PAP password for the user account. UCP authenticates the user with CiscoSecure ACS and then allows the user to specify a new password. UCP changes both the PAP and CHAP passwords for the user to the password submitted.

> Communication between UCP and CiscoSecure ACS is protected with 128-bit encryption. To further increase security, we recommend implementing SSL to protect communication between web browsers and UCP.[1]

To install and run the UCP module, the system that it is placed on must run Microsoft Internet Information Services (IIS) 5.0. It does not need to be on the same server as ACS, but it must be able to reach the ACS device on the network.

Preparing the Web Server

Before you can install the UCP module, you must prepare your web server. The web server needs to perform Secure Sockets Layer (SSL) encryption, or the users' passwords can be seen in clear text when changed.

In addition to the server enrolling and obtaining certificates to be used for the encryption, you also need to prepare the server by creating two virtual directories. By creating two virtual directories, one called *secure*, the other named *securecgi-bin*, the *secure* directory includes the HTML code for the UCP and the *securecgi-bin* directory includes the executable files for the UCP.

After you have prepared your web server, you need to do a little more configuration in ACS if the UCP module is not going to be installed on the same device. You also need to assign permissions to the personal directories. If permissions are set incorrectly, the UCP module might not operate correctly.

The following steps from the *Installation and User Guide for Cisco Secure ACS User-Changeable Passwords*[2] guide you through the process of preparing the web server:

Step 1   Make sure the web server uses Microsoft IIS 5.0. IIS 5.0 is included with Windows 2000.

Step 2   In the file system directory that the web server uses as its home directory, create the following two directories:

— **secure**—This directory contains the HTML files used by UCP. You can use a name different from *secure*. You use the name you choose later in Step 3 of this procedure and twice more in "Installing UCP the Module."

— **securecgi-bin**—This directory contains the executable CGI files used by UCP. You can use a name different from *securecgi-bin*. You use the name you choose in Step 4 of this procedure and twice more in "Installing UCP Module."

If the home directory of the web server is C:\Inetpub\wwwroot, use My Computer to add the directories to C:\Inetpub\wwwroot.

NOTE	To determine the home directory, see the properties of the default web site for Microsoft IIS.

Step 3 In Microsoft IIS, add a virtual directory for the HTML files used by UCP. Use the following information when you create the virtual directory:

— **Virtual Directory Alias**—A name for the virtual directory, which corresponds to the secure directory created in Step 2. We recommend that you use *secure*. This alias is a component in the URL used to access UCP, so a short but descriptive alias can help users remember the URL.

— **Web Site Content Directory**—The directory specified must match the secure directory created in Step 2. The default directory from Step 2 is C:\Inetpub\wwwroot\secure.

— **Access Permissions**—Give this virtual directory read permissions. No other permissions are necessary. For information about creating virtual directories, see Microsoft IIS documentation, available at http://www.microsoft.com/windows2000/en/server/iis/.

Step 4 Add a virtual directory for the CGI executable files used by UCP. Use the following information when you create the virtual directory:

— **Virtual Directory Alias**—A name for the virtual directory, which corresponds to the securecgi-bin directory created in Step 2. We recommend that you use *securecgi-bin*.

— **Web Site Content Directory**—The directory specified must match the securecgi-bin directory created in Step 2. The default directory from Step 2 is C:\Inetpub\wwwroot\securecgi-bin.

— **Access Permissions**—Give this virtual directory read and execute permissions. No other permissions are necessary. For information about creating virtual directories, see Microsoft IIS documentation, available at http://www.microsoft.com/windows2000/en/server/iis/.

Step 5 If the web server runs IIS 6.0, you must configure IIS to allow unknown CGI extensions. To do so, use the Web Service Extension page in the IIS Manager window and set the status of Allow Unknown CGI Extensions to "Allowed."

Step 6 If you use the IIS Lockdown Tool to help secure your Microsoft IIS 5.0 web server, be sure that the Lockdown Tool allows executable files to run. If its executable files cannot run, UCP fails and users cannot change passwords.

Preparing ACS for UCP

If you are placing the UCP on a different device, you need to enable the ACS to accept password change requests from the server with the UCP installed. To do so, these steps guide you through the process[3]:

Step 1 Log in to the HTML interface of the CiscoSecure ACS that you want UCP to send user password changes to.

NOTE   If you are using the CiscoSecure Database Replication feature, the CiscoSecure ACS that UCP sends user password changes to should be a primary CiscoSecure ACS; otherwise, if the user database is replicated, user password changes are overwritten by the older information from the primary CiscoSecure ACS.

Step 2   Click **Interface Configuration**, and then click **Advanced Options**. Result: The Advanced Options page appears.

Step 3   Make sure the **Distributed Systems Settings** check box is selected. This enables the AAA Servers table to appear in the Network Configurations section. This is seen in Figure 7-4.

Figure 7-4   *Selecting Distributed System Settings*

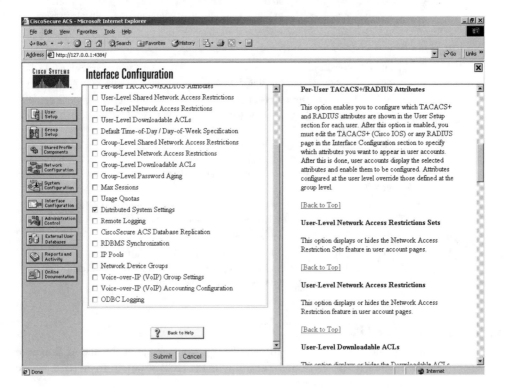

Step 4   Click **Submit**.

Step 5   Click **Network Configuration**.

Step 6   If Network Device Groups (NDGs) are enabled, click the NDG that you want to add the UCP web server to.

Step 7   In the AAA Servers table, click **Add Entry**.

Step 8   In the AAA Server Name box, type the name you want to give to the UCP web server. We recommend using the web server host name; however, you can include additional useful information, such as *UCP* to readily identify the UCP web server. For example, if the web server host name is *wwwin*, you could type **UCP-wwwin** in the AAA Server Name box. This page is illustrated in Figure 7-5.

Figure 7-5   *Adding an AAA Server to ACS*

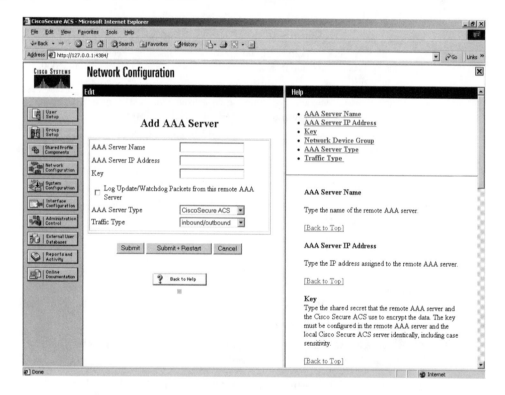

Step 9   In the AAA Server IP Address box, type the IP address of the UCP web server. Use dotted decimal format.

NOTE   The other settings on the Add AAA Server page are irrelevant to proper functioning of UCP.

Step 10   Click **Submit + Restart**.

Result: CiscoSecure ACS is configured to recognize and respond to password change information from the web server you plan to install UCP on.

Enabling SSL on the Web Server

In the section titled "User Changeable Passwords" earlier in the chapter, SSL was briefly mentioned. For those of you that are unfamiliar with SSL, SSL is a means of encrypting communication between the web server and the user that is changing their password. If the users that change passwords with the UCP exist on a trusted network, it might not be necessary to encrypt this traffic. It is my general recommendation to encrypt it anyhow. To configure the SSL portion on the web server, perform the following tasks[4]:

Step 1   Obtain a certificate from a certificate authority.

After you have received your certificate from the certificate authority, install the certificate on your web server. For information about installing a certificate, see Microsoft IIS documentation, available at http://www.microsoft.com/windows2000/en/server/iis/.

Following your Microsoft IIS documentation, activate SSL security on the web server. Keep in mind the following points when enabling SSL security:

— You can enable SSL security on the root of your web site or on one or more virtual directories.

— After SSL is enabled and properly configured, only SSL-enabled clients can communicate with the SSL-enabled WWW directories.

— URLs that point to documents on an SSL-enabled WWW folder must use https instead of http in the URL. Links that use http in the URL do not work.

Installing the UCP Module

Now it's time to install the UCP module. This section assumes that you are installing the UCP from the ACS CD-ROM or the folder that ACS was extracted to. To begin the setup of the UCP module, follow these steps:

Step 1   Browse the ACS CD or the folder that ACS was extracted to for the folder named User Changeable Password.

Step 2   Double-click the **Setup.exe** icon to begin the install of the UCP module. You must have administrative rights on this machine to install the UCP module.

Step 3   When you begin the install, a dialog box appears to confirm your preparations. This is seen in Figure 7-6. Select all check boxes and then select **Next**.

Step 4   Enter the path to the *secure* virtual directory that you created and select **Next**. This is seen in Figure 7-7.

Figure 7-6   *Before You Begin (UCP)*

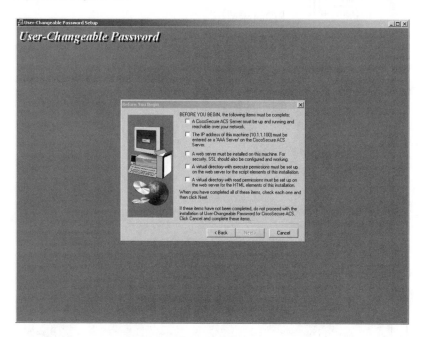

Figure 7-7   *Enter the Path to the secure Virtual Directory*

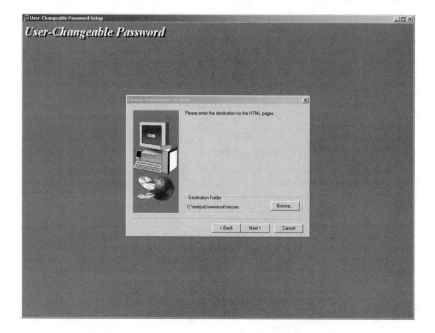

Step 5   Enter the path to the *securecgi-bin* virtual directory that you created and select **Next**. This is seen in Figure 7-8.

Figure 7-8   *Enter the Path to the securecgi-bin Virtual Directory*

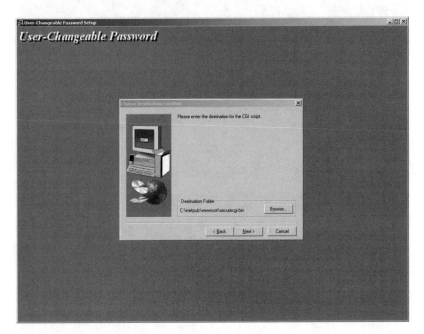

Step 6   Enter the URL for the HTML virtual directory. You might want to choose the default, which is the *secure* directory that you created. You usually do this if you are not using SSL. If you decide to use SSL, you need to change the beginning of the URL from HTTP:// to HTTPS://. This is seen in Figure 7-9.

Step 7   Select **Next**.

Step 8   You are then prompted for the URL to the *securecgi-bin* folder. You can choose the default; however, if you are using SSL, follow Step 3 and select **Next**. This is seen in Figure 7-10.

Step 9   You then see a dialog box that indicates "Connecting to Cisco Secure Server." Enter the IP address to the ACS device here. Select **Next**.

Step 10   You then see the **Setup Complete** box and can select **Finish** to end the installation process.

Figure 7-9   *Enter the URL for the HTML Virtual Directory*

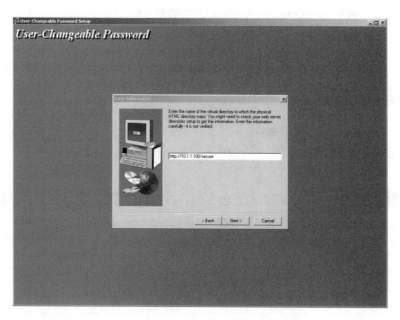

Figure 7-10   *Enter the URL for the securecgi-bin HTML Virtual Directory*

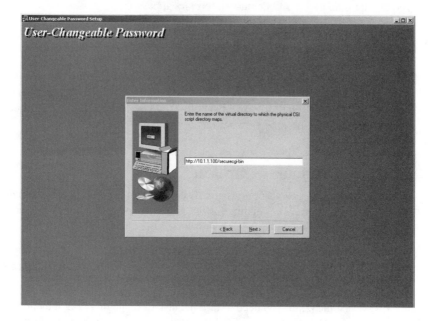

Now that the UCP module is installed, you can test the functionality of the UCP module by creating a new user account in ACS. Then from a web browser on the network, access the URL of the UCP server. It should look something like this:

```
http://10.1.1.100/secure/login.htm
```

This is the URL that users must access to change passwords. The users see a page that accepts a login, redirects them to a change password page, and applies the changed password. This works well; however, in a company with numerous employees the task of having users change their passwords becomes difficult. It might be a good idea to use corporate e-mail as a reminder to change passwords or to even include the change password URL on a commonly viewed intranet site.

Authenticating Users to a Windows NT/2000 Database

If you have a Windows NT/2000 domain, your users probably already have a domain username and password. If this is the case, it is probably an easier task on a network administrator to configure ACS to use a remote database. The point here is that having a Windows domain opens up additional features of ACS. Having a Windows domain allows such configurations as Unknown User Policy.

If you recall, in Chapter 4, "Enterprise Authentication Servers," you installed the ACS on a server in your network. One of the steps of the install was to enter the IP address of the Windows server. For the time being, this is the server that we are going to use to authenticate users, rather than go the ACS database for a local password.

Authenticating to a Windows Domain

To configure ACS to perform in this manner, you simply access the user account that you want to authenticate to the Windows NT/2000 domain and select Windows NT/2000 in the Password Authentication drop-down list below the User Setup heading. This causes the user to authenticate with the password on the Windows domain.

Authentication and Password Options

Authentication and password options greatly depend on the network environment that ACS is deployed in. As seen earlier in this chapter, you can choose to implement local passwords in ACS and allow users to change passwords with the UCP module.

Of course, your network security might be at such a high priority that you choose to implement an ACS device in conjunction with a token server. You might also choose strict lockout policies in the ACS device or on a Windows NT/2000 domain.

Either way, at some point, you need to face the task of managing user authentication and password options. The User Setup of ACS enables you as the administrator to choose separate passwords for the Challenge Handshake Authentication Protocol (CHAP), Microsoft-Challenge Handshake Authentication Protocol (MS-CHAP), or AppleTalk Remote Access Protocol (ARAP). These protocols never send the actual username and password over the network but rather a hash that can be re-created and authenticated on either side. Because it would be foolish to use a protocol such as Password Authentication Protocol (PAP), which sends the username and password in clear text across a network and then uses the same password for devices requiring CHAP/MS-CHAP, or ARAP authentication, you can choose to create separate passwords in the ACS database.

User Callback and Client IP Assignment

ACS also provides for user callback. This sends a string to the access server that allows a user to be called back at a predefined number. This is also a security measure that ensures authentication. The options for callback follow:

- **Use group settings**—This uses the group settings configured for callback.

- **No callback allowed**—Select this option if you want to disable the callback feature for this user.

- **Callback using this number**—This is the option that you select to specify the number to always call this user back at. This is very secure; however, the user cannot roam.

- **Dialup client specifies callback number**—This can be used if you want users to be able to roam and specify their own callback number.

- **Use Microsoft NT/2000 callback settings**—This option can be selected if you want to inherit the callback settings in Windows NT/2000.

Another authentication option that can be configured is client IP address assignment. The following list contains the options for client IP assignment:

- **Use group settings**—This option is selected if you want to use the group configured settings to assign IP addresses to users.

- **No IP address assignment**—If you have group settings that are assigning addresses to users in that group and you do not want a particular user to be assigned addressing from that group, you select this box. This overrides the group IP addressing assignments.

- **Assigned by dialup client**—You select this if you want to use the IP address from the dialup client. This again overrides the group IP addressing assignments.

- **Assign static IP address**—This can be used in situations where administrators are making dial-in connections and you want to assign them a specific IP address. The reason this works well for administrators is because this gives you the ability to filter network access based on IP address.

- **Assigned by AAA client pool**—You can configure a client address pool on the AAA client. You can then choose this option and enter the name of the AAA client address pool in ACS. When the user authenticates, ACS assigns an address from that client address pool.

- **Assigned from AAA pool**—This is an alternative to configuring address pools on the AAA client. This creates the pool on the ACS device itself. You can see how this is configured in the step sequence after this list. Select the AAA server IP pool name in the Available Pools list and by clicking the right arrow button, that pool moves into the Selected Pools list. If more than one pool exists in the Selected Pools list, the users in this group are assigned to the first available pool in the list. You can also change the order that the pool is selected by selecting the pool name and clicking the Up or Down button until you are satisfied with the selections in place. This changes the order of the pool. The pool at the top of the list is used first. Once again, keep in mind that the IP assignment in User Setup overrides the IP address assignment in Group Setup.

To set up a local AAA pool, follow these steps:

Step 1 Select **Interface Configuration**.

Step 2 Select **Advanced Options**.

Step 3 Place a check mark in the box marked **IP Pools**, as shown in Figure 7-11.

Figure 7-11 *Enabling IP Pools*

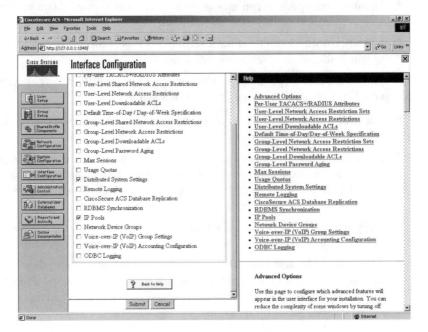

Step 4   Select **Submit**.

This makes the IP Pools portion of the configuration visible in the ACS interface.

Step 5   Select **System Configuration**.

Step 6   Select **IP Pools Server**.

Step 7   Select **Add Entry**.

Step 8   Enter a name for your address pool, as shown in Figure 7-12.

Figure 7-12   *Naming an IP Pool*

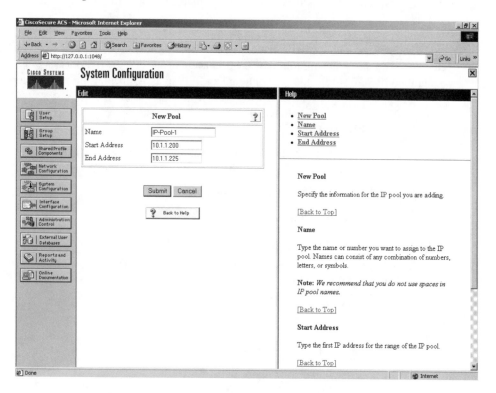

Step 9   Enter a Start address.

Step 10   Enter an End Address.

Step 11   Select **Submit**.

Step 12 You now see an address pool entry in the ACS interface. At this point, you have a few options. You can allow pool addresses to overlap by selecting the button **Allow Overlapping Pool Address Ranges**, you can **Refresh**, or you can **Cancel**. If you note in the chart with your address pool entry, you can determine the percentage of the address pool that is used. Use the **Refresh** button to monitor this value. In this situation, you select the **Cancel** button. This is simply to navigate away from this page without saving settings.

Step 13 From the Select menu, now choose the link **IP Pools Address Recovery**. This is yet another management aspect of IP address assignment. Here you can reclaim addresses after a specified amount of time.

Step 14 Select **Cancel**.

Now that the IP Pool has been created, you next apply it to one of the users that you have created. To do this, you need to access the user account and edit the IP Pool assignment. By default, no IP Pool is selected. To configure an IP Pool assignment, follow these steps:

Step 1 Select **User Setup**.

Step 2 Select **List All Users**.

Step 3 Select the user **aaauser**, which you want to add an IP pool to, from the User List in the right frame. Figure 7-13 demonstrates this list.

Step 4 Scroll to **Client IP Address Assignment**.

Step 5 Select **Assigned from AAA pool**.

Step 6 Select the IP pool from the list of available pools.

Step 7 Select the right arrow to place the available pool into the **Selected Pools** list. (See Figure 7-14.)

Step 8 Select **Submit**.

Figure 7-13 *User List*

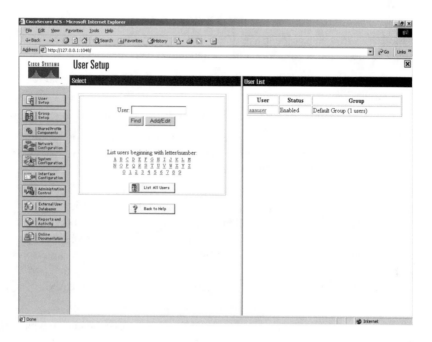

Figure 7-14 *Selecting an IP Pool*

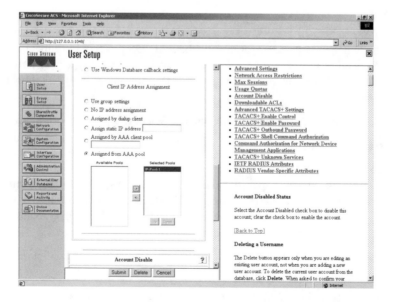

Advanced Configurations

Advanced configurations are those that are a bit more than just authenticating a user with a password. They can be used in a number of ways that you see during the course of this book. Some of these advanced configurations include some of these features:

- First of all, they can be used for PPP parameters. This can be used for IP, IPX, or AppleTalk.

- You can configure Link Control Protocol (LCP) options and so on here.

- You can also configure TACACS+ for command authorization. Command authorization is best used with new administrators that you want to control certain commands and access levels.

A beneficial advanced configuration capability of ACS is the configuration of 802.1x Switchport Authentication. The IEEE 802.1x standard defines a client-server–based access control and authentication protocol that restricts unauthorized clients from connecting to a LAN through publicly accessible ports. This might be a connection directly into a switch or via a wireless network. This is done by the authentication server, in this case ACS, authenticating each client connected to a switchport and assigning that port to a VLAN before making available any services offered by the switch or the LAN.

Until the client is authenticated, 802.1x access control allows only Extensible Authentication Protocol over LAN (EAPOL) traffic through the port to which the client is connected. After authentication is successful, normal traffic can pass through the port.

EAP Support

EAP support can be considered an advanced configuration in ACS. The actual EAP support at the switchport can be performed via the RADIUS protocol by authenticating the user to ACS. In this type of environment, you must determine what type of EAP to use, EAP-TLS or EAP-MD5. To enable switchport authentication support in ACS, follow these steps:

Step 1   Configuration of the RADIUS profile is found in the IETF RADIUS settings of the **Interface Control**.. Select **Interface Configuration**.

Step 2   Select **RADIUS (IETF)**.

Step 3   The attributes that you need to be enabled (check marked) are **[064]Tunnel-Type**, **[065]Tunnel-Medium-Type**, **and [081]Tunnel-Private-Group-ID**. This now makes these RADIUS attributes visible in ACS Group Setup. You begin by placing a check box next to the newly added attributes, as shown in Figure 7-15.

Step 4   Now that the RADIUS options have been enabled, you configure them in the group configuration. Select **Group Setup**.

Step 5   Select the **0:Default Group** in the Group drop-down list.

Figure 7-15 *Enabling RADIUS Attributes 64, 65, and 81*

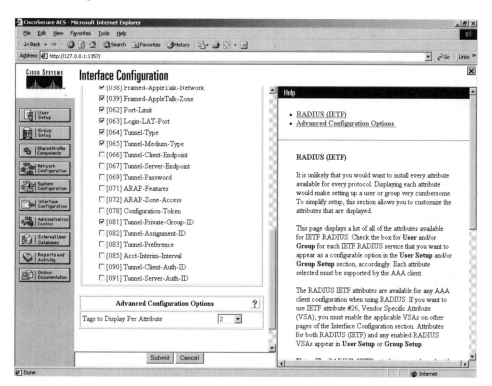

Step 6 Select **Edit Settings**.

Step 7 Using the Jump To drop-down, jump to **RADIUS (IETF)** and scroll until you find attribute 064.

Step 8 Since only 1 VLAN can be passed in a RADIUS packet, the only tag that is valid is **1**. Ensure that the second tag is set to **0**, as seen in Figure 7-16, for both attributes 064 and 065. It will be ignored.

Step 9 In attribute 064, select **TAG 1** with a value of VLAN.

Step 10 In attribute 065, select **TAG 1** with a value of 802.

Step 11 In attribute 081, select **TAG 1** with a value that is equal to the VLAN name that you want to assign when a user authenticates. For our example, we have used the VLAN name *VLAN_AUTHEN*, as seen in Figure 7-16.

Step 12 When this is completed, select **Submit + Restart**.

Figure 7-16 *Configuring 802.1x Support in ACS*

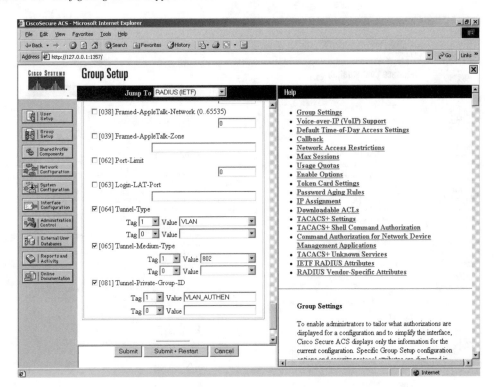

Configuring Switches

The next set of configurations you need to do is configuring the switch to talk to ACS and vice versa. At this point, you should be able to add a new AAA client to ACS. Do this from the **Network Configuration** section. When you add the switch as an AAA client to ACS, ensure that you select **RADIUS (IETF)** as your protocol type. This is seen in Figure 7-17.

Figure 7-17 *Configuring the Switch as an AAA Client in ACS*

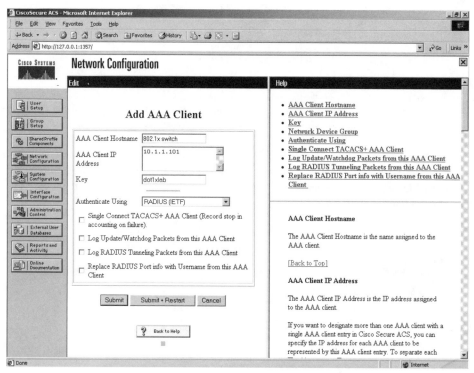

On the Cisco switch, you would enter the commands seen in Example 7-2.

Example 7-2 *AAA Switch Configuration*

```
switch#conf t
switch(config)#aaa new-model
switch(config)#radius-server host 10.1.1.100
switch(config)#radius-server key dot1xlab
switch(config)#aaa authentication dot1x default group radius
switch(config)#dot1x system-auth-control ←This enables dot1x on the switch.
switch(config)#interface Vlan1 ←This is the L3 interface for accessing RADIUS
  server.
```

continues

Example 7-2 *AAA Switch Configuration (Continued)*

```
switch(config-if)#ip address 10.1.1.101 255.255.255.0
switch(config-if)#interface fa0/1 ← The RADIUS server is behind this L2 port.
switch(config-if)#switchport
switch(config-if)#switchport mode access
switch(config-if)#switchport access vlan 1
switch(config-if)#interface range fa0/2 - 12 ←These are the ports where users exist.
switch(config-if)#switchport
switch(config-if)#switchport mode access
switch(config-if)#dot1x port-control auto ←This Enables 802.1x on the interface
```

Example 7-2 is for an IOS-based switch. For set-based switches see the Cisco documentation at http://www.cisco.com/univercd/home/home.htm. The preceding configuration
enables VLAN assignments from the ACS server. The new topology with the 802.1x switch
is seen in Figure 7-18.

Figure 7-18 *New Common Topology with 802.1x Switch*

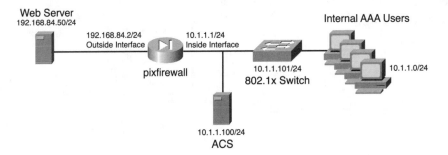

Enable an Administrative Policy

The next configuration enables an administrative policy in ACS for the switch.

Cisco recommends that you separate your users' access to the network from the administrator's access to the network. The simplest way to do so is by using the RADIUS protocol
for average users and TACACS+ for administrative users. To enable this on your IOS-based
switch, you enter the additional commands seen in Example 7-3.

Example 7-3 *Separating Users from Administrators*

```
switch#conf t
switch(config)#tacacs-server host 10.1.1.100
switch(config)#tacacs-server key dot1xlabadmin
switch(config)#aaa authentication login default group tacacs+ local
switch(config)#aaa authentication login not_auth none
```

Example 7-3 *Separating Users from Administrators (Continued)*

```
switch(config)#aaa authentication enable default group tacacs+ enable
switch(config)#ip tacacs source-interface loop0 ←This allows you to add the switch
as another AAA client in ACS with a different IP address.
switch(config)#interface loop0
switch(config-if)#ip address 1.1.1.1 255.255.255.0
switch(config-if)#exit
switch(config)#username administrator password acspassword
switch(config)#line console 0
switch(config-line)#login authentication not_auth
```

As long as you have users configured in the ACS and the AAA client has been defined, the administrator gains access to the switch where the average user that authenticates with RADIUS would fail shell authorization. To configure a host to perform EAP authentication, you can use the following URL as a guide for Windows XP: http://www.cisco.com/en/US/products/hw/switches/ps700/products_tech_note09186a00801d11a4.shtml. Note that URL requires a CCO login.

Summary

At this point, you should be comfortable with maneuvering the ACS interface and adding users. It is important that you become familiar with the different sections that you need to manipulate as you enter users, add access rights, and configure advanced settings. In the next chapter, you begin to configure User Groups and incorporate your policies with numerous users and assign special rights to specific users while other users can inherit groups settings.

If you have deployed the UCP module, you should be able to successfully access the UCP web page from the network, log in as a user, and change that user's password. Remember to select the distributed database option if the UCP is on a server other than the one ACS is installed on.

You should also be able to determine addresses assigned by ACS, whether they be static, from a pool on the AAA client, or from a pool that you have created in ACS. As you proceed, be prepared to determine what users require special rights to the network and how you can separate users into groups.

End Notes

[1]Installation and User Guide for Cisco Secure ACS User-Changeable Passwords, page 2, Mark Wilgus
http://www.cisco.com/en/US/products/sw/secursw/ps2086/
prod_installation_guide09186a00800e6edf.html

[2]Installation and User Guide for Cisco Secure ACS User-Changeable Passwords, page 3, Mark Wilgus
http://www.cisco.com/en/US/products/sw/secursw/ps2086/
prod_installation_guide09186a00800e6edf.html
[3]Installation and User Guide for Cisco Secure ACS User-Changeable Passwords, page 5, Mark Wilgus
http://www.cisco.com/en/US/products/sw/secursw/ps2086/
prod_installation_guide09186a00800e6edf.html
[4]Installation and User Guide for Cisco Secure ACS User-Changeable Passwords, page 7, Mark Wilgus
http://www.cisco.com/en/US/products/sw/secursw/ps2086/
prod_installation_guide09186a00800e6edf.html

In this chapter, you learn the following topics:

- How to modify user groups
- How to use PPP callback configuration
- How to configure Network Access Restrictions
- How to configure max sessions, usage quotas, and password aging rules
- How to configure IP assignment and downloadable ACLs
- How to use TACACS+ for groups configuration of PPP VPDN

## CHAPTER 8

Configuring User Groups

In Chapter 3, "Authentication Configuration on Cisco Routers," you configured a user into the Access Control Server (ACS) database and were able to test authentication to the local ACS database as well as the Windows NT/2000 domain. In this chapter, you explore the group configurations of ACS as well as enable special user-level configurations for particular members of a given group. In this chapter, you also perform configurations that include group settings as well as user-level settings.

NOTE   As with any network, you probably have users that are members of a group, yet still require special network privileges. With the ability in ACS to configure group policy and then override it within User Setup, this task becomes very simple. The understanding that is assumed from here on out is that user-level configuration always overrides group-level configuration.

Group-Level Configuration of ACS

User groups are an easy way to implement control of user and administrative activity on your network without the tedious task of assigning numerous common rights to each individual user. The group-level configuration of ACS has multiple configuration areas, each of which is discussed in the following sections.

Modifying User Groups

When you select the **Group Setup** tab, the main frame of ACS changes to the Select screen. From this screen, you have the ability to choose from and modify a total of 500 user groups. The zero group is the default group. This is where users are added when you do not specify a group assignment in the user setup. You also see the number of users that are currently members of the group. In more advanced configurations, you configure group mappings for external databases, so your group configurations are very important to you.

By selecting the **Users in Group** button, you change the right ACS frame to display the users that are assigned to the group. If you want to assign special settings to users of that group, you can simply select the user by clicking on the username, and it takes you to the User Setup page for that individual user.

The next option that you can use from the Group Setup Select screen is the **Edit Settings** button. This takes you to the configuration area for whatever group is selected in the drop-down list of groups.

The final option that is selectable from this Group Setup Select screen is the **Rename Group** option. By selecting this button, you can rename the group that is selected in the drop-down list of groups.

To begin your configuration of user groups, follow these steps to rename a group and edit that group's settings:

Step 1 In the Group drop-down list, select **1:Group 1**.

Step 2 Select the button labeled **Rename Group**. Your screen should resemble Figure 8-1.

Step 3 Enter the new name for this group, and then select the **Submit** button.

Figure 8-1 *Rename Group*

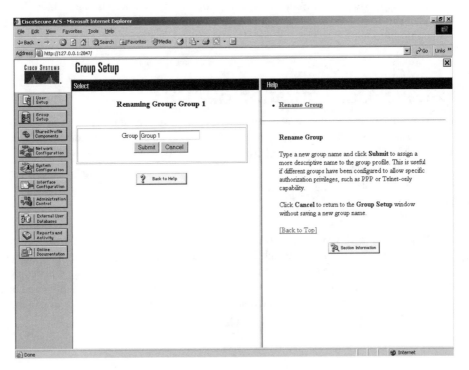

Step 4 Now, your newly named group should appear in the Group drop-down
menu. Select **Edit Settings**.

You have now been placed in Group Setup configuration for the group named FirstUsers.
You can choose to scroll through the group settings by using the scroll bar on the right-hand
side of the center frame, or you can quickly jump to the main settings areas by selecting the
configuration area from the Jump To list, as seen in Figure 8-2.

Figure 8-2 *Using the Jump To List*

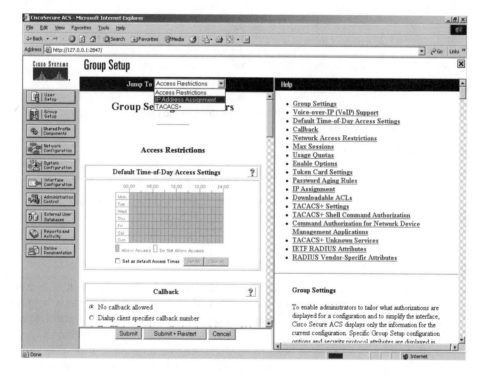

You can use this list to jump to Access Restrictions, IP Address Assignment, TACACS+,
and a few others, depending on your interface configuration and RADIUS protocols that
have been enabled.

You begin your configuration by enabling additional group settings. Follow these steps to
enable advanced group settings:

Step 1 Select **Interface Configuration** from the left frame menu.

Step 2 Select the **Advanced Options** link in the center frame.

Step 3   Place a check mark in the boxes next to the following Group attributes:

      — Default Time-of-Day/Day-of-Week Specification

      — Group-Level Shared Network Access Restrictions

      — Group-Level Network Access Restrictions

      — Group-Level Downloadable ACLs

      — Group-Level Password Aging

      — Max Sessions

      — Usage Quotas

      — Voice-over-IP (VoIP) Group Settings

Step 4   Next, select **Submit**.

You have just enabled more configuration options in the Group Setup section. To verify this, follow these steps:

Step 1   Go to the **FirstUsers** group that you created.

Step 2   Select the arrow to display the Jump To menu.

Step 3   Now select the **Access Restrictions** section in the Jump To list, as shown in Figure 8-3.

Configuring Voice over IP Support

In ACS, you can configure Voice over IP groups. These groups are most likely kept separate from groups with configurations that have actual user-access restrictions in them. This is mainly because a Voice over IP group is going to authenticate with only a username. If this were a Voice over IP group that you were going to configure, you would place a check mark in the Voice over IP Support box. Users of a Voice over IP group authenticate with only a username, which is usually the telephone number of each device for each phone call or session. This option enables a NULL password for all members of this group. This option disables ACS from performing password checking on this group as well as some of other configuration parameters that are available when password authentication takes place. Voice over IP users need enter only the user ID, not a password to authenticate. In this case, the "user" is the phone itself. The person that uses the phone does not even know they are authenticating.

Figure 8-3   *Viewing Changes in the Group Setup*

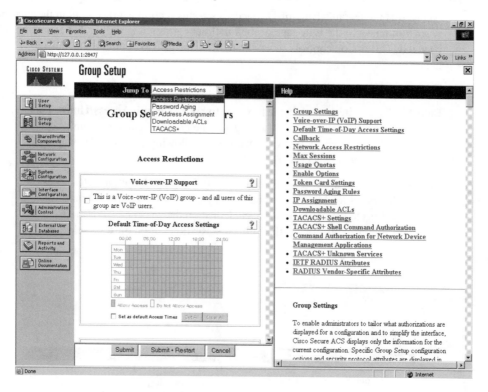

If you are not using Voice over IP in your network, this option is not necessary. To disable this option from view in Interface Configuration, follow these steps:

Step 1   Select **Interface Configuration**.

Step 2   Select the **Advanced Options** link.

Step 3   Deselect Voice-over-IP (VoIP) Group Settings.

Step 4   Select **Submit**.

This removes the Voice-over-IP Support from view in Group Configuration.

Configuring Time-of-Day Access Settings

Notice that the Default Time-of-Day access settings section is grayed out in the interface when you return to the Edit page of the FirstUsers group. It is visible, but cannot be changed. This option controls access hours. Use the grid to configure the desired access hours.

To change the grid, follow these simple steps:

Step 1   Place a check mark in the box next to **Set as Default Access Times**. This then allows you to modify the grid. The grid also changes from a gray color to a green color. A green box is for allowing access, and a white box is for denying access.

Step 2   To change the colors of a box, click it. Figure 8-4 demonstrates access hours set for Monday through Friday from 6:00 a.m. to 6:00 p.m. Also, access to the network has been denied on the weekends. For these settings to take place, the **Submit + Restart** button must be selected.

Figure 8-4   *Time-of-Day Access Restrictions*

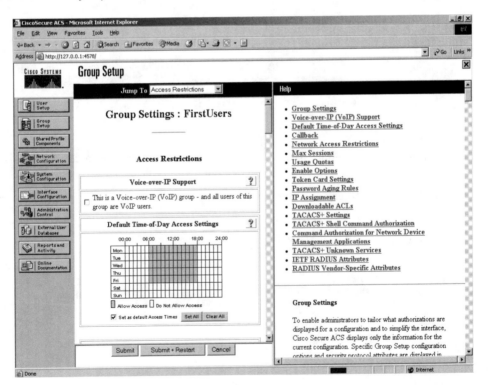

You can scroll through the Group Setup page and note that the only Time-of-Day access restrictions are at the Access Restrictions area. You can actually set Time-of-Day access restrictions for TACACS+ PPP configuration and TACACS+ Shell configuration.

To make the Time-of-Day grid visible in these sections, follow these steps:

Step 1   Select **Interface Configuration** from the left frame menu.

Step 2   Select **TACACS+ (Cisco IOS)**.

NOTE   TACACS+ appears here only if you have added an AAA client that uses TACACS+. This configuration was covered in Chapter 5, "Deploying Cisco Secure Access Control Server for Windows Server."

Step 3   Under the **Advanced Configuration Options** section place a check mark in the box next to **Display a Time-of-Day access grid** for every TACACS+ service where you can override the default Time-of-Day settings.

Step 4   Select **Submit**.

Step 5   Select the **Group Setup** button from the left menu.

Step 6   Select the **FirstUsers** group in the drop-down list.

Step 7   Click the **Edit** button.

A new Time-of-Day grid is then visible under the TACACS+ settings, as seen in Figure 8-5.

You can manipulate service hours for TACACS+ just as you did for access hours. Don't forget that you must select **Submit + Restart** for your changes to take place.

Figure 8-5 *TACACS+ Time-of-Day Restrictions*

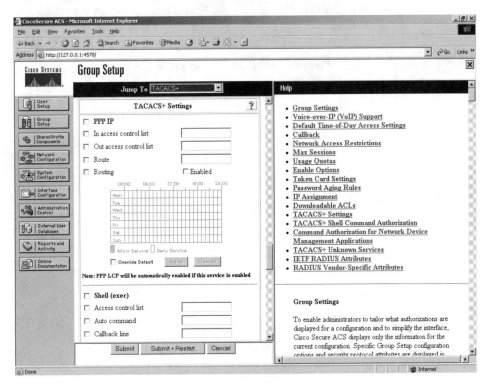

PPP Callback Configuration

Callback passes a command string back to an access server. This provides more security and allows you to initiate a callback string based on parameters given by the dialup client or from parameters in a Windows database. It is used in situations where you require the security of knowing the number you are calling back or even for the reversal of call charges. It is used in PPP connections for a number of reasons. When configuring callback options, you have three options:

- The first is security. You can option to use the Windows NT/2000 callback settings for the entire group. This way you can specify specific numbers to call back. This is one way to ensure network security.

- Another callback option you can choose is to allow the dialup client to specify the callback number. While this is not the most secure method, it allows the reversal of charges and connectivity to roaming users.

- The third option of callback is to select the option **No callback allowed**, which disables callback features for the group.

Configuring Network Access Restrictions

As you begin to explore the group section to apply Network Access Restrictions (NAR), note that you see no current NARs in the left vertical box titled NARs. This is because you must first configure the NAR before you can apply it. In this section, you configure a NAR and then apply it to an interface.

The type of NAR that you configure is called a shared NAR. All users of this group share this common NAR, and you can also use this NAR for other groups. A NAR is simply additional access restrictions that must be met before a user can access the network. By using a NAR, you are going to create an IP-based filter or a non-IP-based filter that provides that additional set of access restrictions. All in all, NARs must match specific attributes sent to the ACS by the AAA client. Understanding how to match these attributes is the key factor when deploying NARs in ACS.

Note the following information from a white paper on NARs:

- A non-IP-based NAR is a list of permitted or denied "calling" or "point of access" locations that you can employ in restricting an AAA client when an IP-based connection is not established. The non-IP-based NAR generally uses the calling line ID (CLID) number and the Dialed Number Identification Service (DNIS) number.

- By entering an IP address instead of the CLID, you can use the non-IP-based filter even when the AAA client does not use a Cisco IOS Software release that supports CLID or DNIS. In another exception to entering a CLID, you can enter a MAC address to permit or deny access when you are using a Cisco Aironet AAA client. Likewise, you could enter the Cisco Aironet access point MAC address instead of the DNIS number. The format of what you specify in the CLID box—CLID, IP address, or MAC address—must match the format of what you receive from your AAA client. You can determine this format from your RADIUS accounting log.

- When specifying a NAR, you can use an asterisk (*) as a wildcard for any value, or as part of any value, to establish a range. All the values and conditions in a NAR specification must be met for the NAR to restrict access. That is, the values are "ANDed."[1]

How a NAR Finds a Match

A NAR creates a rule that is based on a match or no match condition. In other words, permission to the network means that you match the NAR. If you do not match the NAR or if not enough information is provided, you are denied access to the network, provided the NAR is a PERMIT. If your NAR is used to deny access to the network, a match to the statement would invoke action to deny, and no match or not enough information would then permit network access.

It is important to understand what attribute field is used when a NAR is configured. The attribute field used if the TACACS+ protocol is in use is the rem_addr field. If you use RADIUS (IETF), calling-station-id (attribute 31) and called-station-id (attribute 30) are used. An attribute is an indication of what type of data is included; the value is the data.

NOTE   Chapter 13, "Exploring TACACS+ Attribute Values," covers the TACACS+ and RADIUS attribute/value pairs.

You can see the actions performed by a NAR more clearly in Table 8-1, the content of which was taken from a white paper[2].

Table 8-1   *NAR Permit and Deny Conditions*

	Match	No Match	Insufficient Information
Permit	Access granted	Access denied	Access denied
Deny	Access denied	Access granted	Access denied

When the ACS that's proxied to receives the T+ request, it checks to see if it has been sent by an IP address that it recognizes as the IP address of the AAA client in the NAR. Unless, as a workaround, the AAA server is configured as an AAA client, too, so that the NAR is written with this bogus AAA client instead of the real AAA client whose IP address is not associated with the forwarded T+ packet, the NAR will never match.

Configuring the NAR

You can configure a NAR in more than one way. You can configure a NAR in the group configuration, the user configuration, or as a shared NAR by using options available in Shared Profile Components. In this example, you configure a NAR only in the group configuration. In Chapter 9, "Managing Network Configurations," the Shared Profile Components are discussed. Follow these steps to configure the NAR at the group level for the network in Figure 8-6:

Step 1   From the left frame menu, choose the button labeled **Group Setup**.

Step 2   Select the **FirstUsers** group in the drop-down list.

Step 3   Click **Edit**.

Step 4   Scroll to **Per Group Defined Network Access Restrictions**.

Step 5   Select the check box **Define IP-based access restriction**.

Step 6   In the drop-down, select **Permitted Calling/Point of Access Locations**.

Step 7   Select **router14all** in the AAA Client drop-down. If router14all does not appear in your ACS configuration, you need to add it to the network configuration. Figure 8-6 demonstrates this AAA client.

Step 8   Enter **23** in the Port Field.

Step 9   Enter **10.*.*.*** in the Address field.

Step 10 Click **Enter**.

Step 11 Click **Submit and Restart**.

Figure 8-6   *router14all's Network Configuration*

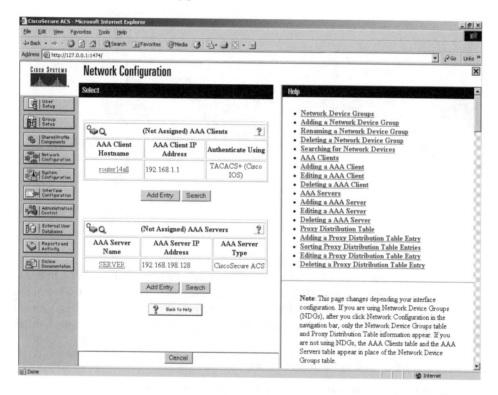

NOTE   In this situation, the default Permitted Calling/Point of Access option is selected in the field labeled Table Defines. Remember that this defines the "match." In other words, if the source IP address matches and the connection to port 23 is to the selected AAA client, the user is permitted access. If the IP address does not match that of the source address and is not destined for the AAA client, router14all, the users are denied access. The other option that you could select is the Denied Calling/Point of Access option. This would behave opposite the example.

Applying a NAR to a User

Now that you have a NAR specified for this group, it's time to look at an extension to the group configuration by adding NARs to the individual user configuration. For this example, you use the network diagram in Figure 8-7.

Figure 8-7 *Simple NAR Topology*

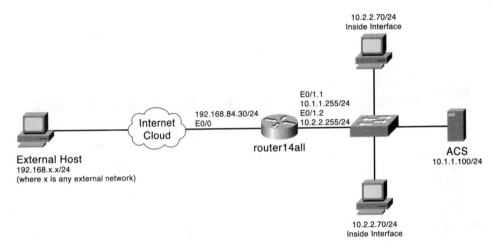

The AAA client router14all is the device that you want to control access to. In this simple network diagram, only two PCs are shown; however, they are in different subnets. The user ADMIN should not be allowed access from any subnet variation of the 10.x.x.x network, and all other users are allowed access to the AAA client on port 23. To accomplish this, you create two NARs.

To apply the NAR to this user, follow these steps:

Step 1 Access the user that you want to apply the NAR to.

Step 2 When in the edit screen of the user, scroll to the Network Access Restrictions (NAR) heading.

Step 3 Select the check box **Define IP-based access restriction**.

Step 4 In the drop-down, select **Denied Calling/Point of Access Locations**.

Step 5 Select **router14all** in the AAA client drop-down. If router14all does not appear in your ACS configuration, you need to add it to the network configuration. Figure 8-6 demonstrated this AAA client.

Step 6 Enter **23** in the Port Field.

Step 7 Enter **10.*.*.*** in the Address field.

Step 8 Click **Enter**.

Step 9 Click **Submit**.

In this configuration, the opposite effect takes place. The user with the deny NAR is not allowed to access port 23 of the AAA client router14all. This configuration is seen in Figure 8-8.

Figure 8-8 *Deny NAR in the User Configuration*

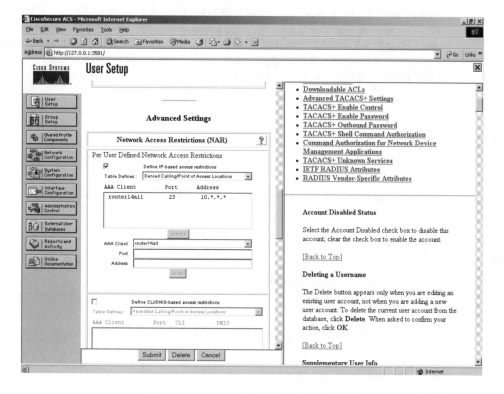

A Look at Shared Network Access Restrictions

By examining the User Setup, you find that user-level Network Access Restrictions are what you used in the preceding example. Although this method works, it is recommended that you create shared Network Access Restrictions in shared profile components. This is a more modular approach and gives you the ability to re-use any NAR that you create. You most likely need to enable shared Network Access Restrictions for both the user and group levels. This is done in Interface Configuration under Advanced Options. This configuration is performed in Chapter 10, "Configuring Shared Profile Components."

Max Sessions, Usage Quotas, and Password Aging Rules

In this section, multiple configuration features are presented. These are essential aspects of a security policy implementation. In particular, max sessions, usage quotas, and password aging rules are covered.

Max Sessions

If you break down the actual function of max sessions, you need to understand that ACS considers a session to be any type of connection that is supported by TACACS+ or RADIUS such as Telnet, PPP, or a NAS prompt. Therefore if you were to specify a max session limit for a group of 10 users to 20 sessions, each user could have only 2 sessions each. Likewise, a single user could establish 20 sessions, and no other users of the group would be allowed a session.

NOTE	The default for max sessions is unlimited for the group.

To restrict a single user from being allowed this many sessions, you could configure the max sessions available to users of this group.

NOTE	To make the max sessions option visible in Group Setup, you might once again need to enable the option in Interface Configuration.

An example of setting max usage options for the FirstUsers group would look something like the following:

- 10 users of FirstUsers group
- 20 sessions max limit set at group level
- 2 sessions available to users of this group

This allows the 20 sessions to be spread evenly across each user of the FirstUsers group. You might also choose to configure the max sessions available to users of this group as well as sessions available to users at the user level. Keep in mind that any configuration at the user level overrides the group-level configuration. Therefore, if you configure two sessions available to users of this group and five sessions available to a specific user, this five-session limit overrides the two-session limit. To track user accounting, you need to enable EXEC accounting on each NAS.

Usage Quotas

The configuration of usage quotas is fairly simple. In this section, you choose to limit each user of this group to a certain number of hours online per day, week, or month. You can also set this as an absolute value. You can also limit each user of this group to a certain number of sessions by day, week, and month or again as an absolute timer. The final option available here is to reset all counters for this group when you select **Submit**. This is always a good idea when you change these values.

As seen in other configurations, you can configure these settings at the user-configuration level. The difference in the configuration section at the user level is that you can see current usage statistics that you cannot see at the group level. This is seen in Figure 8-9.

Figure 8-9   *Current Usage Statistics*

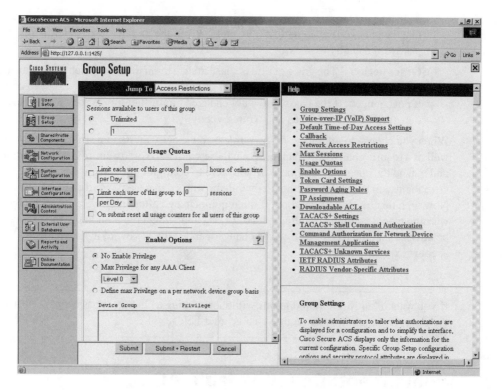

Password Aging Rules

Password aging gets its own Jump To link. To get to this section, choose **Password Aging** in the Jump To menu. As a security administrator, you understand the importance of changing passwords on a regular basis. This area of configuration allows you to force a user to change passwords accordingly.

According to the Cisco documentation, to use this feature, the AAA client must be running the TACACS+ or RADIUS protocol for password aging over dial-in connections. Only password aging over interactive connection (Telnet) is supported with TACACS+. This means that if you are using Telnet or Secure Shell (SSH), you need to use TACACS+. You can choose to apply age-by-date rules and age-by-uses rules and to apply a password change rule, which forces users to change their passwords after an administrator has changed it.

The age-by-date rule has three option boxes as follows:

- **Active period**—The active period is the number of days that you want to allow a user to log in without being prompted to change passwords. The default active period is 20 days. When a user is first prompted to change passwords, the user grace period and warning period begin.

- **Warning period**—The warning period is a length of time in which a user is warned that the password is going to expire and is given the number of days left before the password actually expires.

- **Grace period**—The grace period is a last chance login timer in which a user can login one last time with the original password. The user is warned that the password expires if not changed. If the password is not changed, no further logins are accepted even if the grace period timer has not expired yet.

When you choose to apply age-by-uses rules, you specify an issue warning after value as well as a require change after value. While these seem to be pretty simple, it is important to understand the absolute value here. If you were to configure the issue warning after value at 15 logins, on the 16th login the user would be warned that a password change is required. Now with this same configuration, if the require change after value were set to 20, the warning would continue for attempts 16, 17, 18, and 19. On the 20th login, the user would be advised that the password must be changed, and if the password is not changed, the account expires.

TIP   If you want to allow unlimited logins without requiring a change of passwords, use a -1 in the issue warning after and require change after fields.

IP Assignment and Downloadable ACLs

Certain network configurations are best kept on the network devices. Many agree, however, that from the network management standpoint, it is extremely beneficial to place as much configuration as possible in a central location. This eases the time taken to manage equipment as well as eases in disaster recovery procedures. In this section, we look at two more aspects of ACS that can both be maintained on ACS.

Address Assignment

Address assignment is a very simple configuration that allows you, the administrator, to control the IP assignment of the users of this group. Beginning with the first option in the IP assignment section of the Group Setup, you can opt to not assign IP addresses. You might also want to allow the dial-in client to specify the IP assignment. In either case, the configuration on your part is minimal.

Note that if you choose to assign an IP address from a pool that is configured on the AAA client, ensure that you have configured that pool on the AAA client and reference the name of that pool in ACS. The format for creating this type of pool on a Cisco PIX Firewall is demonstrated in Example 8-1.

Example 8-1 *Configuring an IP Pool on a Cisco PIX Firewall*

```
ip local pool bigpool 192.168.1.1-192.168.1.254
```

In the configuration of ACS, the pool named **bigpool** would be referenced. This pool can be seen in Figure 8-10. Notice that the name referenced matches the name defined in the pool in Example 8-1.

Figure 8-10 *Assignment of IP from AAA Client Pool*

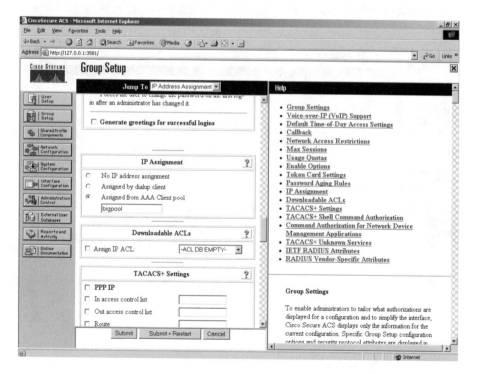

While this configuration works well, you must keep in mind that it is not as easy to manage the range of the pool or pool configuration because it is actually configured on another device. You must also select **Submit + Restart** for your changes to take effect.

For ease of management, you have the ability to configure the pool value on the ACS itself. For this configuration, you must follow these steps:

Step 1 Select the **System Configuration** button in the left frame menu.

Step 2 In the System Configuration select screen, choose the **IP Pools Server** link.

NOTE If this option does not appear in your ACS interface, you need to enable IP Pools in Interface Configuration.

Step 3 Select the **Add Entry** button.

Step 4 In the New Pool screen, enter the information pertaining to your pool. A sample of this configuration is seen in Figure 8-11.

Figure 8-11 *Configuring an IP Pool in ACS*

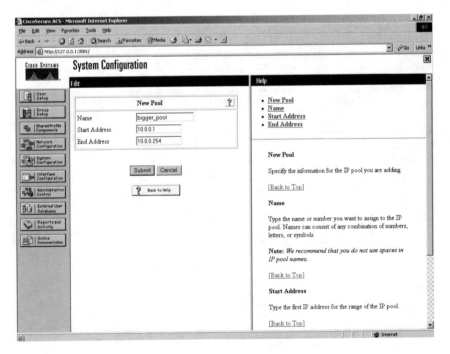

Step 5 Select **Submit**.

Now that the pool has been configured on the ACS server, return to the group configuration to apply this pool to the group. The following steps detail the configuration process in the Group Setup page:

Step 1   Select **IP Address Assignment** in the Jump To at the top of the Group Setup frame.

Step 2   Select the radio button labeled **Assigned from AAA server pool**.

Step 3   From the Available Pools list, select the **bigger_pool** and choose the right arrow button.

NOTE   This places the bigger_pool in the Selected Pools list on the right. You do have the ability to assign multiple pools, in which case the pool at the top of the list would be the first pool of addresses served to users. You cannot change the order that the pools are used in; it is always top to bottom. However, you can change the order of the pools in the list with the up and down buttons.

Step 4   Select **Submit + Restart** for your changes to take effect.

Now, you are all set to assign IP addresses from ACS.

Downloadable IP ACLs

The downloadable IP ACL is a fairly new configuration option in the ACS device. It was specifically designed to work with the PIX Firewalls; however, in ACS 3.2, it works with VPN 3000 series concentrators. In ACS 3.1, you see it in the interface as downloadable PIX ACLs, and in version 3.2, it has been renamed to downloadable IP ACLs.

To use the downloadable PIX ACL, you must use the RADIUS protocol in communication between the PIX and ACS and have authorization configured. This allows an ACL to be downloaded to any PIX Firewall in the network. This is more efficient from a network management standpoint. In this manner, you do not need to configure ACLs within the command line of each PIX Firewall. When a user makes an outbound connection attempt and is authenticated and authorized, the ACL is downloaded. You still need to configure an ACL on outside interfaces to allow inbound connectivity through your firewalls. It is sometimes easier to understand if you see it step by step. Figure 8-12 shows a PIX Firewall and downloadable ACLs. This process is broken out into the following steps:

Step 1   A request to the Internet server from the AAA user is intercepted by the PIX Firewall.

Step 2   An authentication request is sent to the AAA server.

Step 3 An authentication response containing the ACL name and time and date stamp from AAA server is sent back to the PIX Firewall.

Step 4 The PIX Firewall checks to see if the AAA user's ACL is already present in its configuration and looks at the time and date stamp to ensure the ACL, if already present, is current.

Step 5 If the PIX Firewall does not find the ACL present, it requests the ACL from the AAA server.

Step 6 The AAA server sends the ACL to the PIX Firewall.

Step 7 The request from the AAA user to the Internet server matches a permit in the ACL, and the request is forwarded to the Internet server.

Figure 8-12 *Downloadable IP ACLs*

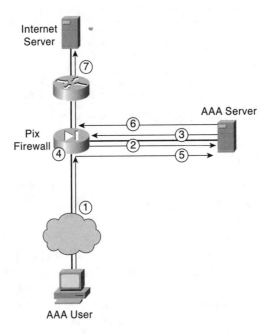

Next, explore the actual configuration of an ACL using the network displayed in Figure 8-13.

Assume that the user at 10.0.7.11 wants to access the HTTP server at 192.168.100.1. If you were to configure an access list on the PIX Firewall itself, it would look something like the following:

```
access-list inside_out permit tcp host 10.0.7.11 host 192.168.100.1 eq www
```

Figure 8-13 *Downloadable IP ACL Examples*

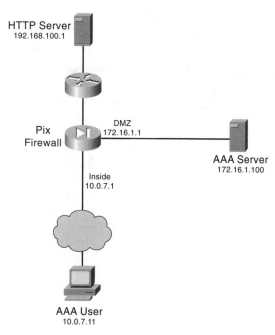

You can further enhance this configuration with object grouping; however, object groups cannot be used when defining PIX ACLs in ACS. Therefore, you configure the ACL just as you would in the aforementioned example; however, you don't include the access list portion of the command, nor does the access list include a name in the configuration. An example of the access list configuration in shared profile components would be as follows:

```
permit tcp host 10.0.7.11 host 192.168.100.1 eq 80
deny ip any any
```

This ACL configuration can be seen in Figure 8-14.

This takes care of the configuration on the ACS device. You can see the ACL being selected in the FirstUsers group configuration page in Figure 8-15.

Figure 8-14 *Configuring the Downloadable IP ACL*

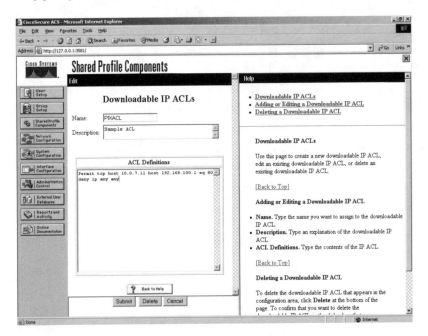

Figure 8-15 *Selecting the ACL for a Group*

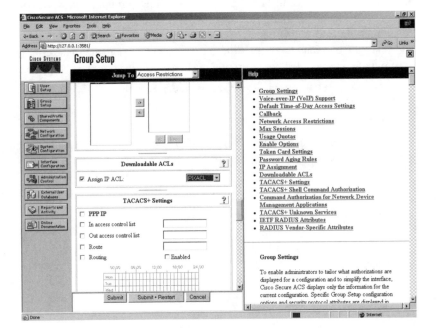

The final step of the configuration is to configure AAA authentication on the PIX Firewall. To configure the PIX Firewall for AAA, perform the following tasks:

Step 1   Define the AAA server group and protocol.

NOTE   You must use RADIUS for downloadable ACLs.

Step 2   Define the AAA server IP address and secret key.

Step 3   Configure AAA authentication outbound.

A sample configuration of AAA for use with downloadable ACLS is seen in Example 8-2.

Example 8-2   *Sample Configuration*

```
pixfirewall(config)#sh aaa
aaa authentication match DOWNLIST inside MYRADIUS
pixfirewall(config)#sh aaa-server
aaa-server TACACS+ protocol tacacs+
aaa-server RADIUS protocol radius
aaa-server LOCAL protocol local
aaa-server MYRADIUS protocol radius
aaa-server MYRADIUS (inside) host 172.16.1.100 secretkey timeout 10
pixfirewall(config)#sh access-list
pixfirewall(config)#access-list DOWNLIST permit ip any any
```

Keep in mind here that you do not need to configure authorization for the Downloadable PIX ACL. It occurs during the AAA authentication in RADIUS.

Using TACACS+ for Group Configuration

TACACS+ is the next generation of the TACACS protocol, which was a lightweight User Datagram Protocol (UDP) designed for access control by BBN, now a Verizon Company for the MILNET.

The TACACS+ protocol enhances the functionality of the TACACS protocol by separating authentication, authorization, and accounting. TACACS+ also encrypts all traffic between the AAA client and the TACACS+ service daemon that runs on a server, such as ACS. TACACS+ uses TCP port 49 in communications. The CSTacacs service of ACS listens on port 49.

To begin your configuration of ACS TACACS+ settings, you need to have a plan as to how you want to implement TACACS+. In this section, you can assign an inbound access control list, an outbound access control list, or a route, or enable routing. The ability to configure time-of-day restrictions can also be enabled in the interface configuration. Each dial-in network varies.

NOTE	You can find more information on PPP configurations on the Cisco website at Cisco.com.

Note that you can configure shell (EXEC) TACACS+ settings to be applied to the group for all users here. You can enable some very basic configurations here, and, of course, you can configure many intermediate to advanced configurations here. The purpose of this section is not to give you the how-to for every configuration available, but rather to give you configuration examples to help you better understand how the ACS reacts with AAA clients using TACACS+ for additional configurations.

NOTE	I have always thought that seeing is believing. Along with believing comes the understanding of how the protocol works. The example that you see here is one of the configurations that actually made that light bulb go off for me. The true test is to just try your ideas.

Basic TACACS+

In this example, you use TACACS+ to perform some authorization and an autocommand. Follow these steps to complete this example:

Step 1 Begin with the goal. In this situation, you have an administrator, that we call junior-admin, log in to a router via the Telnet protocol. This junior-admin is not allowed to make major changes to the router rbb. What you want to happen here is for junior-admin to see a menu when they authenticate to ACS, choose an option from that menu, and have authorization take place for those commands. Example 8-3 shows the configuration of the menu that is accessed by junior-admin upon accessing the command line of rbb.

Example 8-3 *Menu Configuration*

```
!
menu admin1 prompt ^C Please select an Action^C
menu admin1 text 1 Show IP Interface Brief
menu admin1 command 1 show ip interface brief
menu admin1 text 2 Show interface fa0/0
menu admin1 command 2 sh int fa0/0
menu admin1 text 3 Show Run Interface fa0/0
menu admin1 command 3 sh run int fa0/0
menu admin1 text 4 Show ip route
menu admin1 command 4 sh ip route
menu admin1 text 5 Show Arp
```

Example 8-3 *Menu Configuration (Continued)*

```
menu admin1 command 5 show arp
menu admin1 text 6 Clear the Arp table
menu admin1 command 6 clear arp
menu admin1 text 7 EXIT
menu admin1 command 7 logout
```

Step 2   After this menu has been added to the router, you can test it by typing the following command: **menu admin1**.

Step 3   Now that the menu is in place, you want to configure the TACACS+ settings on the router. Basic AAA commands are given in this example; however, for more detailed AAA configuration, see Appendix A, "RADIUS Attribute Tables." You now add the ACS server into the router.

Step 4   Configure the AAA group and protocol by entering the command **tacacs-server host 192.168.1.1.**

Step 5   Next, configure the secret key by entering the command **tacacs-server key cooljive**.

Step 6   To enable authentication, enter the following AAA configuration command: **aaa authentication login default group tacacs+ local**.

NOTE   Note that the tag **local** is added. This is to enable a secondary method of authentication in the event that the server is offline or becomes unavailable. For this to work, you need a local username and password on the router.

Step 7   Next, enable the router to send authorization requests to the ACS server. Do this by entering the command: **aaa authorization exec default group tacacs+ local**.

Note that, once again, the **local** tag is present. With this present, you need to enable the local command authorization on the Cisco router. You also need to add some additional configuration to the router to authorize for the commands in the menu admin1. These commands are seen in Example 8-4.

Example 8-4 *Router Authorization Commands*

```
privilege exec level 5 show ip interface brief
privilege exec level 5 show interface
privilege exec level 5 show run interface
privilege exec level 5 show ip route
privilege exec level 5 show arp
privilege exec level 5 clear arp
```

Figure 8-16 shows a sample of the basic network topology.

Figure 8-16 *Basic Network Topology*

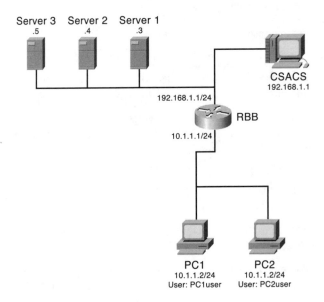

At this point, you need to configure the ACS server to perform the necessary authentication and authorizations. Begin the configuration on the ACS device by defining the router as an AAA client. Figure 8-17 shows an example of this.

After you define the router rbb in the ACS device, you might want to verify that junior-admin has an account on the ACS device. If not, be sure to create the junior-admin account.

Assume that in this network environment, we have also created a group called ROUTER_ ADMINS on our ACS device. At this point, you want to add junior-admin to the ROUTER_ADMINS group in ACS. When a member of the ROUTER_ADMINS group, junior-admin inherits the group settings unless otherwise configured at the user level. With junior-admin added to the ROUTER_ADMINS group, you can configure the group to run the autocommand when a user establishes a Telnet connection into the router.

Figure 8-17 *Adding an AAA Client to ACS*

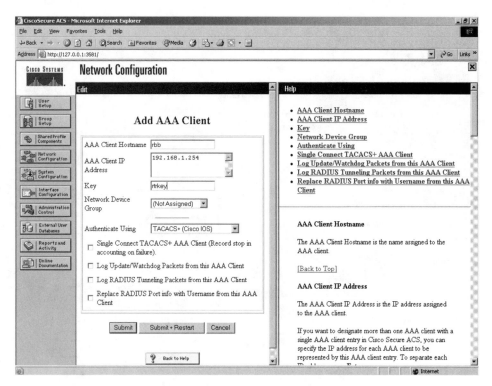

To enable the autocommand, simply follow these steps:

Step 1 Select **TACACS+** in the Jump To list. By selecting **TACACS+** in the Jump To list, you are taken to the TACACS+ Settings configuration screen. See Figure 8-18.

Step 2 From here, scroll to the **Shell (exec)** section. It is here that you enable the autocommand. You could enter any command here that you would like the user to execute. After the command has been executed, the Telnet connection to rbb drops.

Figure 8-18 *Using the Jump To*

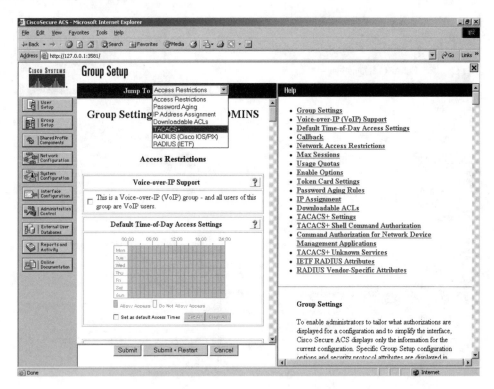

Step 3 Now that you are in the Shell (exec) configuration section, you want to select the check box next to **Shell (exec)**. This enables junior-admin shell authorization.

Step 4 Also, check the **autocommand** option and in the box, enter the command **menu admin1**. This was displayed in Figure 8-18.

Step 5 After the configuration is enabled, you can select **Submit + Restart** to restart the ACS service.

Step 6 Next, you Telnet from the junior-admin workstation where the junior-admin is prompted to enter a username and password. When authentication has been accepted, the autocommand takes place.

junior-admin is now authenticated through ACS, and the autocommand has been issued to the router. Now each command that is executed from the menu system is authorized as well. For some commands, junior-admin does not require any special configuration on the ACS.

For commands that require a level 15 or privileged level access to rbb, the command needs to be entered into ACS in a separate command authorization set.

With this configuration in place, you can now see the entire process by turning on the debug commands on rbb, **debug aaa authentication** and **debug aaa authorization**. Example 8-5 displays the authentication occurring during the login of junior-admin. Here, you see the messages passed between ACS and rbb.

Example 8-5 *Authentication Debug Output*

```
3w6d: AAA: parse name=tty131 idb type=-1 tty=-1
3w6d: AAA: name=tty131 flags=0x11 type=5 shelf=0 slot=0 adapter=0 port=131
  channel=0
3w6d: AAA/MEMORY: create_user (0x62098664) user='' ruser='' port='tty131'
rem_addr='192.168.1.1' authen_type=ASCII service=LOGIN priv=1
3w6d: AAA/AUTHEN/START (2194878578): port='tty131' list='' action=LOGIN
service=LOGIN
3w6d: AAA/AUTHEN/START (2194878578): using "default" list
3w6d: AAA/AUTHEN/START (2194878578): Method=tacacs+ (tacacs+)
3w6d: TAC+: send AUTHEN/START packet ver=192 id=2194878578
3w6d: TAC+: Opening TCP/IP to 192.168.1.254/49 timeout=5
3w6d: TAC+: Opened TCP/IP handle 0x623C7668 to 192.168.1.254/49
3w6d: TAC+: periodic timer started
3w6d: TAC+: 192.168.1.254 req=62098014 Qd id=2194878578 ver=192 handle=0x623C7668
(ESTAB) expire=4 AUTHEN/START/LOGIN/ASCII queued
3w6d: TAC+: 192.168.1.254 ESTAB id=2194878578 wrote 39 of 39 bytes
3w6d: TAC+: 192.168.1.254 req=62098014 Qd id=2194878578 ver=192 handle=0x623C7668
(ESTAB) expire=4 AUTHEN/START/LOGIN/ASCII sent
3w6d: TAC+: 192.168.1.254 ESTAB read=12 wanted=12 alloc=12 got=12
3w6d: TAC+: 192.168.1.254 ESTAB read=55 wanted=55 alloc=55 got=43
3w6d: TAC+: 192.168.1.254 received 55 byte reply for 62098014
3w6d: TAC+: req=62098014 Tx id=2194878578 ver=192 handle=0x623C7668 (ESTAB)
expire=4 AUTHEN/START/LOGIN/ASCII processed
3w6d: TAC+: periodic timer stopped (queue empty)
3w6d: TAC+: ver=192 id=2194878578 received AUTHEN status = GETUSER
3w6d: AAA/AUTHEN (2194878578): status = GETUSER
3w6d: AAA/AUTHEN/CONT (2194878578): continue_login (user='(undef)')
3w6d: AAA/AUTHEN (2194878578): status = GETUSER
3w6d: AAA/AUTHEN (2194878578): Method=tacacs+ (tacacs+)
3w6d: TAC+: send AUTHEN/CONT packet id=2194878578
3w6d: TAC+: periodic timer started
3w6d: TAC+: 192.168.1.254 req=623E5DD0 Qd id=2194878578 ver=192 handle=0x623C7668
(ESTAB) expire=5 AUTHEN/CONT queued
3w6d: TAC+: 192.168.1.254 ESTAB id=2194878578 wrote 25 of 25 bytes
3w6d: TAC+: 192.168.1.254 req=623E5DD0 Qd id=2194878578 ver=192 handle=0x623C7668
(ESTAB) expire=4 AUTHEN/CONT sent
3w6d: TAC+: 192.168.1.254 ESTAB read=12 wanted=12 alloc=12 got=12
3w6d: TAC+: 192.168.1.254 ESTAB read=28 wanted=28 alloc=28 got=16
3w6d: TAC+: 192.168.1.254 received 28 byte reply for 623E5DD0
3w6d: TAC+: req=623E5DD0 Tx id=2194878578 ver=192 handle=0x623C7668 (ESTAB)
expire=4 AUTHEN/CONT processed
3w6d: TAC+: periodic timer stopped (queue empty)
3w6d: TAC+: ver=192 id=2194878578 received AUTHEN status = GETPASS
```

continues

Example 8-5   *Authentication Debug Output (Continued)*

```
3w6d: AAA/AUTHEN (2194878578): status = GETPASS
3w6d: AAA/AUTHEN/CONT (2194878578): continue_login (user='junior-admin')
3w6d: AAA/AUTHEN (2194878578): status = GETPASS
3w6d: AAA/AUTHEN (2194878578): Method=tacacs+ (tacacs+)
3w6d: TAC+: send AUTHEN/CONT packet id=2194878578
3w6d: TAC+: periodic timer started
3w6d: TAC+: 192.168.1.254 req=623E5DD0 Qd id=2194878578 ver=192 handle=0x623C7668
(ESTAB) expire=5 AUTHEN/CONT queued
3w6d: TAC+: 192.168.1.254 ESTAB id=2194878578 wrote 27 of 27 bytes
3w6d: TAC+: 192.168.1.254 req=623E5DD0 Qd id=2194878578 ver=192 handle=0x623C7668
(ESTAB) expire=4 AUTHEN/CONT sent
3w6d: TAC+: 192.168.1.254 ESTAB read=12 wanted=12 alloc=12 got=12
3w6d: TAC+: 192.168.1.254 ESTAB read=18 wanted=18 alloc=18 got=6
3w6d: TAC+: 192.168.1.254 received 18 byte reply for 623E5DD0
3w6d: TAC+: req=623E5DD0 Tx id=2194878578 ver=192 handle=0x623C7668 (ESTAB)
expire=4 AUTHEN/CONT processed
3w6d: TAC+: periodic timer stopped (queue empty)
3w6d: TAC+: ver=192 id=2194878578 received AUTHEN status = PASS
3w6d: AAA/AUTHEN (2194878578): status = PASS
3w6d: TAC+: Closing TCP/IP 0x623C7668 connection to 192.168.1.254/49
3w6d: TAC+: Opening TCP/IP to 192.168.1.254/49 timeout=5
3w6d: TAC+: Opened TCP/IP handle 0x623F0744 to 192.168.1.254/49
3w6d: TAC+: periodic timer started
3w6d: TAC+: 192.168.1.254 req=623E5DD0 Qd id=1466688619 ver=192 handle=0x623F0744
(ESTAB) expire=5 AUTHOR/START queued
3w6d: TAC+: 192.168.1.254 ESTAB id=1466688619 wrote 66 of 66 bytes
3w6d: TAC+: 192.168.1.254 req=623E5DD0 Qd id=1466688619 ver=192 handle=0x623F0744
(ESTAB) expire=4 AUTHOR/START sent
3w6d: TAC+: 192.168.1.254 ESTAB read=12 wanted=12 alloc=12 got=12
3w6d: TAC+: 192.168.1.254 ESTAB read=30 wanted=30 alloc=30 got=18
3w6d: TAC+: 192.168.1.254 received 30 byte reply for 623E5DD0
3w6d: TAC+: req=623E5DD0 Tx id=1466688619 ver=192 handle=0x623F0744 (ESTAB)
expire=4 AUTHOR/START processed
3w6d: TAC+: periodic timer stopped (queue empty)
3w6d: TAC+: (1466688619): received author response status = PASS_ADD
3w6d: TAC+: Closing TCP/IP 0x623F0744 connection to 192.168.1.254/49
3w6d: AAA/MEMORY: free_user (0x62098664) user='junior-admin' ruser='' port='tty131'
rem_addr='192.168.1.1' authen_type=ASCII service=LOGIN priv=1
rbb#
rbb#
```

In the debug outputs, you can see the user is authenticated and you can also see the start/stop accounting taking place.

In Example 8-6, you see the authorization taking place using the **debug aaa authorization** command. In these messages you can see the TACACS+ AV (Attribute-Value) pairs. An AV pair is an Attribute, such as autocmd=, and a Value, such as menu admin1.

Example 8-6 *Authorization Debug Output*

```
rbb#debug aaa authorization
AAA Authorization debugging is on
rbb#
3w6d: AAA: parse name=tty131 idb type=-1 tty=-1
3w6d: AAA: name=tty131 flags=0x11 type=5 shelf=0 slot=0 adapter=0 port=131
  channel=0
3w6d: AAA/MEMORY: create_user (0x62098664) user='' ruser='' port='tty131'
rem_addr='192.168.1.1' authen_type=ASCII service=LOGIN priv=1
3w6d: tty131 AAA/AUTHOR/EXEC (729024685): Port='tty131' list='' service=EXEC
3w6d: AAA/AUTHOR/EXEC: tty131 (729024685) user='junior-admin'
3w6d: tty131 AAA/AUTHOR/EXEC (729024685): send AV service=shell
3w6d: tty131 AAA/AUTHOR/EXEC (729024685): send AV cmd*
3w6d: tty131 AAA/AUTHOR/EXEC (729024685): found list "default"
3w6d: tty131 AAA/AUTHOR/EXEC (729024685): Method=tacacs+ (tacacs+)
3w6d: AAA/AUTHOR/TAC+: (729024685): user=junior-admin
3w6d: AAA/AUTHOR/TAC+: (729024685): send AV service=shell
3w6d: AAA/AUTHOR/TAC+: (729024685): send AV cmd*
3w6d: AAA/AUTHOR (729024685): Post authorization status = PASS_ADD
3w6d: AAA/AUTHOR/EXEC: Processing AV service=shell
3w6d: AAA/AUTHOR/EXEC: Processing AV cmd*
3w6d: AAA/AUTHOR/EXEC: Processing AV priv-lvl=15
3w6d: AAA/AUTHOR/EXEC: Authorization successful
3w6d: AAA/MEMORY: free_user (0x62098664) user='junior-admin' ruser='' port='tty131'
rem_addr='192.168.1.1' authen_type=ASCII service=LOGIN priv=1
```

For the most part, this configuration works well for those new administrators. The problem here is that junior-admin is a member of the same group as the other administrators, those of whom are allowed more extensive access to the routers on the network. When any member of the administrator group Telnets to rbb, they receive the autocommand back from ACS, and no way to break out of the menu exists after they are there.

Some of the options you have here are to edit the menu to allow a break out of the menu to the command line or to move the autocommand from the group configuration to the user configuration. This configuration appears to be a better solution in that when a user graduates to a new level of access, you simply remove the autocommand in ACS.

Figure 8-19 displays the same type of autocommand configuration that you performed in Group Setup, only this is being performed at the user level in ACS. Notice that the configuration area in User Setup does not require a restart to the ACS service. This might be another motivating factor in determining how to approach the placement of the autocommand.

Figure 8-19 *User Level Autocommand*

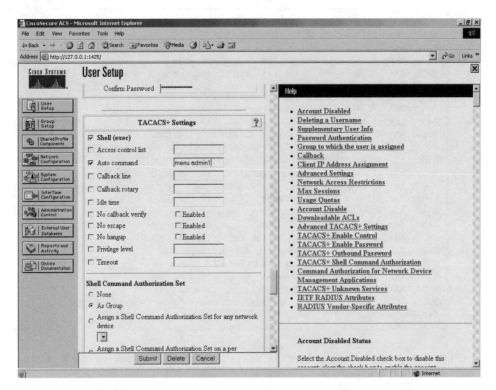

Although this example seems to be very basic, it demonstrates a number of different functions and aspects of ACS. In this example, you can not only see authentication via ACS take place, but also see the "autcmd" AV pair in detail and command authorization.

Shell Command Authorization Sets

Another aspect of TACACS+ in ACS is the Shell Command Authorization Sets. Here you have the ability to utilize shell command authorizations. In this section, you create two configurations using the same configuration areas in ACS. You most likely want to utilize these functions in separate groups. In Figure 8-20, you see the Shell Command Authorization Sets configuration fields.

In this example, you see that the ROUTER_ADMINS group uses shell command authorization, implemented with the Cisco PIX Firewalls running OS version 6.2(2) to authorize command-line entries for junior-admin. Example 8-7 demonstrates the authentication and authorization configuration on the PIX Firewall. Figure 8-21 is a sample of this network.

Figure 8-20 *Shell Command Authorization Sets*

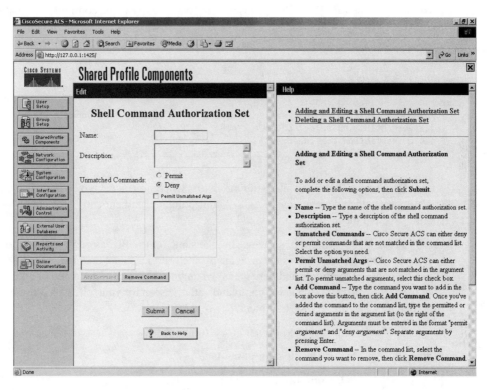

Figure 8-21 *Command Authorization with the PIX Firewall*

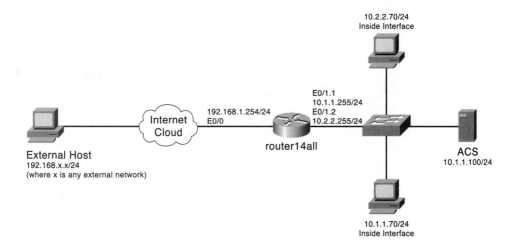

You can configure command-line authorizations with other Cisco devices; however, only examples with the PIX Firewalls are discussed. Example 8-7 is the configuration that is used on the PIX Firewall.

Example 8-7 *PIX Configurations*

```
aaa-server MYACS protocol TACACS+
aaa-server MYACS (inside) host 10.0.1.11 acskey
aaa authentication enable console MYACS
aaa authentication serial console MYACSaaa authentication ssh console MYACS
aaa authentication telnet console MYACS
aaa authorization command MYACS
```

After you have the PIX Firewall configured with this command set, you can then use the **enable** command to authenticate to ACS. At this point, the authentication for junior-admin should pass, but the authorization would fail.

The steps in the following step sequence are the same for the PIX as they would be for the routers and switch shell. This is because the pixshell service is not enabled in the PIX OS. What is important to understand here is that when you enable command authorization for your users, you also need to enable command authorization for yourself. This prevents you from being locked out of the equipment.

To create a basic command authorization set, follow these steps:

Step 1 Select **Shared Profile Components**.

Step 2 Select **Shell Command Authorization Sets**.

Step 3 Select **Add**.

Step 4 Enter a name and description for this set of commands.

Step 5 You have the option to either permit or deny unmatched commands. In this first example, you want to permit everything. Select **Permit** and then select **Submit**.

This creates a "superuser" set. You now need to apply it to the group that this user is a member of. Figure 8-22 shows a sample of this command set.

Figure 8-22 *Shell Command Authorization Set*

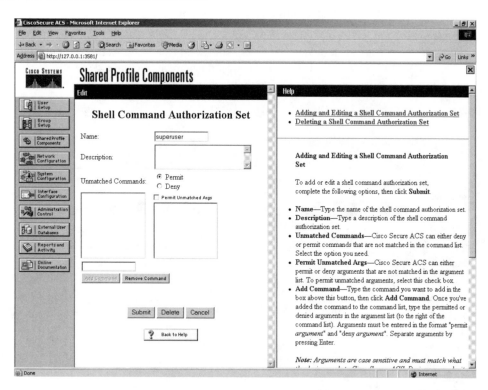

To enable this command authorization set for users of the ROUTER_ADMINS group, follow these steps:

Step 1   Select the **admin** group in group configuration, and scroll to the pixshell option.

NOTE   There is no point in enabling pixshell in the interface configuration as this option is not enabled on the PIX itself. To perform this configuration, you simply need shell command authorization.

Step 2   In the shell section of group configuration, place a check mark in the box next to **Shell Command Authorization Set**.

Step 3   Next, select the option to **Assign a Command Authorization Set for any network device**. Ensure that the Shell Command Authorization Set that you created is seen in the drop-down menu. Figure 8-23 demonstrates the preceding group configuration.

Figure 8-23   *Assigning a Command Authorization Set to the Group*

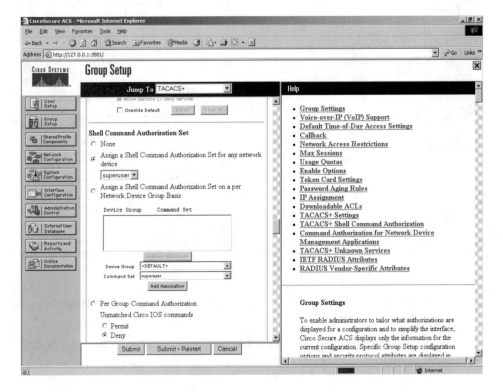

Step 4   Now select **Submit + Restart** for this configuration to take place.

You also need to ensure that advanced TACACS+ options are enabled in Interface Configuration. To enable this, perform the following task:

Step 1   Select **Interface Configuration**.

Step 2   Select **TACACS+ Cisco IOS**.

Step 3   Check **Advanced TACACS+ Features**.

Step 4   Click **Submit**. This makes the advanced TACACS+ settings visible under the user configuration.

Step 5   Select **Group Setup**.

Step 6   Select **ROUTER_ADMINS** in the drop-down list.

Step 7   Use the Jump To to access Enable options.

Step 8   Select the **Max Privilege for any AAA Client** radio button.

Step 9   Select **Level 15** in the drop-down list.

Step 10 Select **Submit + Restart**.

Step 11 Select **User Setup**.

Step 12 Select **List All Users**.

Step 13 Scroll to **TACACS+ Enable Password**.

Step 14 Select **Use CiscoSecure PAP Password**.

Step 15 Select **Submit**.

You can now configure the authorization set. To do so, follow these steps:

Step 1   Go to **Shell Command Authorization Set**, check the **Command** button, and enter **login**.

Step 2   Select **Permit** under **Unlisted Arguments**. Repeat this process for the **logout**, **enable**, and **disable** commands. This is creating a set of commands that is authorized.

Step 3   Go to **Shell Command Authorization Set**, check the **Command** button, and enter **show**. Under **Arguments**, enter **permit clock**, and select **deny** for **Unlisted Arguments**.

Step 4   When you are finished, click **Submit**. This enables some basic command authorization at the Group level.

User-Level Authorization

Although the group-level command authorization provides an amount of security, it is not every situation that everyone in the group is given the same level. For situations such as this, you are going to take your command authorization a step further by configuring user-level command authorization.

Before you begin configuring user-level authorization, ensure that it is enabled in Interface Configuration. Follow these steps to enable the option:

Step 1   Select the Advanced Options link.

Step 2   Select **Per-user TACACS+/RADIUS Attributes**. This enables the visibility of user-level authorization; however, you're not done yet.

Step 3   The next step here is to enable the option at the user level. This is also done at the Interface Configuration section. Select the **TACACS+ (Cisco)** link, and at this point, you should be able to see a new column for enabling user options. Select the **Shell (exec)** option.

From this point on, you can configure user-level command authorization just as you would configure group-level authorization. As a point of reference, you should keep in mind that user attributes override group attributes. Configure a group-level command authorization policy that is relevant to most of the group members and minimizes the amount of configuration you perform at the individual user level.

As a side note, when testing your configuration, create two users and apply the test settings to one individual user so that if by chance you are locked out of the device, you can access it with the other user account. Don't be afraid to experiment with the individual users. By now, you should have a firm understanding on both the ability to configure group items, while integrating other configurations such as downloadable PIX ACLs and Network Access Restrictions, as well as your ability to configure these at a user level for more specific policy settings.

Summary

It is important to understand the correlation between group configurations and user configurations. You can optimize your configurations by using group settings to apply to the larger number of users and allow individual configuration to be done on an "as needed" basis. The ability of ACS to perform similar configuration in both User and Group Setup provides for this.

As you move on into the next chapter, you find that much of the configuration from one section in ACS (e.g., Shared Profile Components) is in other configuration sections. This ties your entire configuration together as you build your ACS foundation. The next chapter discusses managing your network configuration, more specifically the placement of one or many ACS devices. As you can tell, your configurations grow very quickly as you deploy more and more users, groups, and servers.

End Notes

[1] Network Access Restrictions White Paper, *NAR White Paper*, Cisco Systems, page 2, http://www.cisco.com/en/US/products/sw/secursw/ps2086/products_white_paper09186a00801a8fd0.shtml

[2] Network Access Restrictions White Paper, *NAR White Paper*, Cisco Systems, page 1, http://www.cisco.com/en/US/products/sw/secursw/ps2086/products_white_paper09186a00801a8fd0.shtml

In this chapter, you learn the following topics:

- How to manage network configurations
- How to configure Network Device Groups
- How to configure Proxy Distribution Tables
- How to configure remote accounting
- How to work with network device searches
- How to configure AAA clients
- How to troubleshoot network configurations

## CHAPTER 9

Managing Network Configurations

Now that you are comfortable with configuring user groups and user settings, it is time to scale your network by creating a distributed system in an environment where users can authenticate to remote authentication, authorization, and accounting (AAA) servers and still retrieve the AAA privileges, access rights, and restrictions that they would have received on the initial server. It is also time to deploy configurations such as network device groups.

In this chapter, the text covers each aspect of a distributed system, its benefits, and how to troubleshoot a network configuration.

Configuring a Distributed System

Distributed systems are networks that deploy multiple AAA servers. These AAA servers then perform authentication, authorization, and accounting to a primary device, backup device, or numerous devices that are peer systems. This is a way to enable a fallback in the event that one AAA server becomes unavailable. This increases network uptime by decreasing the possible downtime incurred by an unavailable AAA server.

With distributed systems in place, you can also control the user database locally and still authenticate that user, which accesses network services from remote locations, to that local database. This authentication can take place even though they authenticate through a remote AAA server that does not have that particular user account in it. This functionality is accomplished through the use of Proxy Distribution Tables and AAA servers in the Cisco Secure Access Control Server (CSACS) AAA servers table.

When the Distributed Systems Settings check box is selected, your interface (as seen in the HTML front end of CSACS) changes slightly. Figure 9-1 shows the view of the Network Configuration page prior to the Distributed System Settings being enabled in Interface Configuration.

Figure 9-1   *Network Configuration Before Enabling Distributed System Settings*

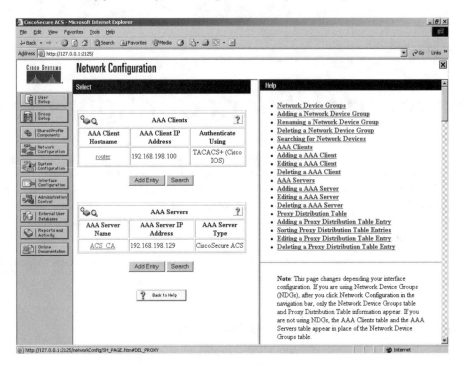

The configurations in this chapter are all enabled by the Distributed Systems Settings check box, the Remote Logging check box, and the Cisco Secure ACS Database Replication check box being selected. Regardless of whether Remote Logging and Cisco Secure ACS Database Replication are enabled, the default action that is implicit is to check the local ACS database for authentication. By checking this option, your existing configuration is not changed.

To enable this functionality, you must check the Distributed Systems Settings check box, under Advanced Options, as shown in Figure 9-2. Also in Figure 9-2, you can see that other options have been selected.

After the Distributed System Settings check box is checked, you see a table for AAA clients, a table for AAA servers, and a Proxy Distribution Table within the Network Configuration page. Note that the Proxy Distribution Table has the default entry of **(Default)**. This is the function previously mentioned for checking the local database. This default function is always enabled to force ACS to check its local database for authentication. The fact is that it is simply not visible until Distributed System Settings has been selected. To add entries to any of these tables, simply select the **Add Entry** button seen at the bottom of each table. Figure 9-3 shows the new view of Network Configuration.

Figure 9-2   *Enabling Distributed Systems*

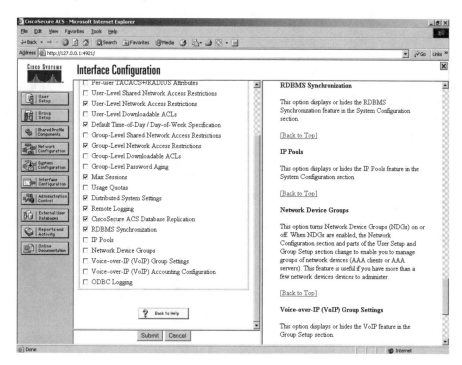

Other aspects of an AAA server that is in a distributed system are the ability to perform database replication and remote or central logging. You might notice a section labeled Proxy Distribution Table when you look at your Network Configuration page now. This is normal, and although there is an entry **(Default)**, all AAA requests are still sent only to the local device. This is discussed later in this chapter.

As you scale your configuration and your network begins to grow, your AAA server table is going to grow as well. Also, your Proxy Distribution Table and your AAA clients table grow. After additional devices have been configured in the AAA server table, ACS can perform other features such as Relational Database Management System (RDBMS) synchronization and database replication, as well as remote logging to any of these other AAA servers that are defined. More of these features and the Proxy Distribution Table are discussed in the following sections of this chapter. RDBMS synchronization is discussed in Chapter 11, "System Configuration."

Figure 9-3 *Network Configuration After Enabling Distributed System Settings*

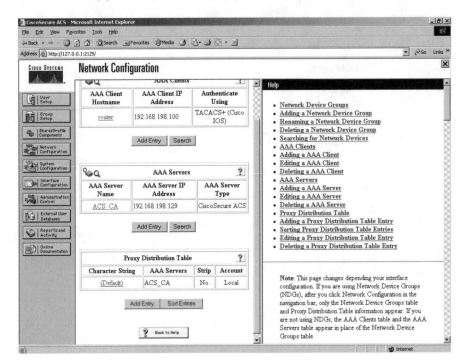

To help further understand the concept of a distributed system, examine Figure 9-4. It shows an ACS server deployed in California with local users, an AAA server deployed in Texas, and an AAA server deployed in New York. By creating a distributed system, you can enable a fallback in the event that one AAA server becomes available. Should an AAA server in California become available, users could authenticate, authorize, and be accounted for based on the server located in Texas or even New York. This configuration is simple on the AAA client device. Simply add the additional AAA servers with the correct AAA statement. For example, if you are using a PIX Firewall, you would simply add another AAA server statement, like so:

```
aaa-server <tag> [<(if_name)>] host <ip_address> [<key>] [timeout <seconds>]
aaa-server MYTACACS (outside) host 64.208.251.xx secretkey timeout 10
```

Figure 9-4   *Distributed System*

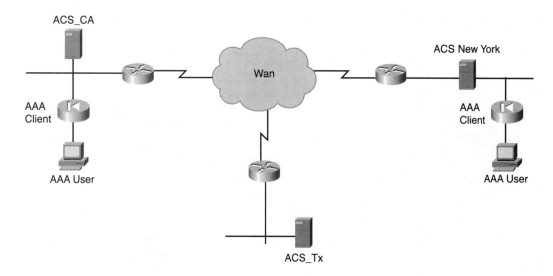

This distributed system increases network uptime and decreases downtime incurred by any unavailable AAA servers. With a distributed system in place, you can control the user database locally and, when users are out of town, still authenticate them to that same local database by using a Proxy Distribution Table configured on the remote ACS device that the user can authenticate through. If a user is in California and the ACS in California goes down, you could use replication functionality to authenticate the user to the ACS in Texas and so on. You could perform many different configurations.

Configuring Network Device Groups

As you can see in Figure 9-5, the Distributed System Settings check box and the Network Device Groups (NDG) check box have been selected in Interface Configuration. When they are selected, a NDG, which is a grouping of AAA servers and AAA clients, is formed. This simply allows you to group AAA clients and AAA servers into groups that might have something in common; for example, you might have a Network Device Group called Routers and another called Firewalls. Of course, you can tell by the name of the group what type of AAA devices is in the group.

Figure 9-5 *Selecting NDGs*

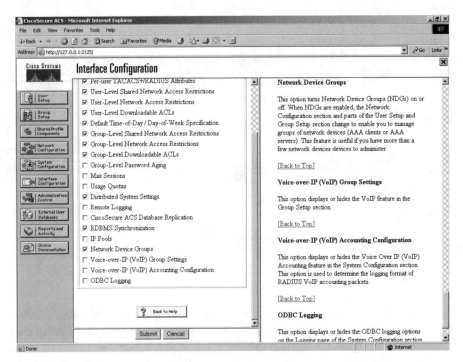

Refer to Figure 9-3, and you don't see any NDGs enabled. You can clearly see an entry for an AAA client named **router** and an entry for an AAA server.

After you have enabled NDGs in Interface Configuration, this view changes in Network Configuration. Figure 9-6 shows this new view.

When you create a new network device group, initially no users are assigned to it. Likewise, before you configure any NDGs, all users are members of the unassigned group. You can clearly see the Not Assigned group in Figure 9-6. To configure a new network device group, other than the Not Assigned group, follow these steps:

Step 1 Select the **Network Configuration** button on the left menu bar of ACS. This opens the Network Configuration page.

Step 2 Under the Network Device Group's table, click **Add Entry**.

Step 3 Select **Add**.

Step 4 Next enter a name for the NDG.

Step 5 Click **Submit**.

Figure 9-6 *New View of Network Configuration After Enabling NDGs*

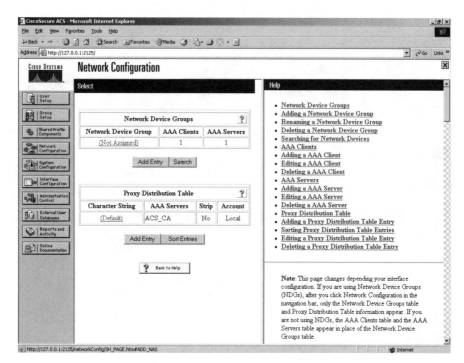

The new NDG that you have just created is now displayed in the Network Device Group table along with the Not Assigned group. Figure 9-7 displays the NDG labeled Perimeter Routers. Note that currently no AAA clients and no AAA servers are in this NDG.

After you have added this new group, you have the ability to assign AAA servers and AAA clients to it as you add them to your configuration.

To add a device to your newly formed NDG, perform the following in ACS:

Step 1 Select **Network Configuration**.

Step 2 Click the NDG you want to add devices to.

Step 3 Select the **Add Entry** button.

Step 4 Enter the AAA client information.

Step 5 Click the **Submit + Restart** button.

Figure 9-7   *Adding a New NDG*

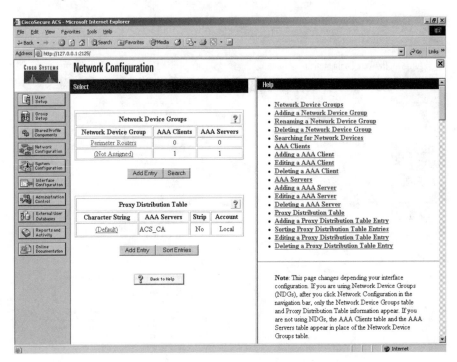

To move an existing AAA client from the Not Assigned NDG to the one you have created, follow these steps:

Step 1   Select the **(Not Assigned)** group.

Step 2   Select the AAA client you want to move.

Step 3   Using the drop-down list, select the NDG you want this AAA client to be placed into.

Step 4   Select **Submit + Restart**.

When you become familiar with NDGs, they can assist you in managing your configurations and making them easier to read, troubleshoot, and keep organized.

Configuring Proxy Distribution Tables

A Proxy Distribution Table allows you to take a request for authentication and forward it to other ACS devices based on the string prefix or suffix that you define. In this manner, you can authenticate a user from a California ACS through a New York ACS using a Proxy Distribution Table. As mentioned in the previous section, this is enabled based on a suffix or a prefix that is added to the username and configured within the Proxy Distribution Table by you.

When a local ACS sees a user request, the first place that ACS looks is into its database for that user. Assume that the ACS that is in New York sees an authentication request from an AAA client of the ACS in New York and the username and password is a user that is in the ACS California database. Because this user does not exist in the ACS New York database, the authentication would fail; however, with a Proxy Distribution Table configured, the ACS in New York could then forward the authentication request to the California ACS.

Proxy authentication can affect authentication by performing a string match. Suppose the string you want to match is **CA\.** You would configure the Proxy Distribution Table in New York with the information necessary to forward the request to California. When a user enters a username preceded or followed by the string, the request is forwarded.

In the Proxy Distribution Table, you define a prefix or a suffix. That prefix or suffix is then associated to another ACS server. For example, a New York ACS has an entry in the Proxy Distribution Table for a suffix of **CA**. When a California user authenticates and that request is sent to a New York ACS, the user then enters his or her username, *username***.CA**. When the New York ACS database determines the string and looks to the Proxy Distribution Table that has an entry for **.CA**, the authentication request is forwarded. The user is then authenticated to the correct database.

With proxy distribution, you also have the ability to configure ACS with multiple options in that Proxy Distribution Table. The character string that you find actually defines the suffix or the prefix. That suffix or prefix can be up to 32 characters long. The string contains a deliminating character, such as a dot (.) or a slash (/) to determine the breaking point, although this is not required. If you choose to use a prefix string, it would resemble the following:

```
Irvine/bcarroll.
```

In the preceding line of code, **bcarroll** is the username. **Irvine/** defines an entry in the Proxy Distribution Table and, more specifically, the prefix that matches. Keep in mind that you don't need to use a / as the deliminating character. You can actually use just about any character you would like. The slash is just an example. You could just as well use the @ symbol. In that case, your string would resemble the following:

```
IRVINE@bcarroll
```

If you choose to use a suffix, it would resemble the following:

```
bcarroll.IRVINE
```

Again, **bcarroll** is the username, and **.IRVINE** is the entry in the Proxy Distribution Table. If the username in the ACS database in Irvine is **bcarroll.IRVINE**, you want to leave things as is. If the user name is simply **bcarroll**, you configure stripping so that when the request is forwarded to the ACS in Irvine, the suffix or the prefix is stripped from the message. When you configure stripping, you must take into account the username format on the destination ACS.

When ACS proxies to another ACS, the second ACS responds to the first using only Internet Engineering Task Force (IETF) Remote Authentication Dial-In User Service (RADIUS) attributes if RADIUS is the protocol used. The ACS that receives the authentication request from the first ACS is unable to use any vendor-specific attributes.

To create entries in the Proxy Distribution Table and enable the entire process, you need to follow three major steps:

Step 1 Configure the local network access server (NAS).

Step 2 Configure the local AAA server.

Step 3 Configure the remote AAA server.

We begin with the local AAA server in California. To demonstrate, refer to Figure 9-8. Here, you can see that a user from New York is on the network in California and would like to retrieve information from the Internet.

Figure 9-8 *Proxy Distribution Table Example Network*

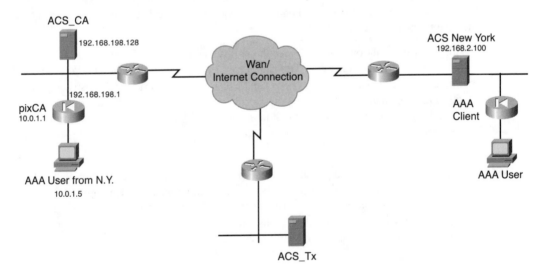

In the California network, the Internet use policy states that you must authenticate to ACS before you are allowed Internet access. Because the user from New York is not in the ACS_CA database, the user's authentication attempt would normally fail.

To cause the attempt to be successful, execute the following steps:

Step 1 Make sure your PIX Firewall is set up with the following configuration:

```
pixfirewall(config)# sh aaa-server
aaa-server TACACS+ protocol tacacs+ <--default config
aaa-server RADIUS protocol radius  <--default config
aaa-server LOCAL protocol local  <--default config
aaa-server MYTACACS protocol tacacs+  <--Defines the Protocol
aaa-server MYTACACS (outside) host 192.168.1.100 acskey timeout 10
  <--Defines the location of the server and the key
pixfirewall(config)#show access-list <- View the ACLs in place
access-list ACS; 1 elements <- This ACL is used in AAA to define what
  to authenticate
access-list ACS line 1 permit tcp host 10.0.1.100 any eq www (hitcnt=7)
access-list INSIDE; 3 elements <-This ACL defines what traffic is
  allowed to pass through the PIX firewall.
access-list INSIDE permit tcp any any eq www
access-list INSIDE permit tcp any any eq 443
access-list INSIDE deny ip any any
pixfirewall(config)# sh access-group <-This displays where the ACL is
  applied.
access-group INSIDE in interface inside
pixfirewall(config)#
pixfirewall(config)#show aaa <- this shows the ACL- ACS applied in the
  authentication statement.
aaa authentication match ACS inside MYTACACS
pixfirewall(config)#
```

Step 2 With the configuration in place on the firewall, you now configure the ACS_CA to view the PIX Firewall as an AAA client. By now you should be pretty comfortable adding AAA clients. Remember that you are using the Terminal Access Controller Access Control System Plus (TACACS+) protocol here.

Step 3 Next configure the ACS_CA with the proxy distribution information. For this example, you use the @ symbol as the deliminating character, and you perform stripping. Start by selecting **Network Configuration**.

Step 4 You need to add the ACS in New York as an AAA server to be able to use it in the Proxy Distribution Table. Select the NDG that you want to work with.

Step 5 Select the **Add Entry** button underneath the AAA Servers table. You can refer to Figure 9-9 to see where this button is. As you can see in Figure 9-9, this configuration is taking place in the Not Assigned NDG.

Figure 9-9   *Network Configuration*

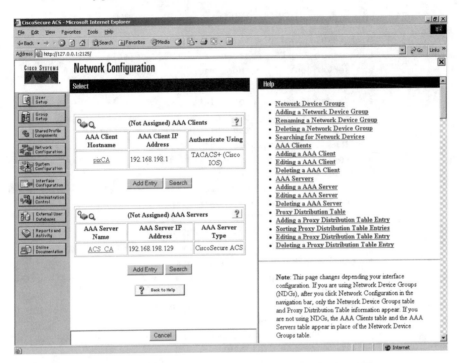

Step 6   Enter the name of the AAA server in New York.

Step 7   Enter the IP address of the AAA server.

Step 8   Enter the key to be used.

Step 9   Select **Submit + Restart**.

Step 10   Next, you use that server in the Proxy Distribution Table to forward
              authentication requests. Start by selecting the **Add Entry** button
              underneath the Proxy Distribution Table. For reference, refer to
              Figure 9-10. This is not in the Not Assigned NDG.

Figure 9-10 *Configuring the Proxy Distribution Table*

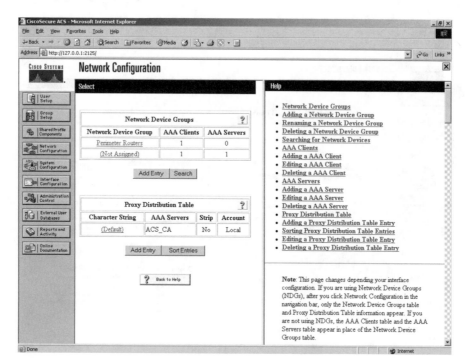

Step 11 Enter the character string.

Step 12 Using the drop-down arrow, select the **p** position. In this example, you use **suffix**.

Step 13 Select **Yes** in the Strip drop-down list.

Step 14 Select the ACS that you want to forward to, in this case ACS_NY, and click the right arrow button to move this server from the AAA server box on the left to the Forward To box on the right.

Step 15 Select **Submit + Restart**.

You can see this configuration in Figure 9-11. In this situation, the user needs to know that when he or she is authenticating when out of town he or she needs to include the suffix **@NY** in his or her username. If the suffix is not included, the authentication fails.

Figure 9-11 *Proxy Distribution Table Parameters*

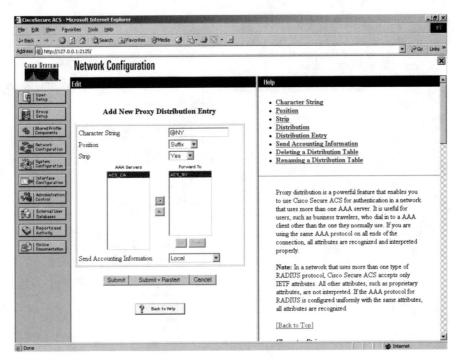

At this point, you would assume that you are done; however, you still have not configured the ACS New York. If you look at this scenario from the perspective of the ACS in New York, when it receives an authentication request from California, it is coming from the ACS_CA and not the pixCA. Therefore, you need to add ACS_CA as an AAA client in the ACS New York. By now, you should be comfortable adding AAA clients to ACS. The configuration is no different than it is with any other AAA client, even though the AAA client, ACS_CA, is an AAA server.

After it is added, you are able to authenticate, and you have just configured a Proxy Distribution Table. Now, you can add more than one server to the table, change the order that ACS proxies, and create a more distributed network.

Using Remote Accounting

When you deploy proxy in your network and you are using a Proxy Distribution Table, you increase the amount of accounting that you can do within your network. You can use accounting in the distributed system in three ways:

- You can log accounting information locally.
- You can forward accounting information to the destination AAA server.
- You can log accounting information locally and forward a copy to the destination AAA server.

The benefits of remote accounting are that the remote AAA server logs an entry in the accounting report for that session on the destination server, thus providing accounting records in another location. ACS also takes the user information for that connection and adds that user's connection information to the list of logged in users. You can view them in the logged in users report.

Another aspect to the remote use of accounting is that the Max Session feature can be enabled. If the remote AAA server is an ACS device and the Max Session feature is implemented, you can track the number of sessions for each user and each group and adjust them accordingly. You also have the option to account for Voice over IP.

To configure remote accounting in the Network Configuration menu, perform the following:

Step 1   Select the entry in the Proxy Distribution Table that you want to perform remote accounting for.

Step 2   Using the drop-down menu, choose **Local**, **Remote**, or **Local/Remote**. Note that if **Local** is chosen, no remote accounting is taking place.

You can see the three options available in Figure 9-12.

Figure 9-12 *Enabling Remote Accounting*

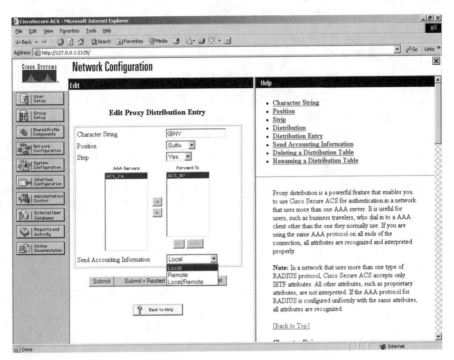

Using Network Device Searches

A network device search is a way to quickly locate network devices. Your ACS configuration grows by adding more AAA servers and more AAA clients to the configuration. Although the new devices are being added to NDGs, this configuration becomes large, and it is difficult to locate AAA servers and AAA clients when you need to verify information or for troubleshooting. Fortunately, ACS has a network device search feature that allows you to search for network devices that are configured in your table based on the name, which is the IP address. In addition to searching for the IP address as a 32-bit address, you can use a wildcard. For example, you could use 192.168.15.*, where the * would be the wildcard that would search the entire range.

You can also search based on the type, on whether it is an AAA server or AAA client, as well as for the NDG that the device is assigned to. For example, if you know it is assigned to a NDG named California and you find so many AAA servers in California's NDG that it is difficult to manage, you can break down the search in that fashion.

To perform a network device search, perform the following:

Step 1   Select **Network Configuration**.

Step 2   Select **Search** under the Network Device Groups table.

Step 3   Enter the host name of the device you are trying to locate. You can leave the asterisk as a wildcard or even enter a partial name with the asterisk appended and search that way.

Step 4   Enter the IP address in dotted decimal notation. You can also enter an asterisk here in place of any octet.

Step 5   Using the drop-down menu, select the type of network device you are searching for. The options are any, TACACS+ (Cisco IOS), RADIUS (IETF), Cisco Secure AAA server, TACACS+ AAA server, or RADIUS AAA server.

Step 6   Using the drop-down menu, select the device group you want to search. The default is any.

NOTE   Any one of the search criteria is sufficient. If you search with the default wildcards, all devices are returned.

In Figure 9-13, a search is performed using the IP address 192.168.*.*. You are asking the search to return all devices that match the IP address of 192.168.*anything-in-this-spot.anything-in-this-spot*.

In Figure 9-14, you see the results of the search. It is apparent that three network devices match the search criteria.

Figure 9-13 *NDG Search*

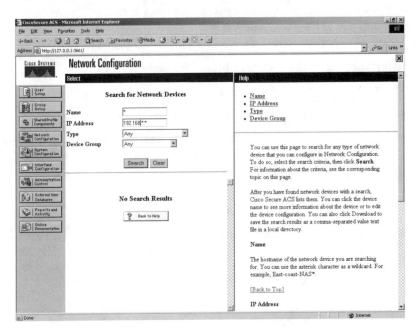

Figure 9-14 *NDG Search Results*

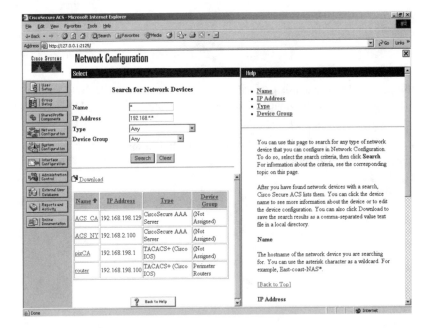

Creating a Complete Distributed Network

You can now tie the configurations discussed in this chapter together and create a complete distributed network. You started out with a network that you wanted to make a distributed system and added a Proxy Distribution Table to forward authentication requests to other ACSs. After your Proxy Distribution Table was created, you were able to configure remote accounting. You also enabled NDGs along the way and discovered how to search them. The following is a recap of all the steps that you performed in this chapter in an order that keeps your ACS configuration clean and easily readable.

The steps required to perform this task include enabling the necessary options in interface configuration, configuring a NDG, moving and manipulating AAA servers and clients, and configuring the Proxy Distribution Table. Finally, you search the NDGs for specific devices for configuration and troubleshooting purposes.

To create a complete distributed network, perform the following tasks:

Step 1   Select **Interface Configuration**.

Step 2   Select **Advanced Options**.

Step 3   Place a check mark next to **Distributed System Settings and Network Device Groups**.

Step 4   Select **Submit**.

Step 5   Select the **Network Configuration** button on the left menu bar of ACS.

Step 6   Under the Network Device Groups table, you click **Add Entry**.

Step 7   You then select **Add**.

Step 8   Next, enter a name for the NDG, in this case **Firewalls**.

Step 9   Click **Submit**.

Step 10 Click **Network Configuration**.

Step 11 Select the **(Not Assigned)** group.

Step 12 Select the AAA client you want to move, in this case the **pixCA** Firewall.

Step 13 Using the drop-down list, select the NDG you want this AAA client to be placed into, in this case **FIREWALLS**.

Step 14 Select **Submit + Restart**.

Step 15 Click **Network Configuration**.

Step 16 Select the **(Not Assigned)** group.

Step 17 Select the AAA server you want to move, in this case the **SERVER** Firewall.

Step 18 Using the drop-down list, select the NDG you want this AAA server to be placed into, in this case **FIREWALLS**.

Step 19 Select **Submit + Restart**.

Step 20 Next, configure the PIX Firewall. The configuration on the PIX Firewall should resemble the following:

```
pixfirewall(config)# sh aaa-server
aaa-server TACACS+ protocol tacacs+ <--default config
aaa-server RADIUS protocol radius  <--default config
aaa-server LOCAL protocol local  <--default config
aaa-server MYTACACS protocol tacacs+  <--Defines the Protocol
aaa-server MYTACACS (outside) host 192.168.1.100 acskey timeout 10
  <--Defines the location of the server and the key
pixfirewall(config)#show access-list <- View the ACLs in place
access-list ACS; 1 elements <- This ACL is used in AAA to define what
  to authenticate
access-list ACS line 1 permit tcp host 10.0.1.100 any eq www (hitcnt=7)
access-list INSIDE; 3 elements <-This ACL defines what traffic is
  allowed to pass through the PIX firewall.
access-list INSIDE permit tcp any any eq www
access-list INSIDE permit tcp any any eq 443
access-list INSIDE deny ip any any
pixfirewall(config)# sh access-group <-This displays where the ACL is
  applied.
access-group INSIDE in interface inside
pixfirewall(config)#
pixfirewall(config)#show aaa <- this shows the ACL- ACS applied in the
  authentication statement.
aaa authentication match ACS inside MYTACACS
pixfirewall(config)#
```

Step 21 You now need to add the ACS New York as an AAA server to be able to use it in the Proxy Distribution Table. Select the NDG that you want to work with.

Step 22 Select the **Firewalls** NDG.

Step 23 Select the **Add Entry** button underneath the AAA servers table. Enter the name of the AAA server in New York.

Step 24 Enter the IP address of the AAA server.

Step 25 Enter the key to be used.

Step 26 Select **Submit + Restart**.

Step 27 Next, you use that server in the Proxy Distribution Table to forward authentication requests. For this example, you use the @ symbol as the deliminating character, and you perform stripping. Start by selecting **Network Configuration**.

Step 28 Start by selecting the **Add Entry** button underneath the Proxy Distribution Table.

Step 29 Enter the character string.

Step 30 Using the drop-down, select the position. In this example, you use **suffix**.

Step 31 Select **Yes** in the Strip drop-down list.

Step 32 Select the ACS that you want to forward to, in this case **ACS_NY**, and click the right arrow button to move this server from the AAA server box on the left to the Forward To box on the right.

Step 33 Using the drop-down menu, choose **local**, **remote**, or **local/remote** to enable remote accounting. Note that if **local** is chosen, no remote accounting is taking place.

Step 34 Select **Submit + Restart**.

Step 35 To search for network devices, select the **Search** button under the Network Device Groups table.

Step 36 Enter the host name of the device you are trying to locate. You can leave the asterisk as a wildcard or even enter a partial name with the asterisk appended and search that way.

Step 37 Enter the IP address in dotted decimal notation. You can also enter an asterisk here in place of any octet.

Step 38 Using the drop-down menu, select the type of network device you are searching for. The options are any, TACACS+ (Cisco IOS), RADIUS (IETF), Cisco Secure AAA server, TACACS+ AAA server, or RADIUS AAA server.

Step 39 Using the drop-down menu, select the device group you want to search. The default is any.

Step 40 Select **Search**.

This completely creates the configuration from each section. Figure 9-15 shows the end result.

Figure 9-15 *Final Network Topology*

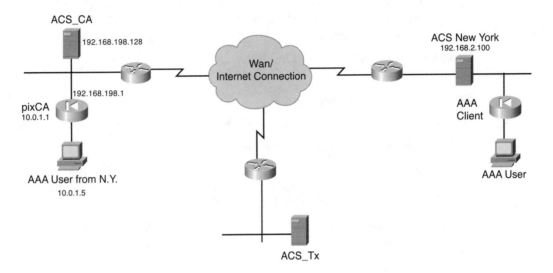

As you can see in the figure, the AAA user from New York attempts to access the Internet. The username with the suffix is included in the authentication request. The ACS_CA device sees the suffix and references the Proxy Distribution Table to determine where to send the request. The Proxy Distribution Table has an entry that points to ACS New York with the corresponding suffix, and the request is forwarded to ACS New York. The authentication is passed, and the user is off and surfing the Internet.

Client Configuration

Numerous network and security devices have become a part of the Cisco product family through many acquisitions. Due to this fact, you might encounter a few different operating systems across the Cisco platforms. Because the operating systems differ, so does the configuration of AAA across different platforms.

To begin configuring devices for AAA, you need at least one entry for every network device in your network if you want ACS to communicate. Likewise, you need to configure those network devices to communicate with ACS.

To add an AAA client to the ACS database and enable communications using the TACACS+ or RADIUS protocols, you use the following steps. After you have completed the following steps for an AAA client, you can then configure that AAA client using the appropriate commands to communicate as well.

Step 1 Select **Network Configuration**.

Step 2 Select the NDG that you place this device in. You should already be able to configure NDGs.

Step 3 Select **Add Entry** under the AAA client table.

Step 4 Enter the host name of the AAA client, or if this is going to be a group of devices, enter a name that makes it easily recognizable.

NOTE The use of the word *group* in the preceding step does not mean a NDG; instead, it means the ability to specify more than one IP address in an entry.

As you can see in Figure 9-16, the host name is set to EAST_COAST_RTRs.

Step 5 Enter the IP addresses of each router that is an AAA client to ACS. To delimitate them, use the Enter key. While you lose some management visibility here by adding more than one AAA client to an entry, this is helpful in adding hundreds or thousands of clients. Also, wildcards per octet and numeric ranges per octet are legal characters. For example, a valid entry would be 10.1.80.* or 10.1.0.12–36.

Step 6 Enter a secret key to be used for encryption. In this configuration, every router in the entry needs this same key configured. This is not necessarily the best security practice.

Step 7 Select **Submit + Restart**.

Upon completion of this configuration, you now have a number of devices defined in the ACS device as AAA clients.

The next step would be to configure the AAA client devices, as discussed in the following subsections.

Figure 9-16 *Adding AAA Clients*

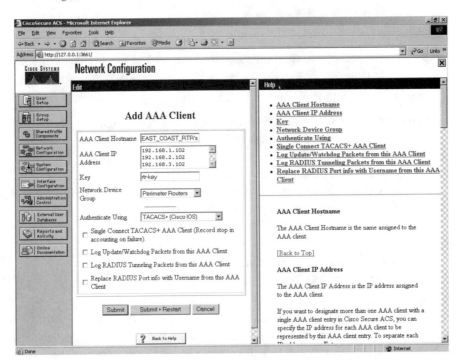

Cisco IOS Routers

To configure a Cisco router for AAA, follow these steps:

Step 1 Begin your router configuration by enabling AAA with this command:

```
aaa new-model
```

Step 2 To add an AAA server to a Cisco IOS router using TACACS+, use the following configuration commands in global configuration mode:

```
tacacs-server host hostname [single-connection] [port integer] [timeout
    integer] [key string]
```

or

```
tacacs-server host ip_address [single-connection] [port integer]
    [timeout integer] [key string]
```

You can use the **no** form of the command in the previous step sequence to delete the specified name or address. This is seen in Example 9-1.

Example 9-1 *Removing a TACACS Server*

```
no tacacs-server host hostname
```

Note that the single-connection switch in the configuration command is optional and specifies that the router keeps a single open connection for confirmation from an AAA/TACACS+ server. This command fails if ACS is not running.

You can optionally define a port number using the port tag. This option then overrides the default port 49. If the port is changed on the router, it needs to be changed on the server as well. You also have the capability of specifying a timeout on the router using the timeout tag. This overrides the timeout only for this server.

The key that you can optionally define is an authentication and encryption key. This must match the key used by the TACACS+ daemon in ACS that you define in the AAA client configuration. Specifying this key overrides the key set by the global command **tacacs-server key** for this server only. This command was first available in Cisco IOS Release 10.0. The Cisco IOS Software searches for hosts in the order in which you specify them. Therefore, you have the ability to define multiple TACACS+ servers.

You use only the single-connection, port, timeout, and key options when running an AAA/TACACS+ server. In RADIUS, there is no connection, so these options are not available. Also, because some of the parameters of the **tacacs-server host** command can be modified to override global settings made by the **tacacs-server timeout** and **tacacs-server key** commands, you can use this command to enhance security on your network by creating a unique policy on each device in your network. As seen in Example 9-2, each tag changes all aspects of the TACACS server 10.1.1.1.

Example 9-2 *Defining Additional TACACS+ Options*

```
tacacs-server host 10.1.1.1 single-connection port 789 timeout 5 key mykey
```

When you use RADIUS, both sets of ports, 1645/1646 and 1812/1813, are in use on ACS. Also, if you use the host name in the command statement, you need to have DNS resolution enabled. To add AAA to a Cisco IOS router using the RADIUS protocol, use the following configuration command in global configuration mode:

```
radius-server host hostname|ip-address [auth-port port-number] [acct-port
    port-number][timeout seconds] [retransmit retries] [key string]
```

Cisco IOS Switches

To add an AAA server to a Cisco IOS switch using TACACS+, add the following configuration commands in global configuration mode:

```
tacacs-server host hostname [single-connection] [port integer] [timeout integer]
   [key string]
```

or

```
tacacs-server host ip_address [single-connection] [port integer] [timeout integer]
   [key string]
```

Note that this command and arguments are similar to the router configurations.

To add an AAA server to a Cisco IOS switch using RADIUS, add the following configuration commands in global configuration mode:

```
radius-server host hostname|ip-address [auth-port port-number] [acct-port
   port-number][timeout seconds] [retransmit retries] [key string]
```

Note again that this command and arguments are similar to the router configurations.

Cisco Set-Based Switches

To add an AAA server to a Cisco set-based switch using TACACS+, add the following commands into enable mode:

```
set tacacs server ip_address primary
set tacacs key key
set tacacs attempts n
set tacacs timeout n
```

To add an AAA server to a Cisco set-based switch using RADIUS, add the following commands into enable mode:

```
set radius server ip_address primary
set radius key key
set radius attempts n
set radius timeout n
```

Cisco PIX Firewalls

To add an AAA server to a Cisco PIX Firewall using TACACS+, add the following commands in configuration mode:

```
aaa-server MYACS protocol TACACS+
aaa-server MYACS (interface_name) host 10.1.1.1 secretkey
```

To add an AAA server to a Cisco PIX Firewall using RADIUS, add the following commands in configuration mode:

```
aaa-server MYACS protocol RADIUS
aaa-server MYACS (interface_name) host 10.1.1.1 secretkey
```

Cisco 3000 Series VPN Concentrators

To add an AAA server to a Cisco 3000 series virtual private network (VPN) concentrator for administrator authentication using the TACACS+ protocol, follow these steps:

Step 1 Select **Administration > Access-Rights > AAA Servers > Authentication**.

Step 2 Select **Add** in the right panel.

Step 3 Enter the server IP, port, timeout, retries, and server secret.

Step 4 Select **Add**.

NOTE   You can use TACACS+ only for administrative authentication on the 3000 series concentrators. This discussion is beyond the scope of this book. For user authentication, use a RADIUS server.

To add an AAA server to a Cisco 3000 series VPN concentrator for user authentication using the RADIUS protocol, follow these steps:

Step 1 Select **Configuration > System > Servers > Authentication > Add**.

Step 2 Select **RADIUS** as the server type.

Step 3 Enter the IP address of the RADIUS server, the server port, timeout, retries, and server secret.

Step 4 Select **Add**.

Cisco Wireless Access Points

To add an AAA server to a Cisco Wireless access point, follow these steps:

Step 1 From the **Summary Status** page, click **Setup**.

Step 2 In the **Services** menu, click **Security**.

Step 3 Click **Authentication Server**.

Step 4 Select the version of 802.1x to run on this Access Point (AP) in the **802.1x Protocol Version** drop-down menu. Please note that Draft 7 is no longer supported.

Step 5 Configure the server IP, server type, port, shared secret, and Retran_Int, and Max Retran.

Step 6 Select **EAP Authentication**.

Step 7 Select **OK**.

Although many other devices in the Cisco product line support TACACS+ or RADIUS, it is beyond the scope of this book to give explicit examples of each device. The idea in mind is more toward giving an understanding of some common network devices and their configurations. For more information on configuring TACACS+ or RADIUS on a device that is not listed here, please see the Cisco website.

Troubleshooting Network Configurations

Probably the most common configuration problem we have ever seen in ACS for initial communications between an AAA client and ACS is the configuration of the shared secret key. The following items might help in troubleshooting problems with the shared secret key:

- Ensure that the shared secret key on the AAA client matches the shared secret key that is configured on the ACS.

- The shared secret key is case sensitive. Ensure that the case of the shared secret key is the same both on the ACS and the AAA client.

- Make sure that the AAA client has been defined in the ACS. If it is not, all packets from it are discarded by the ACS.

- If the AAA client is in a group of clients defined on the server and you are using an IP range rather than individual IP addresses, ensure that the IP address of the AAA client is within the range defined on the ACS.

- Ensure that the protocol used to communicate, TACACS+ or RADIUS, is the same on both the ACS and the AAA client.

- If you have verified the items in the preceding bullets and you are still experiencing communication failures, ensure that the AAA client has basic connectivity to the ACS via ping.

- Ensure that no firewall policy is blocking communications between the ACS and the AAA client.

- If communications are not reliable, ensure that the "Single TCP session" option is not selected.

- Use the reports in ACS. Although they have not been discussed yet, you could use the Passed and Failed Attempts reports in the ACS interface. These are discussed in Chapter 12, "Reports and Logging for Windows Server."

If you have verified everything in the preceding list and you are still having problems, you might want to check the Cisco Network Professionals Connection on CCO, or open a Cisco TAC case at Cisco.com.

Summary

In the ACS Network Configuration section, you can find many powerful tools to assist in enabling a distributed system. From a Proxy Distribution Table to NDGs, the configuration here in ACS is the foundation for network availability and network uptime. The tools provided here help to encompass the full functionality of ACS in a distributed system environment and pay mind to the configurability of the device. As you configure ACS in future examples, you can clearly see where a distributed system environment can better increase the availability of these networks. If nothing else, you have to try it to see what it can do for you.

In this chapter, you learn the following topics:

- Downloadable ACLs
- Network Access Restrictions
- Configuring Network Access Restrictions
- Command authorization sets
- Troubleshooting extended configurations
- Common issues of network access restrictions
- The importance of documentation

## CHAPTER 10

Configuring Shared Profile Components

In Access Control Server (ACS), Shared Profile components can consist of downloadable IP access control lists (ACLs), Network Access Restrictions (NARs), and command authorization sets for both shell commands and PIX shell commands. These configurations can sometimes prove to be more difficult to configure and maintain because of their complexity. This chapter provides a more extended look into the configuration and management of these components than the examples seen in other chapters.

To begin this chapter, we look at downloadable IP ACLs. Specifically, you look at the configuration of downloadable IP ACLs and how to apply them to a PIX Firewall. After configuring downloadable ACLs, you then take a look into the workings of NAR, which help you to configure policy based on the entry point of a network, and finally command authorization sets are discussed to assist you in better understanding and controlling administrative access to the command-line interface (CLI) of PIX Firewalls and Cisco IOS routers in your network.

Figure 10-1 illustrates the common topology used for all examples in this chapter. As you can see, the topology used here is the same as the topology used in previous chapters, with a few devices added the network. Two perimeter routers sit at the forefront of this sample network. These routers are named "Perimeter Router 1," and "Perimeter Router 2." Inside the perimeter routers sit two PIX Firewalls, "Pixfirewall 1" and "Pixfirewall 2," and inside the PIX Firewalls sits a private network with multiple users and ACS.

The examples in this chapter using this topology have been configured according to the policy that states that users that access the Internet through Pixfirewall 1 and Pixfirewall 2 are to be authenticated and have an ACL applied with their restrictions. Users accessing the routers for administrative purposes are restricted access to certain devices based on whether they access from Pixfirewall 1 or Pixfirewall 2. Finally, command authorization is configured on both PIX Firewalls and the perimeter routers to control administrative access.

Figure 10-1 *Common Topology*

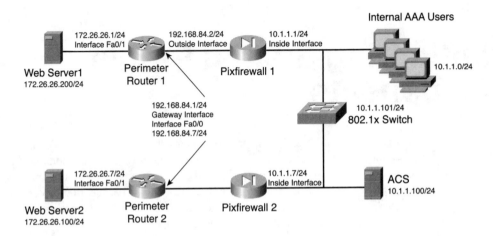

Downloadable ACLs

As seen in earlier chapters, downloadable ACLs can provide a powerful tool to network administrators for the restriction of individual users. In this section, you see more examples of the downloadable ACL and create ACLs that can be assigned to groups and individual users.

Understanding Downloadable ACLs

You don't have a lot to understand about downloadable ACLs. The basic principle behind it is that an access list is configured on the server instead of the PIX. This provides the benefit of a single point of configuration when changes need to be made to the ACL. Additionally, you need to configure the ACL only once, on one device, and you can apply the same ACL on numerous devices.

With authentication configured, when a user establishes a connection and authenticates, the PIX downloads the ACL and applies it to the user's *uauth*. A uauth is the user's authentication information as stored in the PIX Firewall cache. This access list functions just like a normal access list.

To give you a better understanding of how you use this type of configuration, Figure 10-2 shows the equipment that is involved with the next few examples.

Figure 10-2 *Downloadable ACLs*

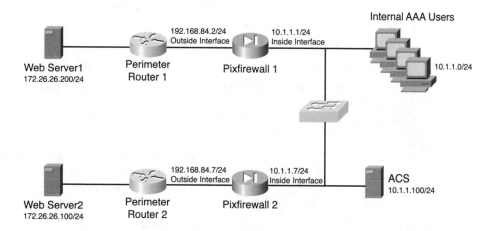

To accomplish a successful configuration, you first determine the policy that you want to have applied to your users. In this example, the users on the 10.1.1.0/23 network are accessing the server 172.26.26.100 and 172.26.26.200 via Hypertext Transfer Protocol (HTTP); however, no other traffic is to be allowed out of the network. A special case has been made by the user "aaauser" to access File Transfer Protocol (FTP) on 172.26.26.100. When this user authenticates, a different access list is applied that allows HTTP and FTP. If the user were to move to another PC on the 10.1.1.0/24 network, the same policy should be applied.

The commands to enable the PIX to perform authentication and download the access list are as follows:

- **aaa-server MYRADIUS protocol RADIUS**
- **aaa-server MYRADIUS (inside) host 10.1.1.100 secretkey**
- **aaa authentication match AUTHENTICATE-TCP inside MYRADIUS**
- **access-list AUTHENTICATE-TCP permit tcp any any**

Creating an ACL

The next step of the process is to create the access list in the ACS. The way that you create your access list is important to the way that traffic is processed. When an access list is searched, most Cisco devices perform a linear search, as does the PIX. This means that the first match that the PIX comes across in the list is the one that is acted upon, regardless of whether a more specific statement exists later in the list.

Other considerations to building your access list should be the following:

- In an access list, the source IP address comes before the destination IP address.
- The PIX Firewall does not use wildcard masks; rather, a standard subnet mask in the access list does the job.
- The two options that an access list can perform are permit or deny.
- The protocol that you define can be Transmission Control Protocol (TCP), User Datagram Protocol (UDP), Internet Control Message Protocol (ICMP), Encapsulating Security Payload (ESP), Generic Routing Encapsulation (GRE), or any, to name a few. You could also use an IP protocol number here.
- Beyond protocols, you can place port numbers or services in the access list. Some examples of port numbers are 23 (Telnet), 80 (HTTP), 443 (SSL [Secure Sockets Layer]), 500 (Internet Security Association Key Management Protocol [ISAKMP] and 25 (SMTP [Simple Mail Transport Protocol]).

The following is the general PIX syntax of an IP access list:

```
access-list acl_ID deny | permit protocol source_addr source_mask [operator
    port[port]]destination_addr destination_mask operator port [port]
```

It is good to be familiar with this format as the configuration of access lists in the downloadable IP ACL is very similar. The format of a downloadable IP ACL is as follows:

```
{Permit|deny} protocol_type source_ip source_mask destination_ip destination_mask
    [protocol specific options]
```

The major difference here is that in entering the ACL definitions in the ACS interface, you do not use **acl_ID**; rather, you begin with a **permit/deny**.

An example of a downloadable IP ACL is shown in Example 10-1.

Example 10-1 *Downloadable IP ACL*

```
permit udp any host 11.0.0.254
permit icmp any host 11.0.0.254
permit tcp any host 11.0.0.253
permit tcp any host 11.0.0.254
```

Using standard RADIUS Cisco AV pairs permits you to enter a maximum of 4 kilobytes of ACLs; the downloadable PIX ACLs can be of unlimited size. This 4-kilobyte limit is a RADIUS limitation.

Working with ACLs After They Are Created

Access lists entered into ACS are protected by whatever backup or replication regime you have established for the ACS. Chapter 11, "System Configuration," discusses this in detail.

After you configure an access list as a named shared profile component, you can include that access list in any Cisco Secure ACS (CSACS) user, or user group, profile. This feature makes for a very modular configuration. This also saves configuration time when the access list applied is common to numerous users or groups.

When CSACS returns an attribute with a named access list as part of a user session RADIUS access accept packet, the PIX Firewall applies that access list to the session of that user. CSACS employs a versioning stamp for ensuring that the PIX Firewall has cached the latest access list version. If a PIX Firewall responds that it does not have the current version of the named access list in its cache, CSACS automatically uploads the current version of the access list to the PIX Firewall cache. When this ACL is downloaded to the PIX Firewall, it is applied to a user's uauth; however, if an ACL exists on an interface, the interface ACL takes precedence over the ACL applied to the uauth.

After you configure a downloadable PIX ACL, it can be applied against any number of single users or user groups. The option needs to be enabled in interface configuration to make this visible in the interface.

Network Access Restrictions

Network Access Restrictions (NARs) are additional authorization conditions that must be met before ACS grants a user access on to the network.

Types of NARs

In the shared profile components configuration page, you can add a new named access restriction, or you can access an existing named NAR to delete or edit it.

Two types of access restrictions exist:

- IP-based filters where the originating request relates to an IP address
- Non-IP–based restrictions for all other cases where automatic number identification (ANI) can be used

When configured, a NAR can be applied to a single user in the users profile or a group in the group setup page.

Working with NARs

NARs enable you to define additional authorization and authentication conditions that must be met before a user is granted access to the network. These restrictions are in addition to authentication credentials supplied by the user.

NARs are based on attributes that come from the AAA client through which the user is accessing the network. To properly configure NARs, you must understand the types of attributes that are passed from the AAA client. Once you understand the attributes passed, you determine a conditions action. In other words, you determine an action to be taken when an attribute is matched. Possible actions include permit or deny. If an attribute is passed that does not include sufficient information, the default rule is to deny access. These possible actions are seen in Table 10-1.

Table 10-1 *NAR Actions*

	Match	No Match	Insufficient Information
Permit	Access granted	Access denied	Access denied
Deny	Access denied	Access granted	Access denied

When you configure NARs, you have two options to choose. One is IP-based restrictions and the other is non-IP–based restrictions. The IP-based access restrictions are where the originating request is related to an existing IP address. The non-IP–based NARs are filters for all other cases where ANI can be used.

IP-Based NARs

IP-based NARs are based on one of two sets of attribute fields, depending on the protocol you are using. The following is a list of attributes:

- If you are using TACACS+, the rem_addr field is used.

- If you are using RADIUS IETF, the calling-station-id (attribute 31) and called-station-id (attribute 30) fields are used.

Again, if AAA clients do not provide sufficient IP-address information to ACS, the default rule is to deny access. This might happen when using NARs where the AAA client is a firewall. Some firewalls do not send sufficient IP information to the ACS, so full NAR functionality might not be supported.

Non-IP–Based NARs

A non-IP–based NAR is a list of permitted or denied "calling"/"point of access" locations that you can employ in restricting an AAA client when you do not have an IP-based connection established. The non-IP–based NAR generally uses the calling line ID (CLID) number and the dialed number identification service (DNIS) number. The CLID is the number that identifies where a call is coming from, and a DNIS is the number that is being dialed. You can use the non-IP–based filter when the AAA client does not use a Cisco IOS release that supports CLID or DNIS by entering an IP address in place of the CLID.

Another exception to entering a CLID is to enter a MAC address to permit or deny access. An example of a situation where a MAC address is used is with a Cisco Aironet AAA client. Enter the Cisco Aironet Access Point (AP) MAC address in place of the DNIS. The format you specify in the CLID box—be it CLID, IP address, or MAC address—must match the format of what you receive from your AAA client. You can determine this format from your RADIUS accounting log.

Configuring Network Access Restrictions

You can configure multiple shared NARs to restrict access to particular AAA clients, all AAA clients, or to named Network Device Groups (NDGs). This section provides the configuration steps for NARs, as well as edit and delete steps.

Creating Shared NARs

To add a shared NAR, follow these steps:

Step 1   Select **Shared Profile Components** in the left navigation bar. This opens the Shared Profile Components page.

Step 2   Select **Network Access Restrictions**.

Step 3   Select **Add**. This opens the Network Access Restrictions page.

Step 4   In the Name box, type a name for the new shared NAR. This can be up to 32 characters and cannot contain any leading or trailing spaces, nor can the following special characters be used:

- [
-]
- ,
- /

Step 5   In the Description box, type a description of the new shared NAR.

Step 6   To create an IP-based NAR, follow Steps 7 through 10. To create a non-IP–based NAR, follow Steps 1 through 7 in the step sequence in the section titled "Creating a Non-IP–Based NAR."

Step 7   Select the Define IP-based access restrictions check box.

Step 8   To specify whether you are listing addresses that are permitted or denied, from the Table Defines list, select the applicable value.

Step 9   Select or type the applicable information in each of the following boxes:

— **AAA Client**—Select **All AAA clients**, or the name of the NDG, or the individual AAA client, to which access is permitted or denied.

— **Port**—Type the number of the port to which to permit or deny access. You can use the wildcard asterisk (*) to permit or deny access to all ports on the selected AAA client.

— **Src IP Address**—Type the IP address to filter on when performing access restrictions. You can type multiple entries separated by a comma or use the wildcard asterisk (*) to specify all IP addresses.

Step 10 Click **Enter**.

Step 11 To enter additional IP-based line items, repeat Steps 8 and 9.

Configuration Details and Tips

This section details some options that are available to you during the configuration:

- When you specify a NAR, you can use asterisks (*) as wildcards for any value, or as part of any value to establish a range. All the values and conditions in a NAR specification must be met for the NAR to restrict access. These values are "ANDed" to determine the result.

- NARs can be applied to a user profile or a group profile.

- When you create the NAR, you don't need to specify if it is to be used for a user profile or a group profile. It is tied to either in their respective configuration page.

- When you name a NAR, use some type of keyword that will be easy to recognize later and provides some info as the specifics of the NAR.

- You can use multiple NARs in one profile.

- When you specify the application of multiple shared NARs to a user or user group, you choose one of two access criteria: either "All selected filters must permit" or "Any one selected filter must permit."

- Shared access restrictions are kept in the ACS user database.

- Shared access restrictions can be backed up/restored by the ACS backup and restore features and replicated to secondary CSACS servers along with other configurations.

Creating a Non-IP–Based NAR

The following steps apply to non-IP–based NARs rather that IP-based NARs:

Step 1   Select the Define CLID/DNIS-based access restrictions check box.

Step 2   To specify whether you are listing addresses that are permitted or denied, select the applicable value from the Table Defines list.

Step 3   To specify the applicability of this NAR, select one of the following values from the AAA Client list:

— The name of the NDG

— The name of the particular AAA client

— All AAA clients

At this point, if you have not configured any NDGs, they do not appear in the list. Subsequently, only the NDGs that you have created appear in the list.

Step 4   To specify the information on which this NAR should filter, fill in the following boxes, as applicable:

— **Port**—Type the number of the port on which to filter.

— **CLID**—Type the CLIDs number on which to filter. You can also use this box to restrict access based on values other than CLIs, such as an IP address or MAC address.

— **DNIS**—Type the number being dialed into on which to filter.

Step 5   Click **Enter**. By clicking Enter, the information is placed as a NAR line item and appears in the table.

Step 6   To enter additional non-IP–based NAR line items, repeat Steps 3 through 5.

Step 7   To complete your configuration, select **Submit**. This saves the NAR that you have created and displays it in the Network Access Restriction Sets table.

This completes your configuration. A sample of an IP-based NAR can be seen in Figure 10-3. This is intended only as an example. The output on your screen might differ.

Figure 10-3 *Configuring an NAR*

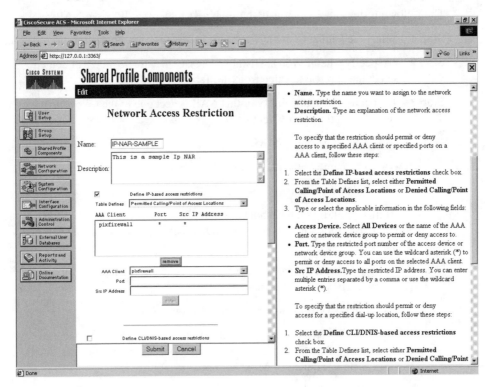

Editing Shared NARs

After you have configured a NAR, it is fairly simple to edit it. To edit a NAR, perform the following steps:

Step 1   Select **Shared Profile Components** in the left navigation bar. This opens the Shared Profile Components page.

Step 2   Select **Network Access Restrictions**.

Step 3   In the Name column, select the shared NAR you want to edit.

Step 4   To edit the name or description of the filter, type and delete information, as needed.

To edit a line item in the IP-based access restrictions table, follow these steps:

Step 1   Double-click the line item to be edited.

Step 2 Edit the information, as applicable.

Step 3 Click **Enter**.

To remove a line item, follow these steps:

Step 1 Select the line item.

Step 2 Below the table, select **Remove**. This removes the line item.

Step 3 Click **Submit**. These changes take effect immediately.

To edit a line item in the CLID/DNIS access restrictions table, follow these steps:

Step 1 Double-click the line item to be edited.

Step 2 Edit the information, as applicable.

Step 3 Click **Enter**.

Step 4 Click **Submit**. These changes take effect immediately.

To remove a line item from the CLID/DNIS access restrictions table, follow these steps:

Step 1 Select the line item.

Step 2 Below the table, click **Remove**. This removes the item.

Step 3 Click **Submit**. These changes take effect immediately.

Deleting a Shared NAR

To remove a shared NAR, follow these steps:

Step 1 Select **Shared Profile Components** in the left navigation bar. This opens the Shared Profile Components page.

Step 2 Select **Network Access Restrictions**.

Step 3 Select the name of the shared NAR you want to delete.

Step 4 At the bottom of the page, select **Delete**. This causes a dialog box to warn you that you are about to delete a shared NAR.

Step 5 To confirm that you intend to delete the shared NAR, select **OK**.

Step 6 The selected shared NAR is deleted.

The warning message that appears when you are deleting a NAR is seen here in Figure 10-4.

Figure 10-4 *NAR Delete Warning*

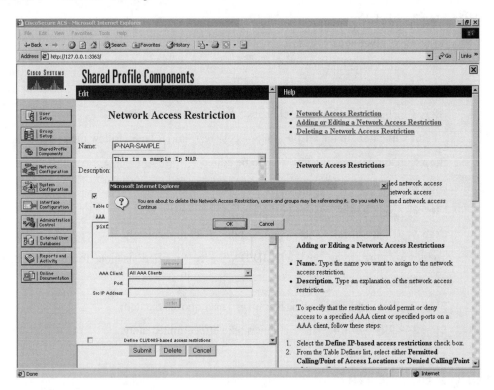

Command Authorization Sets

Command authorization sets create a central depository for command authorization. The capability of command authorization is available in most Cisco routers and PIX Firewalls at the local level. This section discusses how to move command authorization to the ACS.

Working with Command Authorization Sets

The ACS provides command authorization sets to be configured in the Group Setup section, as well as via the Shared Profile Components section. While the functionality of command authorization is the same in both areas, the benefit to configuring command authorization sets within Shared Profile Components is that you can configure the entire command set at once without continuously having to submit each command before configuring the next. Another benefit to configuring command authorization sets within Shared Profile Components is that you can configure multiple levels of command sets and apply them either at the group or the user-profile level.

PIX Command Authorization Sets Versus Shell Command Authorization Sets

Although the ACS gives you the option for configuring PIX command authorization sets or shell command authorization sets, the PIX Firewall never implemented the pixshell, which is what the PIX command authorization sets are based on. Therefore, the workaround to configure command authorization sets on a PIX Firewall is to use the shell command authorization sets.

Configuration Considerations for Command Authorization Sets

When beginning to configure command authorization, take the following into consideration:

- How many users will be accessing the shell of your network devices?
- How many levels of privilege will you need?
- Will you apply the privilege to the user profile or the group?
- If you will apply the privilege to the user, is there a default group privilege?

In addition to asking these questions, you might also consider writing out what commands you want to be available at each level as well as who is assigned each level. This is beneficial because it gives you a more visual approach to creating your command authorization sets.

Router Preparation for Command Authorization

To prepare a router to perform command authorization with ACS, you need to enter the following commands:

```
Router(config)# aaa new-model
Router(config)# tacacs-server host ip-address key key I radius-server host
   ip-address key key
Router(config)#radius-server host 10.1.1.100 key secretkey
```

or

```
Router(config)# tacacs-server host 10.1.1.100 key secretkey
Router(config)# aaa group server {radius I tacacs+} group-name
Router(config-sg-tacacs+)# server 10.1.1.100
Router(config)# aaa authentication login default group [group-name I
   {radius I tacacs] }
Router(config)# aaa authorization commands level {default I list-name} group
   group-name
Router(config)# aaa authorization exec default group {tacacs+Iradius}
```

PIX Firewall Preparation for Command Authorization

To prepare the PIX Firewall for command authorization, enter the following commands at the config prompt on the PIX:

```
pixfirewall(config)# aaa-server MYTACACS protocol tacacs+
pixfirewall(config)# aaa-server MYTACACS (inside) host  ip address  secretkey
  timeout 10
pixfirewall(config)# aaa authentication telnet console MYTACACS
pixfirewall(config)# aaa authentication enable console MYTACACS
pixfirewall(config)# aaa authorization command MYTACACS
```

NOTE   To perform command-line authorization on a PIX Firewall, you *must* run Finesse OS version 6.2 or greater.

Configuring Shared Profile Components for Command Authorization

To configure command authorization sets for either the PIX or a Cisco IOS router, perform the following steps:

Step 1   Select **Shared Profile Components** from the left menu screen.

Step 2   Select **Shell Command Authorization Sets**.

Step 3   Select the **Add** button.

Step 4   Enter a name.

Step 5   Enter a description.

Step 6   Select a permit or deny option for this command set.

The option to select a permit action versus a deny action here is determined based on the amount of commands you want to allow a user to have access to. For example, if you want a user with this command level to have access to all except for the **erase** and **reload** commands, it makes sense to make a deny authorization list for just the two commands. This would mean the **Permit Unmatched Commands** option would be selected. Follow these steps to create this authorization set:

Step 1   Select **Shared Profile Components**.

Step 2   Select **Shell Command Authorization Sets**.

Step 3   Select the **Add** button.

Step 4   Enter a name for your shell command authorization set.

Step 5   Enter a description for your shell command authorization set.

Step 6   You have two options in the form of radio buttons for unmatched commands. Select the **Permit** radio button.

Step 7   The large box on the left is populated as you enter commands in the small text box below it. In the small text box, enter the word **write**.

Step 8   Select the **Add Command** button.

After performing Step 8, you can see the **write** command placed in the large box on the left side of the configuration page.

Step 9   Select the command with your mouse. This highlights the command in blue.

Step 10   Place a check mark in the box next to the words **Permit Unmatched Arguments**. This causes any argument that is not listed in the box below the check mark to be permitted. If the box is empty, all arguments are permitted.

Step 11   To lock in the command **write erase** as a command that is to be matched, you need to place a permit statement with the command argument in the box below the check mark. Place the statement **permit erase** in the box.

At this point, your command authorization set reads like this: Any command that does NOT match "write erase" will be permitted. This accomplishes the task of denying a **write erase** from being performed. To include the **reload** command as a denied command, simply follow Steps 7 through 11 in the preceding step sequence, replacing the command **write** with the command **reload**. Do not perform Steps 10 and 11. This causes the configuration to include the **reload** command and any argument.

On the other hand, if you are going to create a level that is very restrictive, you would want to then select the option to **Deny Unmatched Commands**. In your list, you would then enter the commands that you want to allow. You can create this list by following these steps:

Step 1   Enter either the commands you want to have permitted or denied. A sample of a command you want to permit is seen in Figure 10-5. You do not enter the entire command here, only the beginning or type of command. For example, if the command you wish to permit is **show running-config**, the command you enter is **show**.

Figure 10-5 *Entering a permit Command*

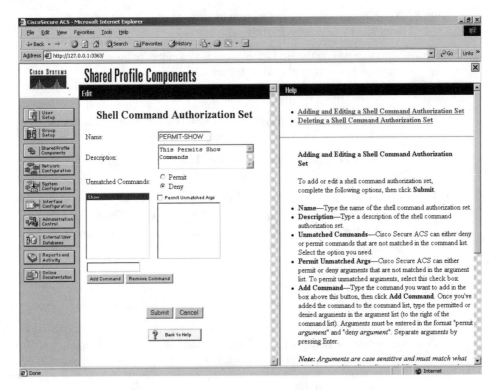

Step 2   In the field directly under the option **Permit Unmatched Args**, enter the rest of the command that you want to allow. This is in a permit format. For example, using the command seen in Step 1, in this field you enter **permit running-config**. Figure 10-6 shows an example of this.

Step 3   When your list is complete select the **Submit** button.

Deleting Command Authorization Sets

Use the following steps to delete a command authorization set:

Step 1   Select **Shared Profile Components** from the left menu screen.

Step 2   Select **Shell Command Authorization Sets**.

Step 3   Select the shell command authorization set that you want to delete.

Step 4   Select the **Delete** button.

Figure 10-6 *Permitting Sub-Arguments*

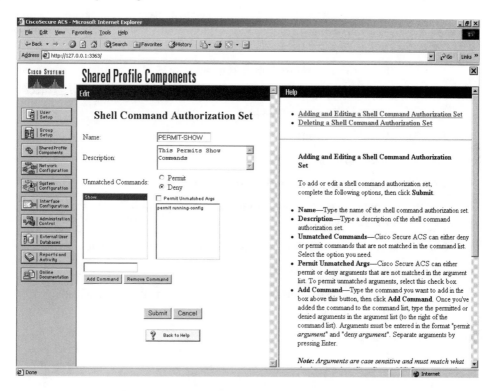

Editing Shell Command Authorization Sets

To edit a shell command authorization set, perform the following:

Step 1   Select **Shared Profile Components** from the left menu screen.

Step 2   Select **Shell Command Authorization Sets**.

Step 3   Select the shell command authorization set that you want to edit.

Step 4   Make the necessary modifications.

Step 5   Select **Submit**.

Configuring the Group Profile

Now that the command set is completed, you need to apply it to either a user or a group. To apply a configured command authorization set to a group profile, complete the following steps:

Step 1   Select **Group Setup** from the left menu in ACS.

Step 2   Using the drop-down menu, select the group that you want to apply the command authorization set to.

Step 3   Select **Edit Settings**.

Step 4   Using the **Jump To** drop-down menu, select **TACACS+**.

Step 5   Scroll to **Shell Command Authorization Set**.

Step 6   Select the **Assign a Shell Command Authorization Set for any network device** radio button.

Step 7   Select **Command Authorization Set** in the drop-down menu.

Step 8   Select **Submit + Restart**.

A sample of this can be seen in Figure 10-7. In the figure, the command authorization set **PERMIT-SHOW** is applied.

Figure 10-7 *Applying Command Authorization to the Group*

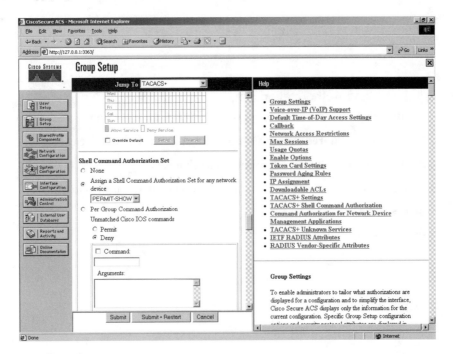

This command authorization set applies to all users that belong to this group. You can assign only one command authorization set this way. Suppose that you want to have separate command authorization sets for each type of equipment, one set for firewalls and one set for routers. To accomplish this, you would create two network device groups. To create network device groups, refer to Chapter 9, "Managing Network Configurations." In one network device group, you would place your firewalls, and in the other, you would place the routers. Once in **Group Setup**, you would apply your command authorization set to a network device group. Figure 10-8 gives you an example of the process.

Figure 10-8 *Applying Multiple Command Authorization Sets to a Group Profile*

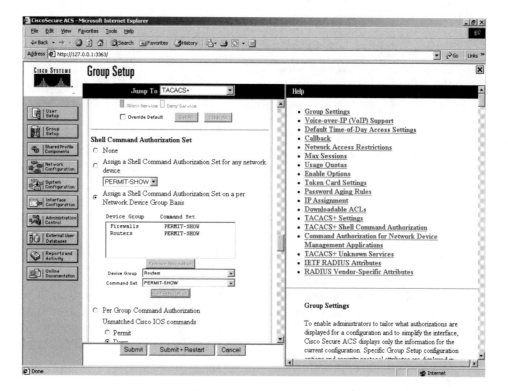

To complete this configuration, follow these steps:

Step 1   Select **Group Setup** from the left menu in ACS.

Step 2   Using the drop-down menu, select the group that you want to apply the command authorization set to.

Step 3   Select **Edit Settings**.

Step 4 Using the **Jump To** drop-down menu, select **TACACS+**.

Step 5 Scroll to **Shell Command Authorization Set**.

Step 6 Select **Assign a Shell Command Authorization Set on a per Network Device Group Basis**.

Step 7 In the **Device Group** drop-down menu, select the device group to which you want to add command authorization.

Step 8 In the **Command Set** drop-down menu, select the command set you want to apply to this group.

Step 9 Select the **Add Association** button.

This places an entry into the Device Group/Command Set table. Repeat Steps 6 through 9 to add the second device group.

Step 10 Select the **Submit + Restart** button when you are finished.

NOTE To remove an association, simply select the association and then select the remove association button. Don't forget to submit and restart in ACS. Also, keep in mind that if you still have the router or firewall configured for command authorization, all subsequent connections to the shells of those devices might be refused. You should remove the AAA authorization for commands prior to removing a command authorization set from the group.

Configuring the User Profile

Situations might prevent themselves when you want a specific command authorization set to be applied to a user. In the user profile, you have the ability to get command authorization from the group, to assign a single command authorization set, to apply a command authorization set associated with a network device group, or to select none. To configure a single command authorization set in the user profiles, perform the following steps:

Step 1 Select **User Setup** from the left menu.

Step 2 Enter the username you want to add command authorization to in the field provided.

Step 3 Select **Add/Edit**.

Step 4 Scroll to **Shell Command Authorization Set**.

Step 5 Select the **Assign a Shell Command Authorization Set for any network device** radio button.

Step 6   Using the drop-down menu, select the command authorization set you want to apply.

Step 7   Select **Submit**.

Assigning command authorization sets associated with a network device group is the same process as when it is done in a group profile. The major difference here is that you have no need to restart the ACS services. This allows for better on-the-fly changes that do not affect other user authentications.

Testing Command Authorization

Testing command authorizations is a very important step in the implementation. In my experiences, I have found that often times certain commands that are common are often overlooked. Try to test when you have local access to the devices, or whenever possible, try to test in a controlled environment prior to deployment. A Cisco PIX 501 and Cisco 800 series router are economical devices that can be used to test a number of the AAA features available in the Cisco IOS and PIX OS.

Troubleshooting Extended Configurations

Troubleshooting can be a difficult task as your network grows and your ACS configuration becomes more complex. This section provides tips to help minimize the difficulty of troubleshooting extended configurations.

When troubleshooting a new configuration, the steps you might take sometimes differ from the steps taken in troubleshooting an existing configuration. Because a new configuration has never worked, you often times have more points of origin for the error. Thus, the following subsections give you hints for situations including both new and existing configurations.

Troubleshooting New Downloadable ACL Configurations

If you experience difficulties when configuring downloadable ACLs for the first time, here is a list of possible issues and verification checks you should make:

- Verify that you have communication between ACS and the firewall.
- Verify that the firewall and the ACS device are using the RADIUS protocol for communications. Downloadable ACLs depend on this.
- Verify that the downloadable ACL is applied to the user or group profile.
- Ensure that once applied to a group the ACS service was restarted.
- Use the **debug radius all** command on the firewall to gain valuable information.

- Ensure that the user can authenticate through ACS without a downloadable ACL applied.
- Use the **show uauth** command to ensure that the ACL is applied to the user that is authenticated.
- If the ACL is being downloaded and the user is unable to access the desired service, ensure that the ACL is created properly. Also ensure that an ACL on an interface is not conflicting with the downloaded ACL.
- Ensure that AAA authentication is configured on the firewall.

NOTE   You do not need to configure AAA authorization. Authorization is a function that is performed during authentication in RADIUS. If you attempt to configure authorization with RADIUS, you receive the following error message: "Authorization is not supported in RADIUS."

Troubleshooting Existing Downloadable ACL Configurations

If you are troubleshooting an existing configuration of downloadable ACLs, here are some tips and steps that you can use:

- Verify that you have communication between ACS and the firewall.
- Verify that the username and password entered are correct.
- Ensure that the downloadable IP ACL is still applied to the user or group.
- Use the **debug radius all** command on the firewall to gain valuable information.
- Use the **show uauth** command to ensure that the ACL is applied to the user that is authenticated.
- If the ACL is being downloaded and the user is unable to access the desired service, ensure that the ACL allow that service.

Troubleshooting New NAR Configurations

If you experience difficulties when configuring NARs for the first time, here is a list of possible issues and verification checks you should consider:

- Ensure that the IP address in the NAR match that of the AAA client, and not the user that attempts authentication.
- If you are using non-IP–based NARs, ensure that the CLID and DNIS match that of the AAA client, and not the user that attempts authentication.

- Ensure that the NAR is assigned to the group of which the user authenticating is a member.
- If applying a NAR to a user, ensure that the option is configured in the user profile.

Troubleshooting Existing NAR Configurations

If troubleshooting an existing configuration of NARs, here is a list of possible issues and verification checks you should make:

- Ensure that the AAA client still has connectivity to the ACS device.
- Ensure that the secret keys match on both the AAA client and ACS.
- Ensure that the user is authenticating through the correct AAA client.

Troubleshooting New Command Authorization Set Configurations

When configuring command authorization for the first time, you have a great chance of getting locked out of your network devices. In this section, you can find a number of tips to help minimize the risk of needing to perform password recovery procedures:

- If you are on a router and the router is remote, set the configuration register value to 0x2002. This allows you to issue a break into ROMMON if you do get locked out of the device. *Do not leave the configuration register set to this value. This is a potential security risk.*
- Try to use a lab or nonproduction network to configure command authorization. A PIX 501 or Cisco 800 series router provides an economical means for testing features of both the Cisco IOS and PIX OS.
- Don't save your AAA configuration until after command authorization is successful.
- Ensure that the AAA server has connectivity to ACS.
- Ensure that the secret key matches on both the AAA client and ACS.
- If configuring PIX command authorization, ensure that you are using shell command authorization sets, and not PIX command authorization sets.
- Ensure that the authorization set is applied to the group profile.
- If performing command authorization for a specific user, ensure that the authorization set is applied to the user profile.
- Authorization must be configured on the AAA client.

Troubleshooting Existing Command Authorization Set Configurations

If you are troubleshooting an existing configuration of command authorization sets, here are tips to assist in troubleshooting:

- Ensure that the authorization set is applied to the group profile.

- If performing command authorization for a specific user, ensure that the authorization set is applied to the user profile.

- Ensure that the AAA server has connectivity to ACS.

- Ensure that the secret key matches on both the AAA client and ACS.

- Ensure that the AAA commands are configured on the AAA client.

- It is a good idea to refrain from saving your configuration during command authorization configurations until command authorization is successful. If you make a mistake, you can recover by reloading.

Common Issues of Network Access Restrictions

Most issues that you run into when configuring NARs are common issues experienced by most when they configure the ACS in conjunction with the AAA client. Far too many possibilities exist to cover in one chapter. Use the Cisco website to find valuable information that might be more specific to the network environment that you are in.

For AAA specific information, check the Cisco Technical Assistance. If you are unable to find the answer online, submit a Technical Assistance Center (TAC) case. Cisco TAC engineers are highly trained in AAA and can give you valuable insight into getting your configuration up and running again.

And Do Not Forget the Importance of Documentation

Overall, I cannot stress the importance of documentation in a network, especially when adding extended features such as downloadable ACLs, shared NARs, and command authorization. It might also help to draw a picture of your network to include protocol addressing, routing information, and device names. Sometimes, it takes a more visual approach to solve even the most miniscule issue.

Summary

This chapter has provided information to configure some of the enhanced options in ACS, including the following topics:

- Downloadable PIX ACLs can add functionality to a network by providing a central repository for policy against multiple firewalls, as well as a policy that follows a user as opposed to a machine.

- Shared NARs add another layer of authorization based on the AAA client that users access a network through.

- Command authorization sets allow a network administrator to protect the availability of the command line on network devices. This can prove to protect new administrators from the embarrassment of issuing an incorrect command, and the network from possible down time.

These options can be used together or as standalone configurations. They can greatly enhance the control of a secure network.

In the next chapter, "System Configuration," you will learn about external database configuration, database replication, database backup, and synchronization.

In this chapter, you learn the following topics:

- How users interact with your external database configuration
- External database configuration
- Database group mappings
- Unknown user policy
- Database replication
- Database synchronization

## CHAPTER 11

System Configuration

This chapter deals with the configuration of Access Control Server (ACS) to facilitate authentication to external databases, as well as the backup and restoration of ACS. In particular, the chapter covers the following:

- External database configuration
- Database group mappings
- Unknown user policy
- Database replication and backup
- Synchronization

The following sections discuss each of these topics in further detail.

How Users Interact with Your External Database Configuration

Different types of users exist in the perspective of ACS. A user might be a known user, meaning that the user was explicitly added to ACS or that ACS learned about the user from a database replication, database synchronization, or by using the CSUtil.exe tool. Other types of users are unknown users and discovered users. When an unknown user attempts an authentication request, he or she becomes a discovered user if he or she is found in one of the configured external databases. To facilitate the process of authentication, you need to add an external database configuration and a database group mapping.

The process of authentication is quite simple. ACS first checks its internal database and, if the user is not found there, proceeds to check the list of external databases and, if the user is not found there, finally fails the authentication request.

If the user is, in fact, found in an external database, the "discovered" user is added to the ACS database, with a pointer to the external server that served back the authentication reply. The next time this user authenticates, ACS checks this external server again, but only for authentication. At this point, all authorizations take place on the ACS by the group the user was placed in at the time of authentication.

External Database Configuration

For most database configurations, Windows NT/2000 databases excluded, ACS supports only one instance of a username and password. If you have multiple user databases with common usernames stored in each, you must take care in your database configurations because the first database to match the authentication credentials is the one that ACS uses from that point on for the user.

Take the following occurrence as an example; assume that you have a user on an Lightweight Directory Access Protocol (LDAP) server with the username of **user1** and a password of **cisco123.** You also have a similar user on an external Open DataBase Connectivity (ODBC) database with the username of **user1** and a password of **ocsic321.** The first database that matches with the username **user1** and properly authenticates is the one that is used from that point on. If the external ODBC database were the one that was matched, **user1** with a password of **cisco123** would no longer be used by ACS.

After a user has been authenticated to an external database, the authorization that can take place is up to ACS. This can complicate things a little more because users authenticated from a CRYPTOCard Token server might require different authorizations on the network than those authenticated by the LDAP server.

Because of this need for different authorizations, you should place users authenticated by the CRYPTOCard server in one group and users authenticated by the LDAP server in another group. To do this, you use database group mappings. This is a way to map an authentication server, VASCO, CRYPTOCard, ODBC, and so on, to a group that you have configured in ACS. For some databases, a user can belong to only one group. For other databases, such as LDAP, Netscape Directory Server (NDS), and Windows, support for group mapping by external database group membership is possible.

To configure ACS for use with external databases, you begin in the External User Databases configuration tab from the left menu. Follow these steps to select an option:

NOTE   Until further noted in this chapter, we assume this to be the starting place for all configurations.

Step 1 Select the **External User Databases** button on the left menu.

The result of the preceding step is that you are placed in the configuration screen for external user databases. In this configuration page seen in Figure 11-1, you can select between unknown user policy, database group mappings, and database configuration.

Figure 11-1 *External User Databases Configuration*

You are probably asking yourself why you would ever want to configure a policy for unknown users. It seems pretty straightforward that if you don't know a user, you would want them to fail authentication. The fact is that when you deal with multiple databases, not knowing a user only means that ACS does not know the user. You might trust another database that does know the user. Unknown user policy is where you configure the authentication procedure for users that are not located in the ACS database.

Database group mappings is where you configure what group privileges external database users inherit when authenticated in ACS. This means that in most cases when a user is authenticated by an external user database, his or her actual privileges are drawn from the ACS and not the external database.

You begin your configuration with the database configuration link. This is where you define all the external servers that you work with and authenticate users against. The Database Configuration page is seen in Figure 11-2 and is detailed in the list that follows:

- Windows NT/2000

- Novell NDS

- Generic LDAP

- External ODBC Database
- LEAP Proxy RADIUS Server
- RADIUS Token Server
- VASCO Token Server
- ActivCard Token Server
- PassGo Defender Token Server
- CRYPTOCard Token Server
- SafeWord Token Server
- RSA SecurID Token Server

Figure 11-2 *Database Configuration*

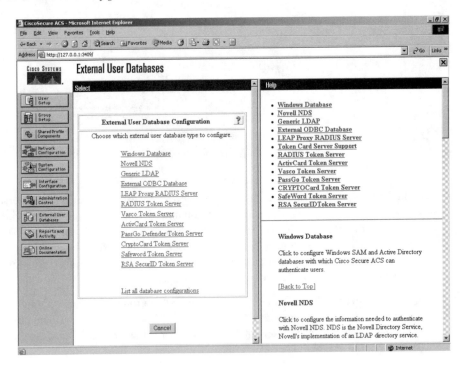

The following sections cover configuration of each of these databases in ACS. For each database that you configure, you must provide certain information, and you want to have the actual database configured before you begin.

Windows NT/2000

The Windows NT/2000 external database configuration is somewhat different from any other external database configuration. Because the ACS server is native to the Windows operating system, it has added functionality therein that you cannot get out of other databases. For example, with Windows NT/2000, you can map databases to domains, so you can have the same username across different domains, all with different passwords. Figure 11-3 shows the configuration of the Windows NT/2000 database. If you want to have more control over who is able to authenticate, you can select the **Grant Dial-in Permissions** check box in the Windows profile, and then select the option in ACS to verify that it is selected. It is important to understand that the Grant Dial-in Permissions option in ACS applies to any access that a user with the option enabled tries to make. The Grant Dial-in Permissions option does not just mean dialup.

Figure 11-3 *Windows NT/2000 Configuration*

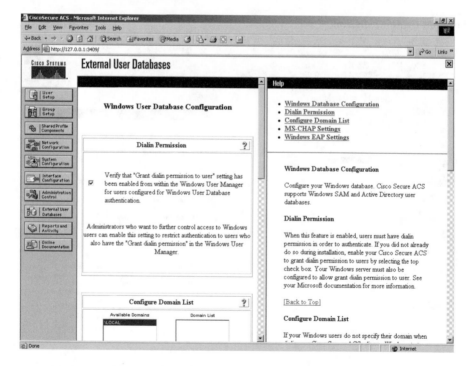

In addition to the capability to check for dial-in permission, ACS can search a list of trusted domains. In this scenario, a user would enter their domain\username and password, and the configuration of an external Windows NT/2000 database would search that domain. If you use a domain-qualified username, the domain list is irrelevant. ACS attempts to authenticate a domain-qualified username only against the domain it is specified as belonging to.

If you do not use a domain-qualified username, ACS submits the user credentials to Windows for authentication. If Windows rejects the user and the domain list is configured, ACS submits the user credentials again in a domain-qualified format, once per each domain in the domain list, until a domain authenticates the user or all explicitly queried domains have rejected the user credentials.

If the authentication request is denied, ACS logs the failed attempt and fails the request. If the credentials submitted by the user do not match the credentials associated with the first matching username that Windows finds, authentication fails.

This is the normal processing procedure; however, using the domain list is not required to support Windows authentication.

You can also see the domain list in Figure 11-4. Additionally, you can configure Microsoft Challenge Handshake Authentication Protocol (MS-CHAP) settings as seen in Figure 11-4. This allows for password changes using MS-CHAP version 1 or 2.

Figure 11-4 *MS-CHAP Configuration*

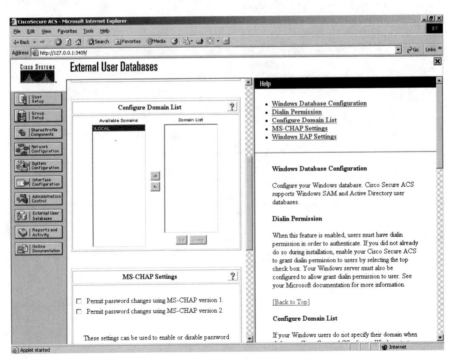

Novell NDS

The following steps configure most external databases. Here, they are seen in a generic form. You will find that you can use these steps time and time again when configuring multiple external databases. The generic steps to create the external server configuration are as follows:

Step 1 Select the external database that you want to use with ACS to authenticate users. In this case, you select the **Novell NDS** link.

Step 2 From the Database Configuration Creation page, select the **Create New Configuration** button.

Step 3 From the Create a New External Database Configuration page, enter a name for your server and select **Submit**.

Step 4 From the External User Database Configuration page, select the **Configure** button to configure server-specific parameters or the **Delete** button to delete the server configuration.

Figure 11-5 demonstrates the results. From this point on, these steps hold true for all other database configurations discussed in this chapter, unless further noted.

Figure 11-5 *Novell NDS Server Creation*

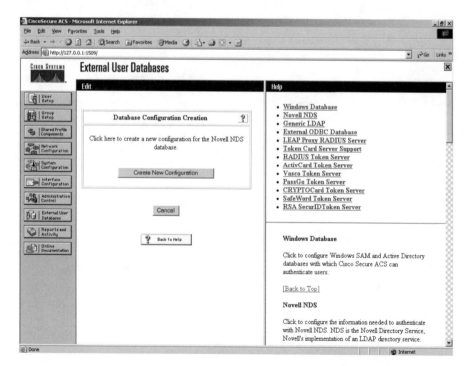

ACS supports ASCII, PAP, PEAP (EAP-GTC), and EAP-TLS authentication with Novell NetWare Directory Services (NDS) servers.

To facilitate the communications between the ACS and Novell NDS server, you need to install Novell Requestor software on the same server as ACS. The Novell Requestor software is available by downloading the Novell client and installing it. Without this client, you cannot proceed, and you get an error in ACS. Once the Authenticator is installed, you are able to access the configuration page seen in Figure 11-6.

Figure 11-6 *Novell NDS Database Authentication Support*

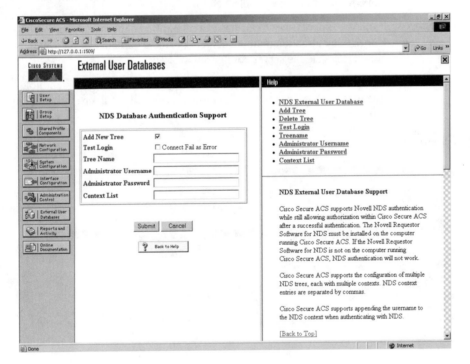

To configure ACS for NDS, perform these tasks:

Step 1 You must select the check box indicating that you want to **Add New Tree**.

Step 2 Choose the **Test Login** option if you want ACS to test the tree's administrative login when you click **Submit**.

Step 3   Enter a tree name.

Step 4   Enter an administrator username.

Step 5   Enter an administrator password.

Step 6   Enter a context list. A context list is similar to the path where the user information is located.

Step 7   Click the **Submit** button to complete your configuration.

After you have named a tree, you can't change it, so you must completely remove the entry by deleting the tree. Also notice that for Novell NDS, you can create only one configuration. This differs from other external databases such as the Generic LDAP database, where you can configure more than one database entry. However, you can add new trees within the same configuration. A sample of what an NDS configuration might look like is seen in Figure 11-7.

Figure 11-7 *Sample NDS Configuration in ACS*

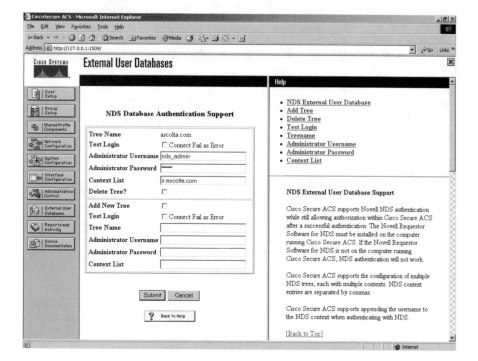

Generic LDAP

For the configuration of a Generic LDAP server, you follow the same generic process as seen in the Novell NDS section earlier in the chapter; however, the configuration parameters are different because of the type of server you are accessing. LDAP is the Lightweight Directory Access Protocol (LDAP), and ACS provides support for ASCII, PAP, EAP-TLS, and PEAP (EAP-GTC) authentication using Generic LDAP.

LDAP configuration can contain more than one subtree for users or groups, and each LDAP configuration supports only one subtree directory for users and one subtree directory for groups. Therefore, you have to configure separate LDAP instances for each user directory subtree and group directory subtree combination for which Cisco Secure Access Control Server (CSACS) submits authentication requests. In Figure 11-8, you can see that an LDAP database is configured already, and also an option to create a new configuration exists.

Figure 11-8 *Database Configuration and Creation of LDAP*

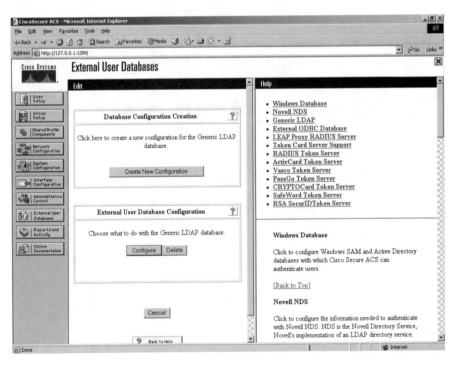

The information required to communicate with the Generic LDAP server includes domain filtering options, common LDAP configuration parameters, and server-specific information.

You can direct authentication in LDAP by utilizing the domain filtering features in ACS. Users can enter a username in the format *username@domainname*. In this case, you might want to filter based on this. Enter the domain qualifier as *@domainname*. This defines what ACS is to look for. The domain filtering options available in ACS are as follows:

- Process all usernames
- Process only usernames that are domain qualified
  - Qualified by suffix or prefix
  - Domain qualifier
  - Strip domain before submitting username to the LDAP server
- Process all usernames after stripping domain name and delimiter
  - Strip starting characters through the last *XX* character, where *XX* is a value
  - Strip ending characters from the first *XX* character, where *XX* is a value

The following parameters are considered common LDAP configuration parameters and are seen in Figure 11-9:

- User Directory Subtree
- Group Directory Subtree
- UserObjectType
- UserObjectClass
- GroupObjectType
- GroupObjectClass
- Group Attribute Name
- Server Timeout
- On Timeout Use Secondary option
- Failback Retry Delay

Figure 11-9 *Common LDAP Configuration Parameters*

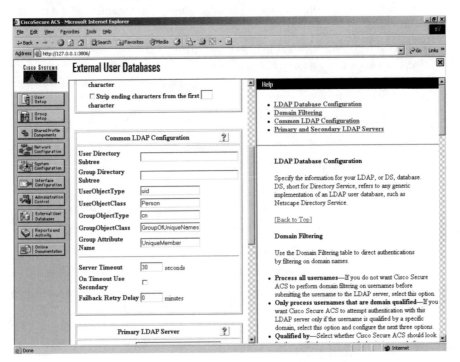

Along with the common configuration parameters, you also need to specify some server-specific options. Figure 11-10 shows the server-specific options. They include the following for both the primary and secondary server:

- Hostname
- Port
- LDAP Version
- Security (Use Secure Authentication)
- Certificate DB Path
- Admin DN
- Password

Figure 11-10 *LDAP Server Configuration Parameters*

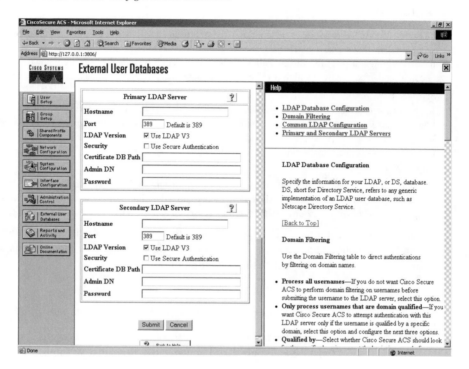

After your configuration has been submitted, you are ready to communicate with the LDAP server.

External ODBC Database

You have the ability to configure ACS to authenticate to an ODBC-compliant relational database. When you authenticate users to a relational database of this type, ACS supports ASCII, PAP, ARAP, CHAP, MS-CHAP (versions 1 and 2), LEAP, EAP-TLS, EAP-MD5, and PEAP (EAP-GTC). This is done through the ODBC Authenticator feature. Other authentication protocols are not supported with ODBC external user databases; however, they might be compatible with other external type databases.

You can also configure the relational database to assign groups to users that have been authenticated to the database. This type of group specification overrides database group mappings discussed in a later section.

The following explains how ACS processes authentication with an ODBC external user database:

[1] Cisco Secure ACS forwards user authentication requests to an ODBC database in either of the two following scenarios. The first scenario is when the user account in the Cisco Secure user database lists an ODBC database configuration as the authentication method. The second is when the user is unknown to the Cisco Secure user database and the Unknown User Policy dictates that an ODBC database is the next external user database to try.

In either case, Cisco Secure ACS forwards user credentials to the ODBC database via an ODBC connection. The relational database must have a stored procedure that queries the appropriate tables and returns values to Cisco Secure ACS. If the returned values indicate that the user credentials provided are valid, Cisco Secure ACS instructs the requesting AAA client to grant the user access; otherwise, Cisco Secure ACS denies the user access.

Cisco Secure ACS grants authorization based on the Cisco Secure ACS group to which the user is assigned. While the group to which a user is assigned can be determined by information from the ODBC database using a process known as "group specification," it is Cisco Secure ACS that grants authorization privileges.

When utilizing an external ODBC database, you can set up only a single configuration. You do not have the option to create a new configuration after the initial configuration is set up; rather, you can configure or delete the configuration.

To configure the database information, follow these steps:

Step 1 Select the **Configure** option from the External User Database screen.

Step 2 You can now enter the information necessary to communicate with the external database. Figure 11-11 shows the options that you must provide, including the following:

  — System DSN:
  - CiscoSecureVarsDB
  - CiscoSecureDBSync

  — DSN Username

  — DSN Password

  — DSN Connection Retries, with a default of 3

  — ODBC Worker Threads, with a default of 1

  — DSN Procedure Type:
  - Returns Recordset (Microsoft SQL)
  - Returns Parameters

  — Support PAP authentication

  — PAP SQL Procedure, with a default of CSNTAuthUserPap

  — Support CHAP/MS-CHAP/ARAP authentication

  — CHAP SQL Procedure, with a default of
  CSNTExtractUserClearTextPw

  — Support EAP-TLS authentication

  — EAP SQL Procedure, with a default of CSNTFindUser

Figure 11-11 *External ODBC Database Parameters*

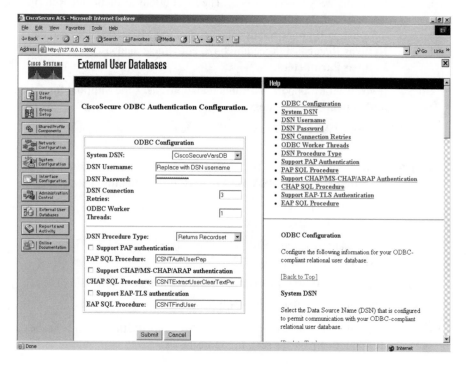

To configure the database parameters, follow these steps:

Step 1 Select the **System DSN**.

Step 2 Enter the Domain Name System (DSN) username.

Step 3 Enter the DSN password.

Step 4 Enter a value for connection retries or leave the default value of 3.

Step 5 Enter the number of ODBC worker threads or leave the default value of 1. The maximum value is 10. You should increase this value only if the ODBC driver you are using is certified thread safe.

Step 6 Select the DSN procedure type. The two options available are Returns Recordset or Returns Parameters. This tells ACS how it receives information from the relational database. For Microsoft SQL, use the **Returns Recordset** procedure type. For Oracle databases, choose **Returns Parameters**.

Step 7 If you want to support PAP authentication, check the **Support for PAP authentication** check box.

Step 8 Enter the PAP SQL procedure type or leave it with the default CSNTAuthUserPap.

Step 9 If you want to support CHAP/MS-CHAP/ARAP authentication, check the **Support CHAP/MS-CHAP/ARAP authentication** check box.

Step 10 Enter the CHAP SQL Procedure. The default is CSNTExtractUserClearTextPw.

Step 11 If you want to support EAP-TLS authentication, check the **Support EAP-TLS authentication** check box.

Step 12 Enter the EAP-SQL Procedure. The default value is CSNTFindUser.

Step 13 When finished, click the **Submit** button.

If the ODBC drivers on the server are configured correctly, the screen refreshes to a successful completion page, as seen in Figure 11-12.

Figure 11-12 *Successful ODBC Database Configuration Screen*

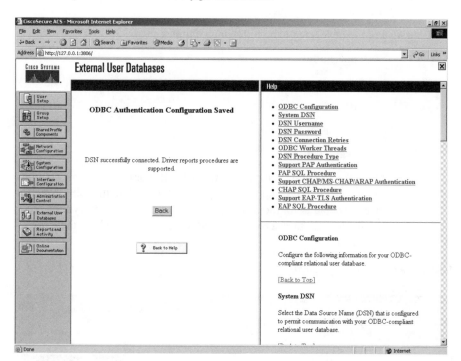

Note that this cannot be successful unless the ODBC drivers are properly configured. After the ODBC drivers are configured, you need to configure the ODBC server. For purposes of simplicity, the following example is the configuration of a SQL server using PAP authentication.

The following steps can be used to configure a simple database in SQL to facilitate PAP authentication:

Step 1   Create a database that you can use for authentication using the SQL Server Enterprise manager.

Step 2   Enter a user for the database that can be authenticated with the ODBC driver.

Step 3   In the database that you have created, create a table. (We call this table *users* for this example.)

Step 4   For the table, create the following columns:

— **username**

— **csacspasswd**

— **dbo**

— **csacsgroup**

— **csacsacctinfo**

Step 5   Make the all columns data type VARCHAR. For the username column, set the length to **64**, and for csacspasswd, set the length to **255**. You can take the defaults for the rest. We also allowed nulls for everything but username and csacspasswd. You can see an example of this table in Figure 11-13.

Figure 11-13   *Table Creation in SQL 2000*

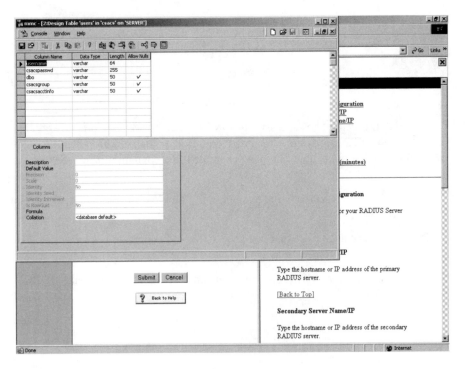

Step 6 Next, using the SQL Server Query Analyzer, you can paste the following:

```
drop procedure dbo.CSNTAuthUserPap
GO

CREATE PROCEDURE CSNTAuthUserPap
@username varchar(64), @pass varchar(255)
AS
SET NOCOUNT ON
IF EXISTS( SELECT username
FROM users
WHERE username = @username
AND csacspasswd = @pass )
SELECT 0,csacsgroup,csacsacctinfo,"No Error"
FROM users
WHERE username = @username
ELSE
SELECT 3,0,"odbc","ODBC Authen Error"

GO
GRANT EXECUTE ON dbo.CSNTAuthUserPap TO Administrator
GO
```

Step 7 Select the database that you are working with from the drop-down menu.

Step 8 Press the **F5** key. (You should receive the following output: "The command(s) completed successfully.")

Step 9 Save your query results and you are done. This completes the process of configuring the ODBC database configuration in ACS. If you need additional guidance, the ACS CD includes stub routines for creating both SQL and Oracle procedures.

LEAP Proxy RADIUS Server

[2] For Cisco Secure ACS-authenticated users accessing your network via Cisco Aironet devices, Cisco Secure ACS supports ASCII, PAP, MS-CHAP (versions 1 and 2), and LEAP authentication with a proxy RADIUS server. Other authentication protocols are not supported with LEAP Proxy RADIUS Server databases.

Cisco Secure ACS uses MS-CHAP version 1 for LEAP Proxy RADIUS Server authentication. To manage your proxy RADIUS database, refer to your RADIUS database documentation.

Lightweight Extensible Authentication Protocol (LEAP) Proxy RADIUS Server authentication allows you to authenticate users against existing Kerberos databases that support MS-CHAP authentication. You can use the LEAP Proxy RADIUS Server database to authenticate users with any third-party RADIUS server that supports MS-CHAP authentication.

The third-party RADIUS server must return Microsoft Point-to-Point Encryption (MPPE) keys in the Microsoft RADIUS vendor-specific attribute (VSA) MSCHAP-MPPE-Keys (VSA 12). If the third-party RADIUS server does not return the MPPE keys, the authentication fails and is logged in the Failed Attempts log.

You should install and configure your proxy RADIUS server before configuring Cisco Secure ACS to authenticate users with it. For information about installing the proxy RADIUS server, refer to the documentation included with your RADIUS server.

To configure a LEAP Proxy RADIUS Server, begin by selecting the LEAP Proxy RADIUS Server link in the External User Database Configuration page. Upon selecting this link, you are taken to the page that creates this configuration in ACS.

To establish a LEAP Proxy RADIUS Server configuration in ACS, follow these steps:

Step 1 From External User Databases, select **Database Configuration**.

Step 2 Select **LEAP Proxy RADIUS Server**.

Step 3 Select the **Create New Configuration** button.

Step 4 Enter a name for your new configuration.

Step 5 Choose **Submit**.

This creates the entry. After the entry is created, you then can configure the parameters required for the connection to take place.

To configure the database parameters, follow these steps:

Step 1 Select the **Configure** button.

Step 2 Enter the primary server name/IP.

Step 3 Enter the secondary server name/IP.

Step 4 Enter the shared secret.

Step 5 Enter the authentication port. This can usually be left as the default of 1812.

Step 6 Enter the timeout (seconds). The default value is 10 seconds.

Step 7 Enter the number of retries. The default is 3.

Step 8 Enter the failback retry delay (minutes). The default value is 5.

Step 9 Click **Submit**.

This enables the database in ACS. You can see an example of this configuration in Figure 11-14. Later in this chapter, you learn how to use this database for user authentication.

Figure 11-14 *LEAP Proxy RADIUS Server Configuration*

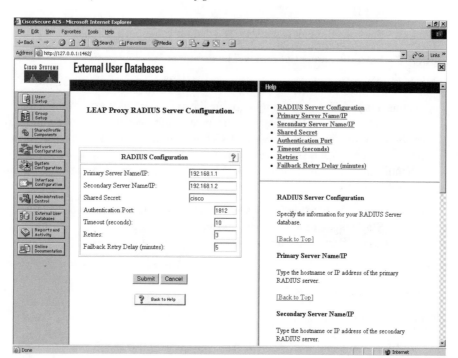

RADIUS Token Server

To configure ACS to work with a RADIUS Token Server, begin with the following steps:

Step 1   From External User Databases, select **Database Configuration**.

Step 2   Select **RADIUS Token Server**.

Step 3   Select the **Create New Configuration** button.

Step 4   Enter a name for your new configuration.

Step 5   Choose **Submit**.

To configure the database parameters, follow these steps:

Step 1   Select the **Configure** button.

Step 2   Enter the primary server name/IP.

Step 3   Enter the secondary server name/IP.

Step 4   Enter the shared secret.

Step 5   Enter the authentication port. This can usually be left as the default of 1812.

Step 6   Enter the timeout (seconds). The default value is 10 seconds.

Step 7   Enter the number of retries. The default is 3.

Step 8   Enter the failback retry delay (minutes). The default value is 5.

You might note that the preceding steps are the same steps as you performed for the LEAP Proxy RADIUS Server. However, you can note a difference in this configuration. You have the ability to configure TACACS+ Shell Configuration options. This enables you to specify how Cisco Secure ACS should respond to TACACS+ authentication requests for users authenticating with this RADIUS Token Server. To configure these options, perform the following tasks:

Step 1   Under the heading Shell Password Prompt, select the radio button for **Static (sync and async tokens)** and enter a prompt, or select **From Token Server (async tokens only)** and enter a password.

Step 2   To complete the configuration, click **Submit**.

This can be seen in Figure 11-15.

Figure 11-15 *Configuring RADIUS Token Server Parameters*

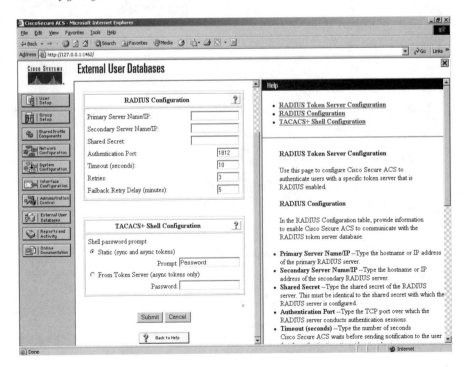

As you can see in Figure 11-16, you can create another RADIUS Token Server entry, or you can configure or delete the one you just made.

Figure 11-16 *Configure/Delete RADIUS Token Server*

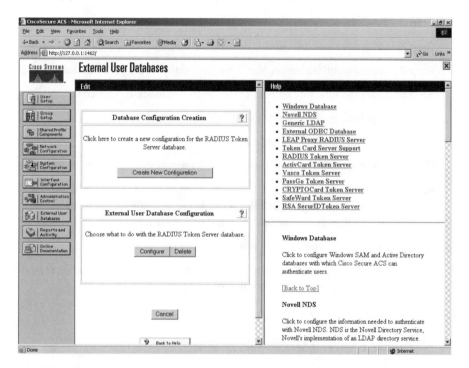

This completes the configuration. To configure another server, repeat the process.

VASCO Token Server

To configure ACS to work with a VASCO Token Server, begin with the following steps:

Step 1 From External User Databases, select **Database Configuration**.

Step 2 Select **VASCO Token Server**.

Step 3 Select the **Create New Configuration** button.

Step 4 Enter a name for your new configuration.

Step 5 Choose **Submit**.

To configure the database parameters, follow these steps:

Step 1 Select the **Configure** button.

Step 2 Enter the primary server name/IP.

Step 3 Enter the secondary server name/IP.

Step 4 Enter the shared secret.

Step 5 Enter the authentication port. This can usually be left as the default of 1812.

Step 6 Enter the timeout (seconds). The default value is 10 seconds.

Step 7 Enter the number of retries. The default is 3.

Step 8 Enter the failback retry delay (minutes). The default value is 5.

To configure these options, perform the following tasks:

Step 1 Under the heading Shell Password Prompt, select the radio button for **Static (sync and async tokens)** and enter a prompt, or select **From Token Server (async tokens only)** and enter a password.

Step 2 To complete the configuration, click **Submit**.

As you can see in Figure 11-17, you can create another VASCO Token Server entry, or you can configure or delete the one you just made.

Figure 11-17 *Configure/Delete VASCO Token Server*

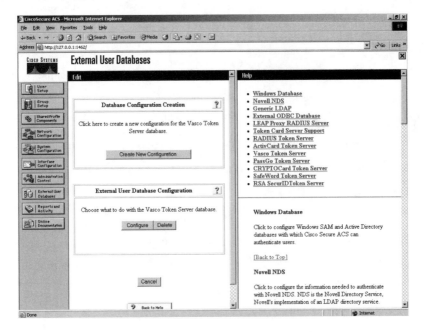

This completes the configuration. To configure another server, repeat the process.

ActivCard Token Server

To configure ACS to work with an ActivCard Token Server, begin with the following steps:

Step 1 From External User Databases, select **Database Configuration**.

Step 2 Select **ActivCard Token Server**.

Step 3 Select the **Create New Configuration** button.

Step 4 Enter a name for your new configuration.

Step 5 Choose **Submit**.

To configure the database parameters, follow these steps:

Step 1 Select the **Configure** button.

Step 2 Enter the primary server name/IP.

Step 3 Enter the secondary server name/IP.

Step 4 Enter the shared secret.

Step 5 Enter the authentication port. This can usually be left as the default of 1812.

Step 6 Enter the timeout (seconds). The default value is 10 seconds.

Step 7 Enter the number of retries. The default is 3.

Step 8 Enter the failback retry delay (minutes). The default value is 5.

To configure these options, perform the following tasks:

Step 1 Under the heading Shell Password Prompt, select the radio button for **Static (sync and async tokens)** and enter a prompt, or select **From Token Server (async tokens only)** and enter a password.

Step 2 To complete the configuration, click **Submit**.

PassGo Defender Token Server

To configure ACS to work with a PassGo Defender Token Server, begin with the following steps:

Step 1 From External User Databases, select **Database Configuration**.

Step 2 Select **PassGo Defender Token Server**.

Step 3   Select the **Create New Configuration** button.

Step 4   Enter a name for your new configuration.

Step 5   Choose **Submit**.

To configure the database parameters, follow these steps:

Step 1   Select the **Configure** button.

Step 2   Enter the primary server name/IP.

Step 3   Enter the secondary server name/IP.

Step 4   Enter the shared secret.

Step 5   Enter the authentication port. This can usually be left as the default of 1812.

Step 6   Enter the timeout (seconds). The default value is 10 seconds.

Step 7   Enter the number of retries. The default is 3.

Step 8   Enter the failback retry delay (minutes). The default value is 5.

To configure these options, perform the following tasks:

Step 1   Under the heading Shell Password Prompt, select the radio button for **Static (sync and async tokens)** and enter a prompt, or select **From Token Server (async tokens only)** and enter a password.

Step 2   To complete the configuration, click **Submit**.

CRYPTOCard Token Server

To configure ACS to work with a CRYPTOCard Token Server, begin with the following steps:

Step 1   From External User Databases, select **Database Configuration**.

Step 2   Select **CRYPTOCard Token Server**.

Step 3   Select the **Create New Configuration** button.

Step 4   Enter a name for your new configuration.

Step 5   Choose **Submit**.

To configure the database parameters, follow these steps:

Step 1   Select the **Configure** button.

Step 2   Enter the primary server name/IP.

Step 3   Enter the secondary server name/IP.

Step 4   Enter the shared secret.

Step 5   Enter the authentication port. This can usually be left as the default of 1812.

Step 6   Enter the timeout (seconds). The default value is 10 seconds.

Step 7   Enter the number of retries. The default is 3.

Step 8   Enter the failback retry delay (minutes). The default value is 5.

To configure these options, perform the following tasks:

Step 1   Under the heading Shell Password Prompt, select the radio button for **Static (sync and async tokens)** and enter a prompt, or select **From Token Server (async tokens only)** and enter a password.

Step 2   To complete the configuration, click **Submit**.

SafeWord Token Server

To configure ACS to work with a SafeWord Token Server, begin with the following steps:

Step 1   From External User Databases, select **Database Configuration**.

Step 2   Select **SafeWord Token Server**.

Step 3   Select the **Create New Configuration** button.

Step 4   Enter a name for your new configuration.

Step 5   Choose **Submit**.

To configure the database parameters, follow these steps:

Step 1   Select the **Configure** button.

Step 2   Enter the primary server name/IP.

Step 3   Enter the secondary server name/IP.

Step 4   Enter the shared secret.

Step 5   Enter the authentication port. This can usually be left as the default of 1812.

Step 6   Enter the timeout (seconds). The default value is 10 seconds.

Step 7   Enter the number of retries. The default is 3.

Step 8   Enter the failback retry delay (minutes). The default value is 5.

To configure these options, perform the following tasks:

Step 1 Under the heading Shell Password Prompt, select the radio button for **Static (sync and async tokens)** and enter a prompt, or select **From Token Server (async tokens only)** and enter a password.

Step 2 To complete the configuration, click **Submit**.

RSA SecurID Token Server

The configuration of an RSA server is somewhat different from the others in that after the server configuration is created, it is the only one available. This means that you can configure only one server. Also, RSA SecurID Token Servers require additional software be installed on the ACS server. If the RSA software is not installed, you receive an error similar to the one seen in Figure 11-18. After the RSA software has been installed, you are then able to configure the ACS parameters. For help installing the software or to obtain RSA software, you can visit www.rsasecurity.com.

Figure 11-18 *RSA Configuration Error*

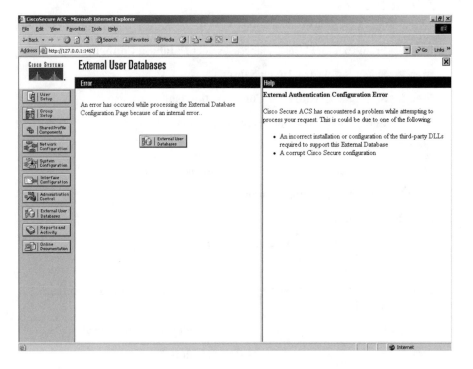

If your installation is correct, ACS displays the name of the token server and the path to the authenticator DLL. This indicates that the installation of the RSA ACE client for Windows 2000 is configured properly. For information on how to install the ACE client, refer to the ACS configuration guides provided with ACS or at www.cisco.com.

Database Group Mappings

After you complete the setup of the database that you want to use with ACS, you can then set up a database group mapping. This maps a group to an external server. This way when users are authenticated by way of one of the external servers, they are placed in the corresponding group in the mapping configuration.

To configure the database group mapping, perform the following steps:

Step 1   Select the **Database Group Mappings** link from the External Database Configuration page.

Step 2   Select the external server that you want to assign a group to.

Step 3   Using the drop-down menu, choose the group to place authenticated users of this database in.

Step 4   Select the **Submit** button. This completes the configuration of unknown user database group mappings.

In addition to this simple mapping, ACS also supports the following:

- Group mapping by external user database group membership
- RADIUS group specification

The group mapping by external user database group membership allows you to map more than a database to a single group for some external database types. An example of this would be a Windows database in which ACS can make use of external group membership to dynamically determine the ACS group membership. The RADIUS group mapping enables you to specify on the RADIUS server the group the user is placed in, and this value is returned in the token server's authentication response. You can also use an ODBC database to specify the group assignment in ACS.

Unknown User Policy

The final aspect of external database configuration is the configuration of how ACS handles an unknown user. At this point, you have the external database in your ACS configuration; you have configured the database to group mapping, but ACS is not sure what to do if it sees a user attempt to authenticate that is not in its local database. This leads you to the unknown user policy configuration.

The first option is to fail the attempt. If this is the case, ACS fails an attempt from a user that attempts to authenticate using credentials from an external database. The second option is to check the external databases that you have configured. To perform this task, you must place the server that is in the left column, titled "External Databases," and place it into the right column titled "Selected Databases." Do this using the right and left arrows. You can also select the order that the databases are searched. Select **Submit** when you are finished.

Database Replication

Database replication is a means of providing a more fault-tolerant network design. This section explains the process of database replication as well as the steps to configure database replication.

Understanding Database Replication

Database replication is a way for you to create a copy of the ACS database on one or more mirror systems. This process allows for the processing of authentication requests if the primary ACS goes down. You can schedule database replication, or you can perform immediate database replications. Another benefit to database replication is that the database is actually compressed before it is sent, and the secondary server has the capability to decompress the information after it has been received.

The following replication process is taken from the user guide for ACS. It details the communication between the primary and secondary ACS.

[3] The database replication process begins when the primary Cisco Secure ACS server compares the list of database components it is configured to replicate with the list of database components each secondary Cisco Secure ACS is configured to replicate. The primary Cisco Secure ACS only replicates those database components that it is configured to send and that the secondary Cisco Secure ACS is configured to receive. If the secondary Cisco Secure ACS is not configured to receive any of the components that the primary Cisco Secure ACS is configured to send, the database replication is aborted.

After the primary Cisco Secure ACS has determined which components to send to the secondary Cisco Secure ACS, the replication process continues on the primary Cisco Secure ACS as follows:

The primary Cisco Secure ACS stops its authentication and creates a copy of the Cisco Secure database components that it is configured to replicate. During this step, if AAA clients are configured properly, those that usually use the primary Cisco Secure ACS failover to another Cisco Secure ACS.

The primary Cisco Secure ACS resumes its authentication service. It also compresses and encrypts the copy of its database components for transmission to the secondary Cisco Secure ACS.

The primary Cisco Secure ACS transmits the compressed, encrypted copy of its database components to the secondary Cisco Secure ACS. This transmission occurs over a TCP connection, using port 2000. The TCP session uses an encrypted, Cisco-proprietary protocol.

After the preceding events on the primary Cisco Secure ACS, the database replication process continues on the secondary Cisco Secure ACS as follows:

The secondary Cisco Secure ACS receives the compressed, encrypted copy of the Cisco Secure database components on the primary Cisco Secure ACS. After transmission of the database components is complete, the secondary Cisco Secure ACS uncompresses the database components.

The secondary Cisco Secure ACS stops its authentication service and replaces its database components with the database components it received from the primary Cisco Secure ACS. During this step, if AAA clients are configured properly, those that usually use the secondary Cisco Secure ACS failover to another Cisco Secure ACS.

The secondary Cisco Secure ACS resumes its authentication service.

To clarify a few items for you, it is important to understand that only those components that the primary is configured to send and the secondary is configured to receive are replicated. The secondary can be configured to receive other components; however, if the primary isn't configured to send them, it won't send them. The primary can be configured to send other components, but if the secondary isn't configured to receive them, it won't receive them. So all that is actually replicated is what the primary is configured to send and what the secondary is configured to receive. This replication occurs as long as they agree on at least one component. If they do not agree, replication is aborted. Additionally, if nothing has changed on the primary server since the last replication, no reason to replicate exists.

Replication Versus Backup

The major difference between database replication and database backup is that database backup creates a backup file on the local drive. This can be copied to other forms of media, or to network shares, and can be used to recover a system that has failed. What database backup does not do is copy the database or portions of the database to other ACSs, known as secondary servers. By using replication, you can provide a redundant server configuration.

Configuring the Primary Server

Database replication is found in the System Configuration section of ACS. To configure the server for database replication, follow these steps:

Step 1 Select **System Configuration**.

Step 2 Select **Cisco Secure Database Replication**.

Step 3 Select **Send** or **Receive** for any or all of the replication components:

— User and group database

— Network configuration device tables

— Distribution table

— Interface configuration

— Interface security settings

— Password validation settings

Step 4 Next, for outbound replication, select the **Scheduling of Outbound Replication** options that you want to employ. Choose **Manually**, **Automatically Triggered Cascade** (meaning when the master receives information it is automatically copied to the others), **Every __ minutes**, or select a specific time using the grid provided.

Step 5 Choose the **Partner server(s)** from the list of AAA servers in the left column of the partners section, and use the **right arrow** button to place them in the replication list to the right.

Step 6 Because this is the primary server, you should not need to configure the Inbound Replication settings; however, a server in a cascade can accept incoming replication, as well as perform outbound replication. If you choose a specific time, select the times from the grid provided.

Step 7 Select the **Submit** button, or to perform immediate replication, select the **Replicate Now** button.

Configuring a Secondary Server

The secondary server must be configured to receive the exact configuration that the primary server is sending.

To configure the secondary server for database replication, follow these steps:

Step 1 From the System Configuration menu, select the **Cisco Secure Database Replication** link.

Step 2 Select the **Receive** check box for each item you want to receive. These include user and group database, AAA servers and AAA clients tables, distribution table, interface configuration, interface security settings, and password validation settings. These should match the options that the primary ACS is sending.

Step 3 Next, from the Inbound Replication section, choose to receive replication from any know Cisco Secure ACS or use the drop-down list to select a trusted server.

Step 4 Select **Submit**.

NOTE Keep in mind that replication can be initiated only by the primary server.

Immediate Replication

You can perform immediate replication from the primary ACS by selecting the **Cisco Secure Database Replication** link and then the **Replicate Now** button at the bottom of the configuration page. This performs an immediate replication.

Backing Up the Cisco Secure Database

Another important aspect of maintaining your ACS configuration is to perform frequent database backups of the ACS database. This section covers the steps needed to perform manual backups, schedule backups, cancel scheduled backups, and recover ACS from a backup.

Under the umbrella of database backup, you have the following options:

- Perform a manual backup
- Schedule a backup to take place at periodic intervals, or at a given time
- Cancel a scheduled backup
- Recover from a backup file

Database backups are performed from the System Configuration subsection ACS System Backup Setup. From this subsection, you can configure manual backups, which requires an administrator to force the backup process into effect or schedule a backup. If you decide to schedule a backup, you have a few options. You can back up based on an interval, the default being 60 minutes, or you can specify times to perform the database backup. To perform a backup, you must tell ACS where to store the backup file. The default location to store backup files in the directory is

C:\Program Files\CiscoSecure ACS v3.1\CSAuth\System Backups

This backup file is stored as a .dmp file. The file is named by date. For example, the file 21-Jul-2003 15-55-12.dmp was created at 3:55 on July 21st. Consider managing this directory if you have ACS perform automatic backups. This directory might get full fast. For this reason, you might want to keep files for a certain period of time or frequently back up this directory to external media.

Manual Backups

To perform a manual backup, select the **ACS Backup** link from the System Configuration section. From here, you simply need to select the **Backup Now** button to perform a manual backup.

Scheduled Backups

To schedule a backup, select the **ACS Backup** link from the System Configuration section. Choose one of the following options:

- Every __ minutes
- At specific times

If you elect to back up at a given time interval, enter an interval or accept the default of 60 minutes. If you choose to back up at specific times, use the time grid provided to select those times. Complete the configuration by selecting **Submit**.

You can manage the directory that backups are performed in by manipulating those options in the ACS interface. The default directory used for backup is C:\Program Files\CiscoSecure ACS v3.2\CSAuth\System Backups. No management is in place for this directory, so it can become very large, very quickly.

Canceling a Scheduled Backup

It is fairly simple to cancel a scheduled backup. Simply access the **ACS Backup** link from the System Configuration section and change from **Every __ minutes**, or **At specific times**, to **Manual backup**. This cancels any further scheduled backups.

Recovering ACS from a Backup file

If you want to recover ACS from a .dmp file, select the **ACS Restore** link from System Configuration, choose the directory that your backup files are stored in, choose the file you want to restore from, opt for restoring user and group database and/or Cisco Secure ACS system configuration, and select the **Restore Now** button.

Synchronization of ACS Devices

ACS supports the use of an external ODBC database for the automation of your ACS configuration. Two components facilitate this process, CSDBsync, which is the process that actually performs the synchronization, and the accountActions table.

The synchronization with an external database allows you to configure the following based on values contained in the External Database table:

- Users
- User groups
- Network configuration
- Custom RADIUS vendors and VSAs

For users, you can configure the following attributes:

- Adding a user
- Deleting a user
- Setting passwords
- Setting user group membership
- Setting max sessions parameters
- Setting network usage quota parameters
- Configuring command authorization
- Configuring network access restrictions
- Configuring time-of-day/day-of-week access restrictions
- Assigning IP addresses
- Specifying outbound RADIUS attribute values
- Specifying outbound TACACS+ attribute values

For user groups, you can configure the following parameters:

- Setting max sessions parameters
- Setting network usage quota parameters
- Configuring command authorization

- Configuring network access restrictions
- Configuring time-of-day/day-of-week access restrictions
- Specifying outbound RADIUS attribute values
- Specifying outbound TACACS+ attribute values

For network configuration, you can configure the following:

- Adding an AAA client
- Deleting an AAA client
- Setting AAA client configuration details
- Adding an AAA server
- Deleting an AAA server
- Setting AAA server configuration details
- Adding and configuring Proxy Distribution Table entries

For custom RADIUS vendors and VSAs, ACS allows you to create up to 10 IETF-compliant RADIUS vendors, and all VSAs that you add for those servers must be sub-attributes of IETF RADIUS attribute number 26.

Components of Synchronization

When you perform database synchronization, two components work together, the CSDBsync process and the accountActions table. This section should help you to better understand what each component's role in synchronization is and how the two work hand in hand to facilitate synchronization.

CSDBSync

CSDBSync is a service that ACS runs to perform automated user and group account management. This functions by gaining access the ODBC driver Data Source Name (DSN) and thereby accessing the accountActions table. The accountActions table holds information that is needed by CSDBSync.

accountActions Table

The accountActions table is a table on the external ODBC server that contains a set of rows that defines what actions CSDBSync performs in ACS.

CSDBSync and accountActions Table Working Together

The basic process of CSDBSync and accountActions table working together is based on an action in the table. The most common actions are SET_VALUE and DELETE_VALUE. The SET_VALUE has an action code of 1 and the DELETE_VALUE has an action code of 2. CSDBSync reads the accountActions table for a configuration item, such as username, and the action code to determine if it is to add or delete a user from ACS. Each record is then deleted from the RDBMS database.

Cisco recommends that for backup purposes, you create another table and mirror each transaction with CSDBSync to that table. Ensure that that table is backed up frequently. Also, ensure that you perform frequent backups of the ACS database.

NOTE   For a complete list of configurations and action codes, see the user guide that came with your ACS.

Preparing for Synchronization

Before you perform synchronization, you need to complete a few tasks. These tasks enable the ACS to use CSDBSync to communicate with the accountActions table:

Step 1   First, determine where you will create the accountActions table and the format you will use.

Step 2   Create the accountActions table on the third-party system.

Step 3   Create any stored procedures that might be necessary to populate the accountActions table. Refer to the user guide for more detailed information on these stored procedures.

NOTE   The mechanism for maintaining your accountActions table is unique to your implementation. For information about the format and content of the accountActions table, see "RDBMS Synchronization Import Definitions" in the ACS user guide.

Step 4   Validate your third-party system to ensure that it updates the accountActions table properly. Rows generated in the accountActions table must be valid.

Step 5   Set up a system DSN on the ACS. This was discussed in the "External Database Configuration" section earlier in this chapter.

Step 6   Schedule RDBMS synchronization in ACS. These steps are discussed in the next section.

Step 7   Configure your external database to begin updating the accountActions table with the information that you want to be imported into the ACS user database.

Step 8   For troubleshooting, use the RDBMS Synchronization report in the Reports and Activity section. Additionally, you can monitor the CSDBSync service log.

RDBMS Synchronization Options

To enable RDBMS synchronization, you must enable it in interface configuration, under the Advanced Options link. Once enabled, you will find an RDBMS Synchronization link in System Configuration. Begin by selecting the **RDBMS Synchronization** link in System Configuration. Under the RDBMS Setup heading, select a DSN from the drop-down menu. (This should already be configured.) Also, you need to enter the username and password for the ODBC connection.

Next, you select the synchronization options from the Synchronization Scheduling heading. Here, you can choose a manual synchronization or schedule synchronization based on a time interval or by choosing timeslots from the time grid provided.

Finally, you need to select the AAA server from the list on the left, and use the right arrow to place them in the Partners column. This allows all partner device information to be synchronized.

Note that you can select the **Submit** button to schedule synchronization, or the **Synchronize Now** button to force a manual synchronization.

This completes the configuration of synchronization. For more detailed information on synchronization, refer to the user guide provided with your ACS as well as the vendor documentation for your ODBC RDBSM system.

Summary

With today's network environments, it is critical that network security equipment remain active and accessible as well as integrate well with databases that are already running in production networks. As you have seen in this chapter, ACS provides a number of functions to facilitate the integration with external databases, the process of backup and recover, and database replication and synchronization.

This chapter is not intended to be the "tell all documentation" on the configurations of these items, but more a guide into the direction that your network requires. For more information and configuration-specific details, refer to the Cisco Secure ACS user guide or the online documentation provided at http://Cisco.com/go/acso.

End Notes

[1] *Installation and User Guide for Cisco Secure ACS*, page 13-48, Mark Wilgus http://www.cisco.com/en/US/products/sw/secursw/ps2086/prod_installation_ guide09186a00800e6edf.html

[2] *Installation and User Guide for Cisco Secure ACS*, page 13-67, Mark Wilgus http://www.cisco.com/en/US/products/sw/secursw/ps2086/prod_installation_ guide09186a00800e6edf.html

[3] *Installation and User Guide for Cisco Secure ACS*, page 9-1, Mark Wilgus http://www.cisco.com/en/US/products/sw/secursw/ps2086/prod_installation_ guide09186a00800e6edf.html

In this chapter, you learn the following topics:

- Reports available in ACS
- Logging attributes in ACS reports
- Working with accounting and administrative reports
- Working with system reports
- Remote logging with ACS

## CHAPTER 12

Reports and Logging for Windows Server

It is important to understand the functionality of reporting made available in Access Control Server (ACS). Likewise, an understanding of the logs that ACS maintains benefits in troubleshooting client/server issues. To better understand this functionality, you need to be able to distinguish between the logs that pertain to the ACS server and the services that ACS runs and the logs that pertain to user interaction with ACS.

This chapter covers the reporting and logging capabilities in ACS for Windows Server only. This chapter also covers how to manage these reports and system logs. This chapter also discusses the configuration of remote logging in ACS for Windows Server. You begin by examining the reporting functionality in ACS.

ACS Reports

ACS has the capability to provide you, the network administrator, with a number of report logs and can give you information about Remote Authentication Dial-In User Service (RADIUS) interaction with authentication, authorization, and accounting (AAA) clients, TACACS+ interaction with AAA clients, and many other aspects of your AAA environment. You can see a list of these reports in the ACS interface by selecting the Reports and Activity page. Your display is seen in Figure 12-1.

The numerous types of reports that ACS is capable of maintaining are stored as either comma-separated value (CSV) files or perhaps as a dynamic report that is not stored at all. These CSV files make it easy to import into other programs that generate custom reports, such as Microsoft Excel or Microsoft Access. Although these are stored as CSV files on the ACS, you can view them in the HTML interface in the form of a web page with tables.

Some of the reports need to interact with accounting configurations on an AAA client while others use information gathered by ACS. Some reports keep track of failed authentication and authorization attempts, while others track the users that have been administratively disabled in ACS.

Figure 12-1 *Reports and Activity*

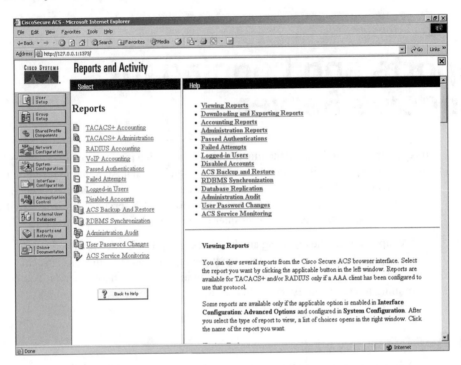

Each of the report logs in the following list can be viewed in the ACS HTML interface, downloaded and viewed in a text editor such as Notepad, or even imported into other programs that are used for custom reporting. If you have access to the file system of the ACS server, you can find them in the following directory locations:

- **TACACS+ Accounting Reports**—Program Files\CiscoSecure ACS v*x.x*\Logs\TACACS+ Accounting

- **TACACS+ Admin Accounting Reports**—Program Files\CiscoSecure ACS v*x.x*\Logs\TACACS+ Administration

- **RADIUS Accounting Reports**—Program Files\CiscoSecure ACS v*x.x*\Logs\RADIUS Accounting

- **VOIP Accounting Reports**—Program Files\CiscoSecure ACS vx.x\Logs\VoIP Accounting

- **Passed Authentications Reports**—Program Files\CiscoSecure ACS v*x.x*\Logs\Passed Authentications

- **Failed Attempts Reports**—Program Files\CiscoSecure ACS v*x.x*\Logs\Failed Attempts

- **ACS Backup And Restore**—Program Files\CiscoSecure ACS v*x.x*\Logs\Backup and Restore

- **RDBMS Synchronization**—Program Files\CiscoSecure ACS v*x.x*\Logs\DbSync

- **Database Replication**—Program Files\CiscoSecure ACS v*x.x*\Logs\DBReplicate

- **Administration Audit**—Program Files\CiscoSecure ACS v*x.x*\Logs\AdminAudit

- **User Password Changes**—Program Files\CiscoSecure ACS v*x.x*\CSAuth\ PasswordLogs

- **ACS Service Monitoring**—Program Files\CiscoSecure ACS v*x.x*\Logs\ ServiceMonitoring

If you don't want to view the report log files that ACS creates in CSV format, you might choose to use the Open Database Connectivity (ODBC)-relational–database compliant form of reporting and logging. This allows ACS to send report log information directly to an ODBC-compliant relational database such as SQL or Crystal Reports. Once in SQL or Crystal Reports, you have the ability to create a much more customized report based on any criteria on which you want to gather information. When this method is used, ACS still creates the local CSV files, and you can still view reports the ACS HTML interface.

Logging Attributes in ACS Reports

When using ACS, you can see special attributes in the ACS reports. These special attributes are designed to give the administrator more information that would not normally be seen in an accounting log on an AAA server. These attributes are special because they are derived from the ACS configuration that you create. These attributes include the following:

- User-Defined Attributes
- Access Device
- Network Device Group
- Device Command Set
- Filter Information
- ExtDB Info

These logging attributes are discussed in greater detail in the next few sections.

NOTE   All attributes for the user are based on the group of which that user is a member. This might be a specific group, or it could be a generic group based on the unknown user authentication policy. The Unknown User Policy is discussed in Chapter 11, "System Configuration."

User-Defined Attributes

User attributes appear in the attributes list for any log configuration page that includes information about the user. The default text box labels are Real Name, Description, User Field 3, 4, and 5 from the user configuration page. Remember that you can change these values to appear with information that is relevant to your users.

To configure user-defined attributes fields, follow these steps:

Step 1   Select **Interface Configuration**.

Step 2   Choose **User Attributes**.

Step 3   From the User Attributes configuration page, enter the attribute field labels as you want them to appear. This is seen in Figure 12-2. Note that this action dictates only how these attribute field labels appear in the user-configuration page; you still need to enter the individual user attributes in each profile.

Figure 12-2   *Configuring User-Defined Fields*

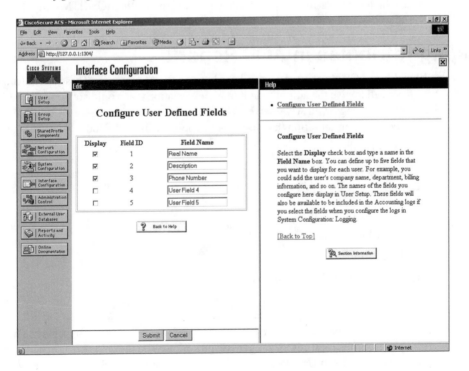

When a user authenticates, these "user-defined" attributes are entered into the report to give you additional information. In Figure 12-3, you can see the attributes as they appear in User Setup, and in Figure 12-4, you can see how they appear in the Passed Authentications report.

Figure 12-3 *User Attributes in User Setup*

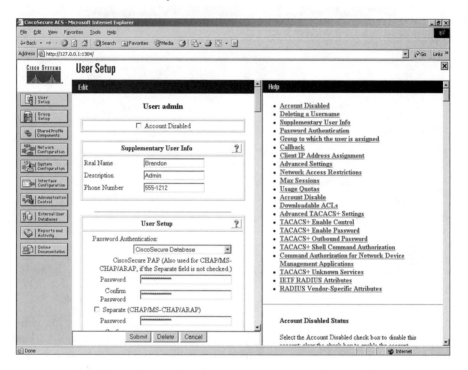

Access Device

The Access Device attribute is an attribute that reflects the name of the AAA client configuration that is sending logging information to ACS. When AAA clients perform a transaction with ACS, the AAA client includes information for authentication to ACS. This is done using a shared secret key. All this information is located in Network Configuration and can be seen in Figure 12-5.

Figure 12-4 *User-Defined Attributes in the Passed Authentications Report*

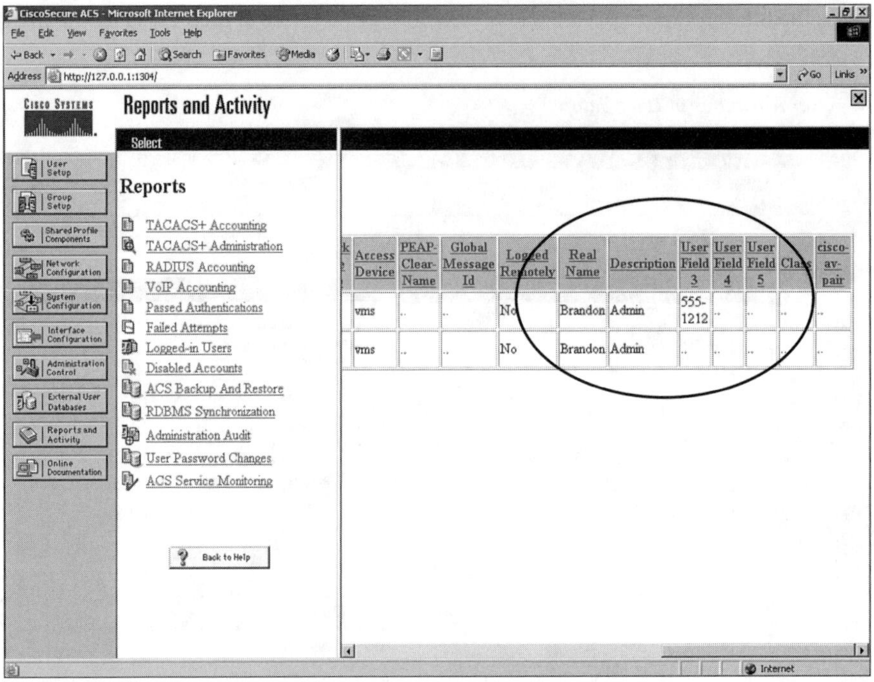

This information is used by ACS to match an AAA client configuration from the list of AAA clients in the Network Configuration page. When a match is found, ACS uses this to log the AAA Client Configuration entry to its report log. This can be seen in Figure 12-6. Notice that the Key entry field has the same name in its entry as the entry found in Figure 12-5.

Network Device Group

The Network Device Group attribute indicates the name of the Network Device Group of which the AAA client is a member. When a user authenticates through different AAA clients, each AAA client is possibly going to be a member of a network device group, depending on your network configuration. In the previous section on the Access Device attribute, you can see that in Figure 12-5 the **vms** access device is not a member of a Network Device Group. In Figure 12-6, you see that the Network Device Group filed in the Passed Authentications log is blank. Adding the **vms** access device to a Network Device Group causes the additional information to be logged to the ACS report. You can see the result in Figure 12-7.

Figure 12-5 *Network Configuration*

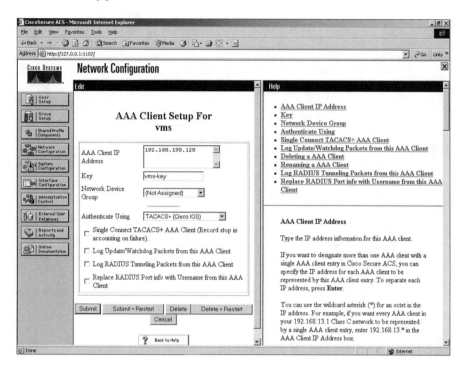

Device Command Set

The purpose of the Device Command Set attribute is to indicate the name of the command authorization set that was used to fulfill a command authorization request. If a command authorization is passed, you *will not* see the name of the command authorization set in a log file. If a command authorization attempt fails, you *will* see the name of the command authorization set that caused the failure, as well as information such as the reason for the failure.

Figure 12-6 *Access Device in the Passed Authentications Report*

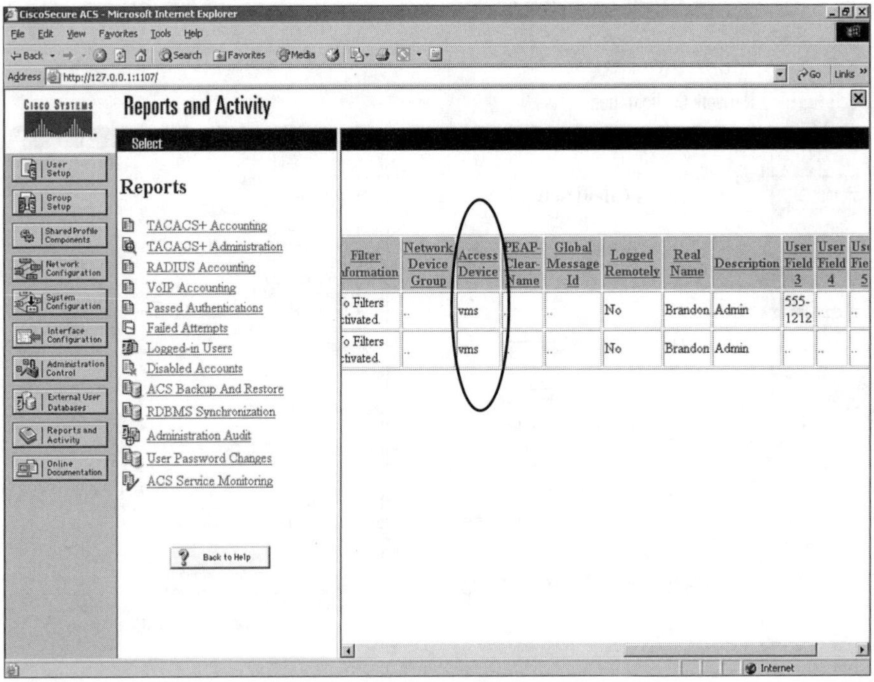

Filter Information

Remember that when you configure Network Access Restrictions (NARs), a user's access can be permitted or denied based on the network access server (NAS) through which they access the network. If an NAR is assigned to a user, this attribute indicates if all the applicable NARs permitted the user access or denied the user access. More specific information is also given that indicates which NAR, if multiple NARs are used, denied the user access. The output can be seen in Figure 12-8. If no NARs are applied, this attribute also indicates that status. As you can tell from the figure, all filters passed. This indicates that the user was allowed access. You can see this attribute information in the Passed Authentications log or Failed Attempts log.

Figure 12-7 *Network Device Attribute in the Passed Authentications Report*

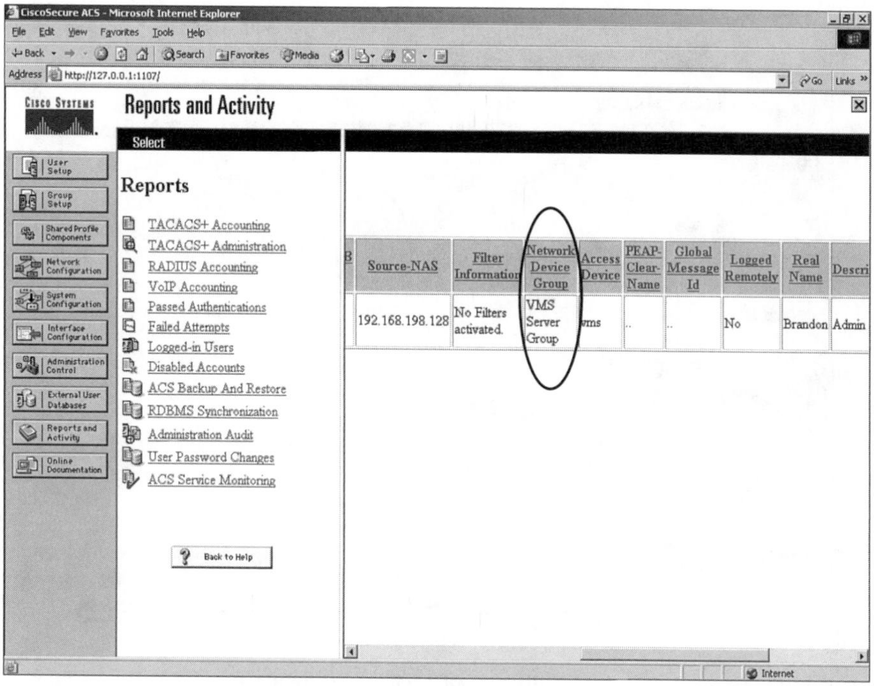

ExtDB Info

If you have configured ACS to authenticate users to an external database, the ExtDB Info attribute contains the information that was returned by that database. For Windows NT/2000 external database authentication, this returns the domain name from which the user authenticated. For other external databases, such as CRYPTOCard authentication servers, RSA's SecurID, LDAP servers, and other external servers that are supported in ACS, the information returned is authentication information. In Figure 12-9, you can see that the username **ext-user** authenticated from an external database called **SERVER**.

Figure 12-8 *Filter Information in the Passed Authentications Report*

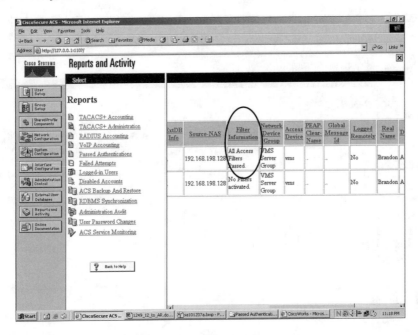

Figure 12-9 *External Database Attribute in the Passed Authentications Report*

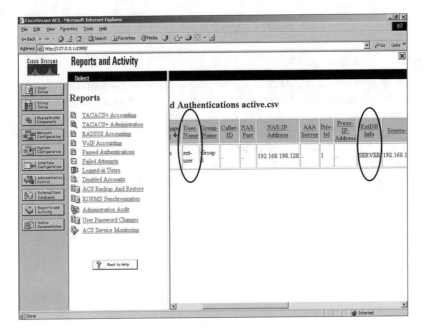

ACS Reports

ACS can provide numerous reports such as accounting reports, administrative reports, and system reports, among others. Some of these reports that ACS maintains might contain information from multiple sources and for multiple reasons. For example, ACS might log a failed password authentication attempt to the Failed Attempts log, and in the same log, you might find a failed attempt caused by an unknown AAA client attempting to communicate with ACS. This is where the third-party reporting programs, such as aaa-reports by Extraxi, SQL, or Microsoft Access can provide enhanced functionality by allowing you to pick the logs apart and see only what you want to see.

Accounting Reports

ACS also maintains TACACS+, RADIUS, and Voice over IP (VoIP) accounting reports, which contain records of successful authentications during selected time periods. In addition to logging successful authentications, these logs contain information such as time/date, username, type of connection, amount of time logged in, and bytes transferred.

Accounting logs contain information about the use of remote access services by users. By default, these report logs are available in CSV format. With the exception of the Passed Authentications log, you can also configure ACS to export the data for these logs to an ODBC-compliant relational database.

TACACS+ Accounting

The TACACS+ accounting report logs contain user sessions' stop and start times, AAA client messages with username, caller line identification information, and session duration. The TACACS+ accounting report is seen in Figure 12-10.

RADIUS Accounting

RADIUS accounting files contain the following information: user sessions' stop and start times, AAA client messages with username, caller line identification information, and session duration. The RADIUS accounting report is seen in Figure 12-11.

Figure 12-10 *TACACS+ Accounting Report*

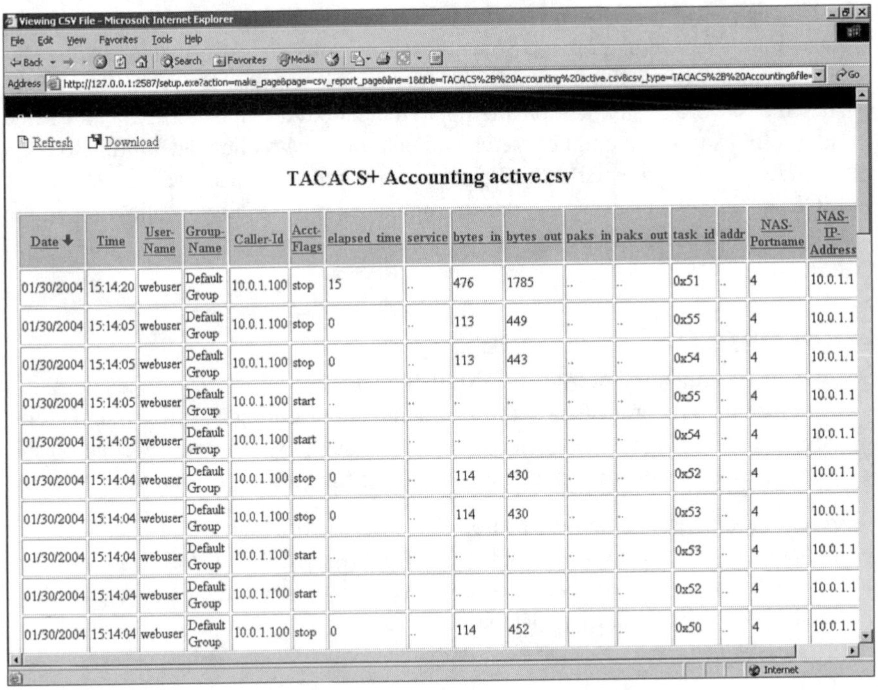

TACACS+ Accounting active.csv

Date	Time	User-Name	Group-Name	Caller-Id	Acct-Flags	elapsed time	service	bytes in	bytes out	paks in	paks out	task id	addr	NAS-Portname	NAS-IP-Address
01/30/2004	15:14:20	webuser	Default Group	10.0.1.100	stop	15	..	476	1785	..	..	0x51	..	4	10.0.1.1
01/30/2004	15:14:05	webuser	Default Group	10.0.1.100	stop	0	..	113	449	..	..	0x55	..	4	10.0.1.1
01/30/2004	15:14:05	webuser	Default Group	10.0.1.100	stop	0	..	113	443	..	..	0x54	..	4	10.0.1.1
01/30/2004	15:14:05	webuser	Default Group	10.0.1.100	start	..	..	..	..	..	..	0x55	..	4	10.0.1.1
01/30/2004	15:14:05	webuser	Default Group	10.0.1.100	start	..	..	..	..	..	..	0x54	..	4	10.0.1.1
01/30/2004	15:14:04	webuser	Default Group	10.0.1.100	stop	0	..	114	430	..	..	0x52	..	4	10.0.1.1
01/30/2004	15:14:04	webuser	Default Group	10.0.1.100	stop	0	..	114	430	..	..	0x53	..	4	10.0.1.1
01/30/2004	15:14:04	webuser	Default Group	10.0.1.100	start	..	..	..	..	..	..	0x53	..	4	10.0.1.1
01/30/2004	15:14:04	webuser	Default Group	10.0.1.100	start	..	..	..	..	..	..	0x52	..	4	10.0.1.1
01/30/2004	15:14:04	webuser	Default Group	10.0.1.100	stop	0	..	114	452	..	..	0x50	..	4	10.0.1.1

You can also configure ACS to include accounting for VoIP in this RADIUS accounting report log or in a separate VoIP accounting log. This is seen in the next section, "VoIP Accounting."

VoIP Accounting

Another type of accounting report that ACS provides is for VoIP. This accounting information can be found in the RADIUS accounting report log or optionally in a separate VoIP accounting report log. You might want to send VoIP accounting to both report logs. These reports can be configured in the System Configuration page under the Logging link.

VoIP accounting reports contain the following information:

- VoIP session stop and start times
- AAA client messages with username
- Calling line identification (CLID) information
- VoIP session duration

Figure 12-11 *RADIUS Accounting Report*

Date ↓	Time	User-Name	Group-Name	Calling-Station-Id	Acct-Status-Type	Acct-Session-Id	Acct-Session-Time	Service-Type	Framed-Protocol	Acct-Input-Octets	Acct-Output-Octets	Acct-Input-Packets	Acct-Output-Packets	Framed-IP-Address	NAS-Port	NA D Add
01/30/2004	15:19:00	webuser	Default Group		Stop	0x00000090	0			113	449				1	10.0
01/30/2004	15:19:00	webuser	Default Group		Stop	0x0000008f	0			113	443				1	10.0
01/30/2004	15:19:00	webuser	Default Group		Start	0x00000090									1	10.0
01/30/2004	15:19:00	webuser	Default Group		Start	0x0000008f									1	10.0
01/30/2004	15:19:00	webuser	Default Group		Stop	0x0000008d	0			114	430				1	10.0
01/30/2004	15:19:00	webuser	Default Group		Stop	0x0000008e	0			114	430				1	10.0
01/30/2004	15:19:00	webuser	Default Group		Start	0x0000008e									1	10.0
01/30/2004	15:19:00	webuser	Default Group		Start	0x0000008d									1	10.0
01/30/2004	15:19:00	webuser	Default Group		Stop	0x0000008a	0			234	895				1	10.0
01/30/2004	15:19:00	webuser	Default Group		Start	0x0000008c									1	10.0

As previously mentioned, you can configure ACS to include accounting for VoIP in this separate VoIP accounting log, in the RADIUS accounting log, or in both places.

Failed Attempts Report

The Failed Attempts report provides you with information related to authentication attempts that were not successful. From this report, you can gather information such as the username attempting to authenticate as well as the IP address that they made the attempt from. You also receive information to guide you in the direction you should look if authentication is not successful. An example of this would be a failed authentication attempt to an external database. In this situation, you receive a message similar to the following: External DB user invalid or bad password.

In cases such as this, you might need to reset the user password in the external database or verify that the password entered is correct. Another example is seen in Figure 12-12. As you can see, authentication has failed for user **admin**. The reason authentication has failed is noted in the Authen-Failure-Code field. In this case, the **CS** in the report stands for Cisco-Secure, so the password the user is entering is being matched to the ACS internal database and is invalid.

Figure 12-12 *Failed Authentications Report with Invalid CS Password*

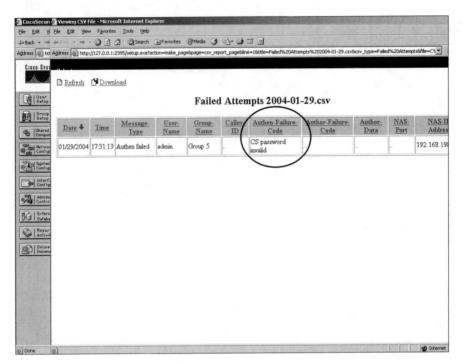

In the Failed Authentications report, you not only see failed authentications by users, but also remember that ACS authenticated the AAA clients that it communicates with using a shared secret key. In Figure 12-13, you see an example that is very common. In the example, the Authen-Failure-Code field tells us that there is a key mismatch. Note here that no user is listed in the User-Name field. This is because the key mismatch is between the AAA client—192.168.198.128 and ACS. This caused the authentication between ACS and the AAA client to fail.

Figure 12-13 *Failed Authentications Report with Key Mismatch*

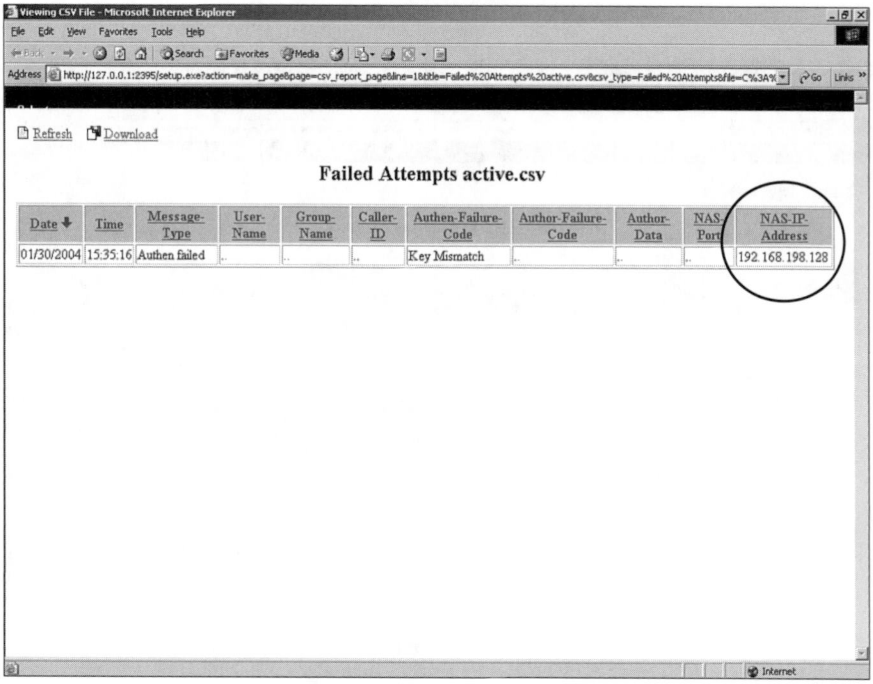

Passed Authentications Report

Passed Authentications gives you information about successful authentications. This report includes the following information:

- Date
- Time
- Message-Type
- User-Name
- Group-Name
- Caller-ID
- NAS-Port
- NAS-IP-Address

An example of the Passed Authentications report is seen in Figure 12-14.

Figure 12-14 *Passed Authentications Report*

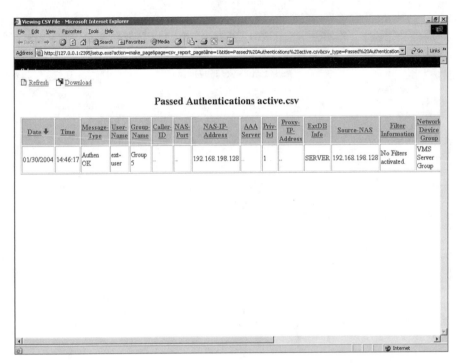

Administrative Reports

Three different administrative reports exist in ACS: TACACS+ Administration, Logged-in Users, and Disabled Accounts. Of the three reports, TACACS+ Administration is not dynamic. It records information as it happens and can be downloaded in CSV format. The other two reports are dynamic.

TACACS+ Administration Report

The administrative report contains information about all the TACACS+ commands requested during the period of time covered in the report. This report is used most often when you are using ACS to control access to network devices or when using command authorization sets.

To use the TACACS+ Administration log, you must configure TACACS+ AAA clients to perform command accounting with ACS. The command authorization configuration is covered in Chapter 10, "Configuring Shared Profile Components." An example of the TACACS+ Administration Report is seen in Figure 12-15.

Figure 12-15 *TACACS+ Administration Report*

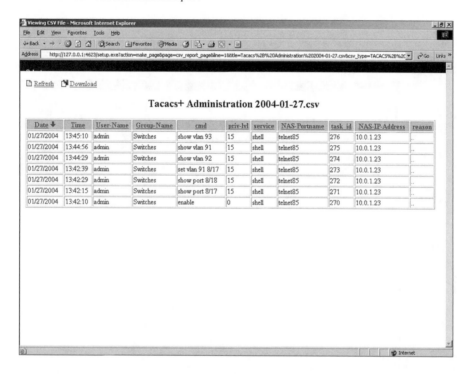

Logged-In Users and Disabled Accounts Reports

The last two administrative reports are dynamic in nature, meaning that they populate based on the current status of ACS. The dynamic administrative reports have the following traits:

- **Logged-in Users**—The Logged-in Users report lists all users receiving services from a single AAA client or all AAA clients with access to ACS. For this log to work, you must configure AAA clients to perform authentication and accounting using the same protocol—either TACACS+ or RADIUS. This log does not work if users access the AAA device using Telnet. In Figure 12-16, you can see that the AAA client **pixfirewall** is logged in to ACS. This means that the AAA client is doing authentication and accounting using the same protocol, which is TACACS+.

- **Disabled Accounts**—The Disabled Accounts report lists all user accounts that are disabled and the reason they were disabled. From here you can re-enable the account by selecting the username link that accesses the user profile. The Disabled Accounts report is seen in Figure 12-17.

Figure 12-16 *Logged-in Users Dynamic Report*

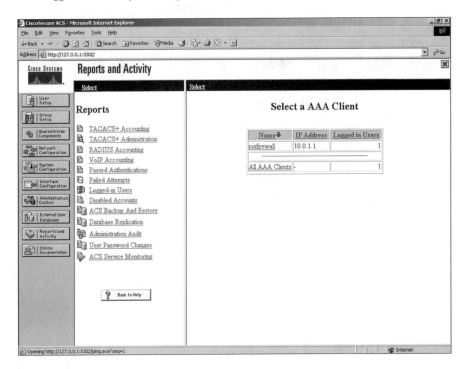

System Reports

System reports are report logs that record events directly related to ACS and actions it has taken. Examples of these reports are as follows:

- ACS Backup and Restore
- RDBMS Synchronization
- Database Replication
- Administration Audit
- User Password Changes
- ACS Service Monitoring

These reports are discussed in further detail.

Figure 12-17 *Disabled Accounts Report*

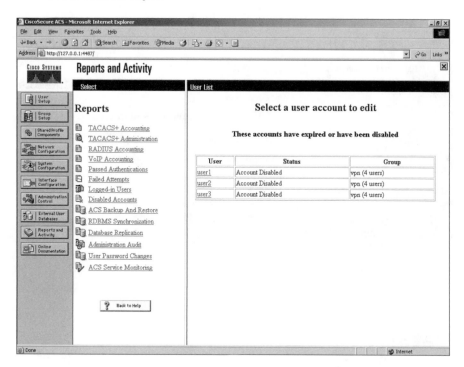

ACS Backup and Restore

The ACS Backup and Restore lists ACS backup and restore activity that ACS has taken. This report is not configurable in the interface. The information that gets populated in this log is placed there automatically when a backup occurs, whether it is a scheduled or manual backup. The report is also populated when a restore occurs. In Figure 12-18, you can see that a backup and a restore has taken place. You can also see the location of the dump file used for backup.

RDBMS Synchronization

The RDBMS Synchronization report lists RDBMS Synchronization activity. This report cannot be configured.

Figure 12-18 *Backup and Restore Report*

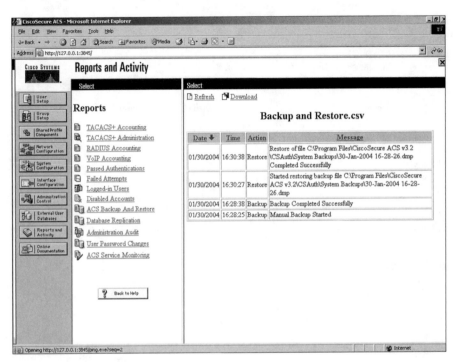

Database Replication

The Database Replication report lists database replication activity. This report also cannot be configured. In Figure 12-19, you can see an example of a replication that was unsuccessful. It is a good idea to check this report from time to time so that you can verify that replication is being performed successfully.

Administration Audit

The Administration Audit report lists actions taken by each system administrator, such as adding users, editing groups, configuring an AAA client, or viewing reports. You can see an example of the Administrative Audit report in Figure 12-20.

Figure 12-19 *Database Replication Report*

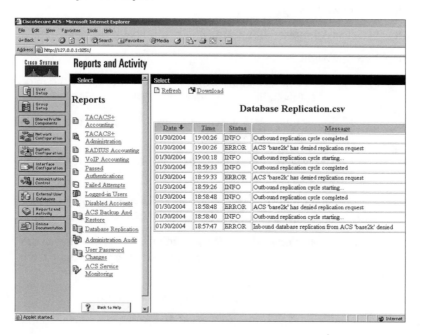

Figure 12-20 *Administrative Audit Report*

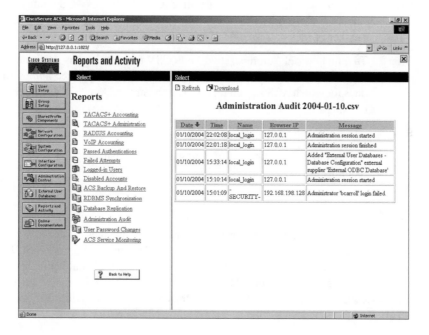

The Administrative Audit report can be modified. You can configure the administration audit report by following these steps:

Step 1 Select **Administration Control**.

Step 2 Select **Audit Policy**.

Step 3 To generate a new Administrative Audit CSV file at a regular interval, select one of the following options:

— **Every day**—ACS generates a new Administrative Audit CSV file at the start of each day.

— **Every week**—ACS generates a new Administrative Audit CSV file at the start of each week.

— **Every month**—ACS generates a new Administrative Audit CSV file at the start of each month.

Step 4 To generate a new Administrative Audit CSV file when the current file reaches a specific size, select the **When size is greater than X KB** option.

Step 5 Type the file size threshold in kilobytes in the X box.

To manage which Administrative Audit CSV files ACS keeps, do the following:

Step 1 Select the **Manage Directory** check box.

Step 2 To limit the number of Administrative Audit CSV files ACS retains, select the **Keep only the last X files** option and type in the X box the number of files you want ACS to retain.

Step 3 To limit how old Administrative Audit CSV files retained by ACS can be, select the **Delete files older than X days** option and type the number of days for which ACS should retain a Administrative Audit CSV file before deleting it.

Step 4 Select **Submit**.

This completes the process of configuring and managing the Administrative Audit reports.

User Password Changes

The User Password Changes report lists user password changes initiated by users, regardless of which password change mechanism was used to change the password. This log contains records of password changes accomplished by the CiscoSecure authentication agent, by the user changeable password HTML interface, or by Telnet session on a network device using TACACS+. It does not list password changes made by an administrator in the ACS HTML interface.

You can configure this log. If you want ACS to generate a new User Password Changes log file at a regular interval, perform these steps:

Step 1   Select **System Configuration**.

Step 2   Select **Local Password Management**.

Step 3   Scroll to the bottom of the page to the Password Change Log File Management section.

In this configuration page, you configure options for your log files. The following options are available:

— **Every day**—ACS generates a new User Password Changes log file at the start of each day. This creates numerous .csv files.

— **Every week**—ACS generates a new User Password Changes log file at the start of each week. These logs are larger than the everyday logs and are easily sorted in third-party software such as Microsoft Access or SQL.

— **Every month**—ACS generates a new User Password Changes log file at the start of each month. This file can be very large depending on your password change policy.

Step 4   If you want ACS to generate a new User Password Changes log file when the current file reaches a specific size, select the **When size is greater than X KB** option and type the file size threshold, in kilobytes, in the X box.

If you want to manage which User Password Changes log files ACS keeps, follow these steps:

Step 1   Select the **Manage Directory** check box.

Step 2   If you want to limit the number of User Password Changes log files ACS retains, select the **Keep only the last X files** option and type the number of files you want ACS to retain in the X box.

Step 3   If you want to limit how old User Password Changes log files retained by ACS can be, select the **Delete files older than X days** option and type the number of days for which ACS should retain a User Password Changes log file before deleting it.

Step 4   Select **Submit**.

This completes the management of ACS User Password Changes log files. These log files can now be viewed in the Reports and Activity section of the ACS HTML interface.

ACS Service Monitoring

The ACS Service Monitoring report is designed to report when the ACS services start and stop. This report is actually built by the CSMon process. When CSMon watches the ACS process and sees the services change, you get a message in this log. You can see an example of this report in Figure 12-21.

Figure 12-21 *ACS Service Monitoring*

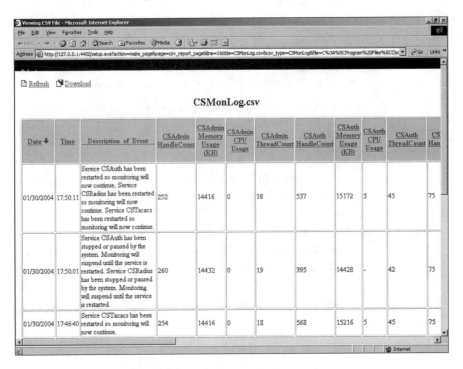

You can also configure this report to log to the Windows Event Log, which is discussed in the next section. To configure ACS service monitoring logs, perform the following tasks:

Step 1 Select **System Configuration**.

Step 2 Select **ACS Service Management**.

To instruct ACS to test the login process, follow these steps:

Step 1   Select the **Test login process every *X* minutes** check box.

Step 2   Enter the number of minutes (up to 3 characters) that should pass between each login process test. You can choose to allow for 2 minutes between each login. In this case, you populate the field with the number **2**.

Step 3   From the **If no successful authentications are recorded** list, select the action that you want ACS to take when the login test fails five times.

Step 4   To have ACS generate a Windows event when a user attempts to log in to your network using a disabled account, select the **Generate event when an attempt is made to log in to a disabled account** check box.

Event logging can also be configured here to either log events to the Windows event log or to generate an e-mail when an event occurs. To configure event logging, continue with these steps:

Step 5   Under the Event Logging header, you can send all events to the Windows event log. To do this, select **Log all events to the Windows Event log** check box.

Step 6   To send an e-mail notification when an event occurs, select the **Email notification of event** check box and enter an e-mail address and SMTP server.

Step 7   Click **Submit**.

Now your ACS sends you an e-mail as well as logs events to the Windows Event log. To view the Windows Event log, you use the event viewer. Follow these steps to access the viewer in Windows 2000:

Step 1   Right-click the **My Computer** Icon on your desktop.

Step 2   Click **Manage**.

Step 3   Double-click in **Event Viewer**.

Step 4   Double-click the **Application** log.

You can now view the service log messages in the Windows Event Viewer. Figure 12-22 shows what this would look like.

Figure 12-22 *ACS Service Monitoring in Windows Event Viewer*

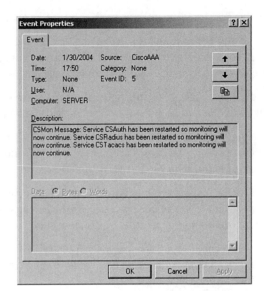

Remote Logging with ACS

Up to this point all the reports that have been discussed are in relation to a local file on ACS, or an ODBC-compliant relational database. In this section, you explore remote logging, which allows you to store your report information on other ACSs.

When configuring remote logging, the first decision to make is which ACS will be the central logging point. This ACS is still able to perform normal AAA function; however, it is also used as a central point that accumulates logs from numerous other ACS devices, so you must ensure it has proper storage space, as well as network connectivity to the other ACS devices.

When remote logging is enabled, and an AAA server receives accounting data from an AAA client, it sends it directly to the CSlog service on the remote logging server. The remote device can save these files as CSV or ODBC. All remote logging is listened for on port 2001. One can tend to think that this is not very secure; however, this information is encrypted by a 128-bit proprietary encryption algorithm.

Configuring Remote Logging

To configure remote logging, you need to perform configuration on the ACS that sends the information and the ACS that receives the information. The order that they are configured in does not matter. The only criteria for performing remote logging are that both devices are running ACS. Therefore, before you can log to server *x,* you must have ACS installed.

Note that a Central Logging Server is the server that receives logging information from remote ACSs. The configuration of the central server is extremely minimal when it comes to remote logging. In fact, you really don't need to do anything. That's right, nothing. Just make sure that the Central Logging Server is running ACS.

There is the chance, however, that you will want to configure the Central Logging Server reports and activity to behave the way you want them to. In this, we are talking about any options to logging and reporting. If you want the Central Logging Server to perform logging to an ODBC-compliant database, you need to configure these options.

Configuring the Remote ACS to Send Logging Information

A few more steps are involved in configuring the remote ACS to send logging information. This information is configured in the Network Configuration section of the ACS HTML interface. Follow these steps to complete your configuration:

Step 1 Verify that Central Logging ACS server is present in network configuration by selecting **Network Configuration** and viewing the AAA server entries.

Step 2 If the Central Logging ACS is not in Network Configuration, you must add it.

Step 3 To add an AAA server to Network Configuration, select **Add** below the AAA Servers table. You can see this in Figure 12-23. If you have Network Device Groups configured, this might be different. Refer to Chapter 9, "Managing Network Configurations," for more information.

Step 4 The next step is to enable remote logging process. Select the **Submit** button.

Step 5 Select **Interface Configuration**.

Step 6 Select **Advanced Options**.

Step 7 Select the **Remote Logging** check box.

Step 8 Select the **Distributed System** check box.

Step 9 Select **Submit**.

Figure 12-23 *Adding the AAA Server*

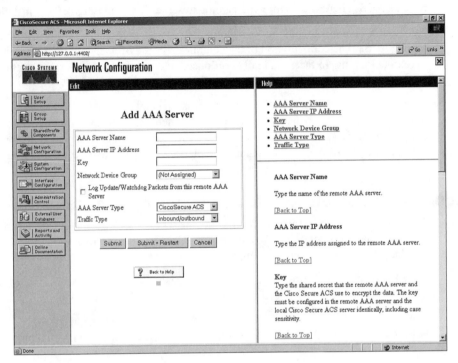

At this point, the remote ACS is capable of performing remote logging. You can see Remote Logging enabled in Figure 12-24.

However, your configuration is not complete. To complete the remote logging configuration on the remote ACS continue with these steps:

Step 1 Select **System Configuration**.

Step 2 Select **Logging**.

Step 3 In the **Local Logging Configuration** table, select **Remote Logging**.

Step 4 If you want ACS to write accounting data for locally authenticated sessions only to the local logs that are enabled, select the **Do not log remotely** radio button.

Step 5 If you want ACS to send accounting data for locally authenticated sessions to all the ACS devices in the Selected Log Services list, choose the **Log to all selected remote log services** radio button.

Step 6 If you want ACS to send accounting data for locally authenticated sessions to the first ACS in the Selected Log Services list that is operational, you should select the **Log to subsequent remote log services on failure** radio button. This provides a backup if your central server is down.

Step 7 Select the ACS in the **Remote Log Services** list that you want to send log data to.

Step 8 Select the right arrow to add the selected ACS to the **Selected Log Services** list.

Step 9 Select the **Submit** button.

At this point, you can see that any messages that are logged to the ACS reports are also seen on the Central Logging ACS.

Figure 12-24 *Enable Remote Logging*

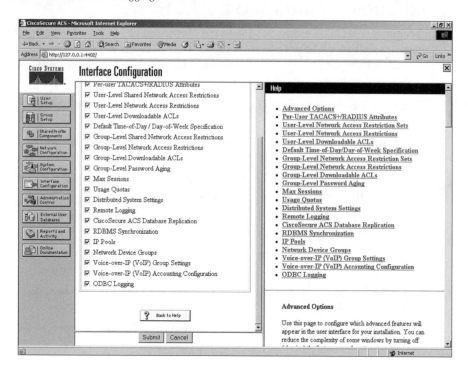

Disabling Remote Logging

Disabling remote logging is a simple process. To disable remote logging, follow these steps:

Step 1   In the navigation bar, select **System Configuration**.

Step 2   Select **Logging**.

Step 3   Select **Remote Logging**.

Step 4   Select the **Do not log remotely** option.

Step 5   Select **Submit**.

That's all there is to it! In no time, you'll have ACS doing exactly what you want it to do when it comes to logging and reporting!

Additional Logs Maintained by ACS

In addition to the CSV logs that ACS maintains for reporting, ACS also maintains what are known as service logs. Service logs are log files stored on the ACS itself that contain information about the process that ACS runs and its activity. The following list contains the service logs kept by ACS and their locations:

- **CSAdmin**—located in the directory **C:\Program Files\CiscoSecure ACS v3.2\CSAdmin\Logs**

- **CSAuth**—located in the directory **C:\Program Files\CiscoSecure ACS v3.2\CSAuth\Logs**

- **CSDBSync**—located in the directory **C:\Program Files\CiscoSecure ACS v3.2\CSDBSync\Logs**

- **CSLog**—located in the directory **C:\Program Files\CiscoSecure ACS v3.2\CSLog\Logs**

- **CSMon**—located in the directory **C:\Program Files\CiscoSecure ACS v3.2\CSMon\Logs**

- **CSRadius**—located in the directory **C:\Program Files\CiscoSecure ACS v3.2\CSRadius\Logs**

- **CSTacacs**—located in the directory **C:\Program Files\CiscoSecure ACS v3.2\CSTacacs\Logs**

NOTE	These directory paths are available only in the ACS for Windows Server and are not available on the Solutions Engine. You can retrieve the service logs on the ACS Solutions Engine by running the **support** command at the command-line interface (CLI) or using the Support page in System Configuration. This is not covered in this chapter.

Each of these directories has a current log designated by the following names:

- ADMIN.log for the CSAdmin service
- AUTH.log for the CSAuth service
- CSdbSync.log for the CSbdSync service
- CSLog.log for the CSLog service
- CSMon.log for the CSMon service
- RDS.log for the CSRadius service
- TCS.log for the CSTacacs service

In each directory, you see additional logs designated by date. These logs take the following format: *Service Year-Month-Day*.log.

If the log file were named AUTH 2003-12-14.log, this would indicate that you are looking at the CSAuth log that was created on December 12th, 2003.

Understanding the Options for Configuring Service Logs

Service logs can be configured in the **System Configuration** tab under the **Service Control** link. The following options are available for managing and configuring log files:

- **Level of detail**—You can set the service log file to contain one of three levels of detail:
  - **None**—No log file is generated.
  - **Low**—Only start and stop actions are logged.
  - **Full**—All services actions are logged.
- **Generate new file**—You can control how often a new service log file is created:
  - **Every Day**—ACS generates a new log file at 12:01 a.m. local time every day.
  - **Every Week**—ACS generates a new log file at 12:01 a.m. local time every Sunday.

— **Every Month**—ACS generates a new log file at 12:01 a.m. on the first day of every month.

— **When Size Is Greater than *x* KB**—ACS generates a new log file after the current service log file reaches the size specified, in kilobytes, by *x*.

- **Manage Directory**—You can control how long service log files are kept:

  — **Keep only the last *x* files**—ACS retains up to the number of files specified by *x*.

  — **Delete files older than *x* days**—ACS retains only those service logs that are not older than the number of days specified by *x*.

Configuring Service Log Options

To configure how ACS generates and manages the service log file, follow these steps:

Step 1   In the left navigation bar, select **System Configuration**.

Step 2   Select **Service Control**.

Step 3   To disable the service log file, under Level of Detail, select the **None** option.

By choosing this selection and restarting ACS, it will no longer generate service logs. Once you have selected this option, items under Generate New File will no longer have any effect.

Step 4   To configure how often ACS creates a service log file, select one of the options under Generate New File.

You can manage the number of log files ACS keeps. To do so, perform these steps:

Step 1   Select the **Manage Directory** check box.

Step 2   To limit the number of service log files ACS retains, select the **Keep only the last *X* files** option and in the *X* box type the number of files you want ACS to retain.

Step 3   To limit how old service log files retained by ACS can be, select the **Delete files older than *X* days** option and in the *X* box type the number of days for which ACS should retain a service log file before deleting it.

Step 4   When all appropriate configurations have been made, select **Restart**.

Summary

For the most part, prior to reading this chapter, you probably were aware that logs are an important part of maintaining a network environment. After reading this chapter, you should clearly see the reporting and logging capability in ACS and have an understanding of how to manage the reports that you use day to day. You should also be able to successfully implement remote logging in a distributed environment. Finally, you should be able to locate and access the ACS service logs, which can help you to assist the Cisco TAC when troubleshooting ACS service issues.

In the remaining chapters of this book, you will see an overview of service provider AAA environments as well as perform an introductory configuration on Cisco's flagship AAA server for the service provider environment—the Cisco CNS Access Registrar (AR).

In this chapter, you learn the following topics:

- How to identify AV pairs
- The attributes of TACACS+ pairs
- Work with an AV pair example
- Understand AV pairs in the ACS interface

## CHAPTER 13

Exploring TACACS+ Attribute Values

Terminal Access Controller Access Control System Plus (TACACS+) as well as the RADIUS protocol use attributes in the messages that are passed between the Access Control Server (ACS) and the authentication, authorization, and accounting (AAA) client. In the next sections, you see what these TACACS+ attributes and values are. It can help to get a better understanding of how Attribute-Value (AV) pairs work, as well as the use of this terminology.

TACACS+ AV Pairs Overview

All TACACS+ values are strings. For the most part, it is very simple to understand. AV pairs are a combination of values. If I said that my name is Brandon Carroll, in this *string* of text the attribute is *name* and the value is *Brandon Carroll*. If you were to write this in the form of a TACACS+ AV pair, it would look like the following:

```
name=Brandon Carroll
```

The "=" indicates that the value of this attribute is mandatory. You could also use the same method in the following format:

```
name*Brandon Carroll
```

In this example, the "*" indicates that the value is optional.

Each implementation of AV pairs, which are a combination of an attribute and the subsequent value of the attribute, is dependent on the version of IOS that you are using in your network. So it's actually a combination of the IOS that you are running and the support in the ACS that is important.

NOTE   In the next section, you can see the AV pairs that are supported by ACS version 3.1.

In combination with the network operating systems (NOSes), you can deploy a very functional AAA configuration. In the forthcoming section, you explore the concept of TACACS+ AV pairs. An explanation of each supported AV pair is also given.

Attributes of TACACS+ AV Pairs

There are many TACACS+ AV pairs. Some TACACS+ AV pairs are not supported by the NOS that you have implemented. Your best bet is to verify supported AV pairs corresponding to the IOS or PIX OS that you intend to use as an AAA client. For a list of AV pairs that specific Cisco devices support, see www.cisco.com.

The following sections are attributes that are supported by the ACS version 3.1. Each of these attributes is discussed in some detail. Note that all of these attributes are TACACS+ authentication and authorization vendor-specific attributes (VSA).

acl=

This attribute is used in EXEC or Apple Remote Access Protocol (ARAP) authorization to indicate an access class number or an access list number. A sample of this would be

```
acl=101
```

With this AV pair, we are referencing access control list (ACL) 101. Access list 101 would then be an extended IP access list configured on the router.

addr=

This attribute is used to assign an address to a user that connects via a service such as PPP/IP (Point-to-Point Protocol/Internet Protocol), or SLIP (Serial Line Internet Protocol). This attribute is available in Cisco IOS Release 11.0 and up. **addr=** is used with a service, for example: **service=ppp** and **protocol=ip**. Although this attribute is supported in ACS, it has been superceded by IP Pools on the group setup page in ACS.

addr-pool=

This attribute specifies a pool that is predefined. To configure this AV pair, enter the following command:

```
addr-pool=bigpool
```

NOTE   Understand that *bigpool* is the name of an IP pool that has been defined. This pool can be defined on the AAA client or the ACS.

This attribute has also been superceded by IP Pools in the group setup page.

autocmd=

This attribute is used to send an autocommand to be issued upon authentication. This is an EXEC service and is used with **service=shell**.

callback-dialstring=, callback-line=, and callback-rotary=

The **callback-dialstring** sets the phone number for a callback. For example, I could call into my network access server (NAS), and when I authenticate, the callback function is determined and the NAS uses the phone number defined here to call me back. This helps me cut down on phone charges.

The **callback-dialstring** can be used with the **callback-line** command, which defines the tty line that is used to call me back. An example of this is **callback-line=3**. You could also use the **callback-rotary** AV pair to define the number of a rotary group between 1 and 100 that is used in the callback. **callback-rotary** is not valid when using Integrated Services Digital Network (ISDN). It is used with **service-arap**, **service=ppp**, **service=slip**, or **service=exec**.

callback-dialstring has been replaced by the callback information in the group setup page.

cmd=

As seen in the attribute configuration in the preceding section, the **cmd** attribute specifies a command. You can create a list of permitted commands for a group, or a user.

cmd-arg=

This AV pair is used to specify any command arguments. For example, I have a user that I want to be able to edit access list 121. In ACS, I would provide the following configuration:

```
service=shell
permit cmd=access-list
permit cmd-arg=121
```

This would allow the users that authenticated with this in their profile to edit access list 121.

dns-servers=

This attribute is used for dial-in Microsoft users to assign the Domain Name System (DNS) servers, primary or secondary. This is negotiated during IP Control Protocol (IPCP) negotiation. Because this is used during a PPP negotiation, it is used with **service=ppp** and **protocol=ip**. When you enter these addresses, enter them in dotted decimal, such as **dns-servers=4.3.2.4**.

gw-password=

This attribute, **gw-password**, is used in Virtual Private Dial-Up Networking (VPDN) to assign the gateway password to a VPDN client. This occurs during the Layer 2 Forwarding (L2F) authentication. The service that **gw-password** is used with is still **service=ppp**; however, the protocol is VPDN, for example, **protocol=vpdn**.

idletime=

This attribute is pretty straightforward. **idletime** sets a timeout value for an established connection. The **idletime** is a value in minutes. For example, **idletime=15** sets a 15 minute timeout once the line goes idle. Additionally, **idletime=0** would enforce no timeout value.

inacl#n

The **inacl#n** indicates the number of an access list that should be applied inbound to an interface for the duration of a PPP connection. This is an ACSII value and doesn't work with ISDN interfaces. This access list is removed when the session terminates. **inacl** is used with **service=ppp** and **protocol=ip** or **protocol=ipx**. The access list assigned here is a per-user access list.

inacl=

inacl= has the same characteristics as the previously discussed **inacl#n**. **inacl=** has been available in Cisco IOS Releases 11.0 and up and **inacl#n** has been available only since release 11.3 and up.

interface-config#<n>

interface-config <n> is an attribute that specifies a specific AAA configuration on an interface, per user, when used with the **service=ppp** and **protocol=lcp**. What happens here is that any IOS interface configuration command can be specified within a virtual profile. For example, an **interface-config <n>** could be **ip route cache**. You can use multiple instances of the same commands; however, they are distinguished by a unique number.

ip-addresses=

The **ip-addresses=** attribute is again used in VPDN configurations where the IP addresses are a list of possible IP address destinations of a tunnel endpoint. This is also used with **service=ppp** and **protocol=vpdn**, as seen in the attribute **gw-password**. This list is created using spaces.

link-compression=

The **link-compression=** attribute determines if "stac" compression is used for a PPP connection. It is a numeric value that ranges from **0** to **3**. A value of **0** indicates that no compression is being turned on. A value of **1** determines that the compression to be used is "stac." A value of **2** determines that the compression is "stac-draft-9," and a value of **3** applies MS-stac compression. This became available in Cisco IOS Release 11.3 and later.

load-threshold=n

In dial situations, you can create multilink bundles. As the load on a connection reaches specified limits, a second connection can be brought up to alleviate some of the load from the initial link. The **load-threshold=n** attribute is used again with the **service=ppp** and **protocol=multilink** to code in the value at which another link in a multilink bundle is to be brought up. The possible value that you can use here can be from **1** to **255** where **255** would be 100 percent load on a link.

max-links=n

load-threshold=n can sometimes pose a problem of one user taking up all the links in a multilink bundle. The **max-links=n** AV pair can fix this problem by again specifying a value between **1** and **255** to determine the number of links that can be used in a bundle. This is also used with the **service=ppp** and **protocol=multilink**.

nas-password

Another VPDN configuration, **nas-password**, specifies the password of the NAS that is used in tunnel authentication during the L2F portion of the connection. This is used with **service=ppp** and **protocol=vpn**.

nocallback-verify

This AV pair designates that no callback verification is required and the only value that you should ever see here is a **1**. This is used with **service=ppp**, **service=arap**, **service=slip**, and **service=shell**.

noescape=

You can use the **noescape=** AV to allow or disallow the user to enter an escape character. The two options that you have here are **true** or **false**. This is used with the **service=shell** AV pair.

nohangup=

The **nohangup=** AV pair determines whether to hang up the line after an EXEC shell has been terminated. For example, you are authenticated to the command line of a Cisco router, and you type **exit**. If the **nohangup=** value is set to **true**, the line will not hang up, but rather return you to a username prompt. The available values are **true** or **false**.

old-prompts=

One of the difficult tasks to accomplish is to migrate to a new version of TACACS without it being apparent to users. The **old-prompts=** allows you to use old TACACS and XTACACS prompts, thus making a migration transparent to the user.

outacl=

outacl= is similar to **outacl#n**. It applies an access list to an interface for the duration of a user's connection. The access list needs to be preconfigured on the router prior to using the **outacl=** attribute. The difference between **outacl#** and **outacl=** is that in this format, the ACL number can be for a SLIP outbound access list.

outacl#n

outacl#<n> is an ASCII access list identifier that applies an access list to an interface for the duration of a user's connection. This attribute uses the **service=ppp**, and **protocol=ip** or **ipx**. The per-user access list does not work on ISDN interfaces.

pool-def#n

This AV pair determines an IP address pool that is defined on the NAS. This is used with **service=ppp** and **protocol=ip**.

pool-timeout=

This is used along with the **pool-def#n** AV pair. It sets a timeout value for the addresses served by the pool that is defined in the **pool-def#n** AV pair. This is used with **service=ppp** and **protocol=ip**.

ppp-vj-slot-compression=

This AV pair determines the use of slot compression if sending VJ-compressed packets across a PPP connection.

priv-lvl=

This AV pair is pretty straightforward. In Cisco routers, you have privilege levels from **0** to **15**, **0** being user-level privileges and **15** being EXEC-level privileges. The numeric values in between can be customized to provide for specific command sets available to certain users. As a user accesses the shell, **service=shell**, a check of privilege level is made. This AV pair sets that value.

protocol=

In the hierarchy, you have a service, such as PPP, SLIP, or shell. Underneath those services, you have a subset, which makes up the protocol. For example, if I am accessing the command line of a Cisco router, the service is shell, and the protocol might be IP. The actual values that you can use are **lcp**, **ip**, **ipx**, **atalk**, **vines**, **lat**, **tn3270**, **xremote**, **telnet**, **pad**, **rlogin**, **vpdn**, **osicp**, **deccp**, **ccp**, **cdp**, **bridging**, **xns**, **nbf**, **bap**, **multilink**, or **unknown**.

route=

When you use the protocol IP and service SLIP or PPP, this AV applies the route that is specified to the interface that is used for access. If a route is not specified, the peer's address is used as the gateway. The configuration of the command is similar to creating a static route. An example of this follows:

```
route="10.1.1.1 255.255.255.255 10.0.1.2"
```

This code enters a static route when the user performs network authorization. This is in all actuality a temporary static route that is removed when the connection is dropped.

route#n

This **route#n** is similar to the **route=** AV pair except for the fact that this route is numbered. By numbering the routes, you now have the ability to add multiple routes.

routing=

This AV determines based on a **true/false** switch whether or not to accept routing information from this interface and to propagate it across the link.

rte-ftr-in#n

This AV pair is actually an input access list that is used to filter routing updates. This filter applies only for the length of the conversation and is removed when disconnected.

rte-ftr-out#n

This AV is similar to the **rte-ftr-in#n**, only it is applied to outbound updates.

sap-fltr-in#n

This AV pair determines an inbound SAP filter to assign based on an input SAP filter access list. This is applied for the duration of the connection and is also used with the **protocol=ipx**.

sap-fltr-out#n

Similar to the input SAP filter, this is applied for the duration of the connection in an outbound direction. It is also used with **protocol=ipx**.

sap#n

This is for static Service Advertising Protocol (SAP) entries to be installed upon connection. This is used with the **protocol=ipx**.

service=

The **service** AV is used to determine what type of service you use. You can use the PPP, SLIP, ARAP, and shell service. Additionally, you can use the tty-daemon, system, and connection service. Probably some of the most common services are PPP and shell. You do not have a choice in using this. It must be included.

source-ip=

This AV pair has the same function as the **vpdn outgoing** global configuration command and is used as the source IP address. All the VPDN packets generated as part of a VPDN tunnel assume this IP address.

timeout=

The **timeout=** AV is used to define a timeout value for EXEC and ARAP sessions and is used with **service=arap**. A value of **0** indicates that there is no timeout. A value of **5** indicates 5 minutes.

tunnel-id

The tunnel-id is actually the username that is passed to authenticate over a VPDN. This is the same as the remote name that is configured in the VPDN outgoing commands.

wins-servers=

This AV pair can identify the Windows server that PPP clients request during PPP negotiations. This is used with service PPP. For example:

```
wins-servers=10.1.1.3
```

zonelist=

This AV pair defines the AppleTalk zonelist. It is used with ARAP and **service=arap**.

AV Pair Example PPP Network

In this section, you look at a very basic dial-in network using PPP. Numerous AV pairs are used in this section. You can guess that the **service=ppp** AV is used, and the **protocol=ip** is used as well. The purpose of this section is not to configure the PPP connection or the AAA configuration on the NAS device, rather to display the TACACS+ AV pair configuration in the ACS HTML interface. (See Figure 13-1.)

Figure 13-1 *PPP Dial-In Network with AV Pairs*

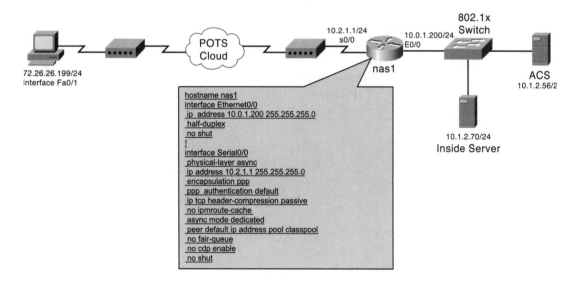

In this example, a dial-in user makes a connection into the NAS1 device and authenticates to ACS. In addition to authenticating to ACS, the user also has the ACS authorize the use of the PPP protocol.

The configuration seen in Example 13-1 is the output from the **show run** command on the NAS device.

Example 13-1 **show run** *Command from NAS1*

```
!
hostname nas1
!
!
aaa new-model
aaa authentication login default group tacacs+ local
aaa authentication enable default group tacacs+ none
aaa authentication ppp default
 group tacacs+ local
aaa authorization network default group tacacs+
!
username admin password cisco
!
clock timezone gmt 0
ip subnet-zero
no ip source-route
no ip finger
no ip domain-lookup
ip host modem 2001 10.0.1.2
!
cns event-service server
!
!
!
!
!
interface Ethernet0/0
 ip address 10.0.1.200 255.255.255.0
 half-duplex
 no shut
!
interface Serial0/0
 physical-layer async
 ip address 10.2.1.1 255.255.255.0
 encapsulation ppp
 ppp authentication default
 ip tcp header-compression passive
 no ip mroute-cache
 async mode dedicated
 peer default ip address pool classpool
 no fair-queue
 no cdp enable
 no shut
```

Example 13-1 **show run** *Command from NAS1 (Continued)*

```
!
interface Serial0/1
 no ip address
 shutdown
!
router rip
 version 2
 network 10.0.0.0
 no auto-summary
!
ip local pool classpool 10.2.1.2
ip classless
ip route 0.0.0.0 0.0.0.0 10.0.1.3
!
access-list 101 permit icmp 10.2.1.0 0.0.0.255 any
access-list 101 permit tcp 10.2.1.0 0.0.0.255 any
!
!
tacacs-server host 10.1.2.56
tacacs-server key cisco123 default
!
line con 0
 exec-timeout 45 0
 logging synchronous
 transport input none
line 1
 autoselect during-login
autoselect ppp
 modem InOut
 modem autoconfigure type usr_sportster
 transport input all
 stopbits 1
 speed 115200
 flowcontrol hardware
line aux 0
line vty 0 4
!
end
```

Completing the Configuration

On the ACS, the user is already configured, as well as the group. For this situation, you assume that the group is already configured, with the exception of the PPP authorization. To configure ACS for authorization of the PPP session, you select the PPP IP TACACS+ option in the group configuration page of the HTML interface. By selecting this option, you are configuring the **service=ppp** and **protocol=ip** TACACS+ AV pairs. Follow these steps to complete the configuration:

Step 1 Select **Group Setup**.

Step 2 Select the group in the drop-down list for which you want to configure the PPP IP TACACS+ option.

Step 3 Select **Edit Settings**.

Step 4 From the group configuration page, select **TACACS+** in the Jump To drop-down list.

Step 5 Place a check mark in the box provided next to the words **PPP IP**.

Step 6 Select **Submit + Restart**.

This completes the configuration of PPP IP; however, your next action here might vary. As long as PPP is selected, the ACS authorizes the service. At this point, you might want to also assign an access list to the interface, configure an idle timeout value, or even push the IP address down to the dialing in user by utilizing other configuration sections of ACS, building an IP Pool, and assigning it to the user.

Whatever you do in the ACS interface determines the TACACS+ AV pairs to be applied and used for the duration of the authenticated and authorized session. A key element to understand is that authentication must take place prior to authorization. If ACS has not already determined who the user requesting service is, ACS does not authorize the requested protocol.

For more information on configuring AAA on the command-line interface of a Cisco IOS device, see Appendix A, "RADIUS Attribute Tables."

Applying an ACL to the Dial Interface

You can further utilize AV pairs with this example by applying an ACL to the dial interface. You can actually do this in two ways. The first way is to define the numbered access list on the router and then reference the numbered access list on ACS. The second method is to create the entire ACL on ACS. For this example, you apply access list 101 to the interface. This is seen in Figure 13-2.

Figure 13-2 *Inbound ACL and PPP*

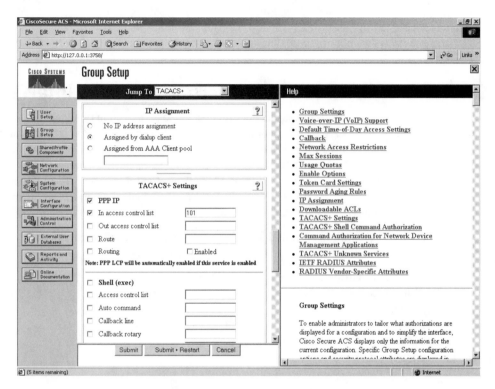

To perform this configuration, simply follow these steps on ACS:

Step 1   Select **Group Setup**.

Step 2   Select the group in the drop-down list for which you want to configure
the ACL.

Step 3   Select **Edit Settings**.

Step 4   From the group configuration page, select **TACACS+** in the Jump To
drop-down list.

Step 5   Ensure that there is a check mark in the box provided next to the words
PPP IP.

Step 6   Place a check mark next to **In access control list**.

Step 7   Enter **101** in the space provided next to **In access control list**.

Step 8   Select **Submit + Restart**.

In this configuration, a user dials in and is authenticated and authorized. An inbound ACL is applied as well. In the next section, "Understanding TACACS+ AV Pairs in the ACS Interface," you take a closer look at how the AV pairs appear in the HTML interface of ACS and are given the opportunity to determine what the AV pairs are in the given examples.

Understanding TACACS+ AV Pairs in the ACS Interface

The AV pair combinations in this chapter are intended to assist you in tying the meaning of them together. Not all AV pairs are configured this way. In fact, many AV pair combinations are configured in ACS using the HTML interface. For example, to configure an autocommand, you would place a check box next to the autocommand and place the command that you want to execute in the given field. The attribute is the **autocmd**, and the value is whatever you place in the field. This makes working with AV pairs much simpler. In fact, many people configure AV pairs and don't even know it.

In the sections that follow, you find five examples of AV pairs configured. For each example, see if you can answer the following questions:

> What is the attribute?
> What is the value?
> Will this work?

AV Pair Discussion #1

Examine Figure 13-3.

In Figure 13-3, there are actually two AV pairs configured. The first AV pair is the **inacl#n** attribute. In the ACS interface, it is simply seen as "In access control list."

The second AV pair in Figure 13-3 is the **routing=** AV pair. The value is **1**, which indicates that routing is enabled. In the ACS interface, you can see that this configuration is accomplished with a simple check box being selected.

This configuration would be useless because the PPP service was not selected.

AV Pair Discussion #2

Examine Figure 13-4.

Figure 13-3 *AV Pair Discussion #1*

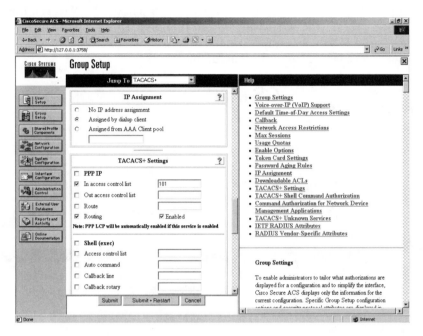

Figure 13-4 *AV Pair Discussion #2*

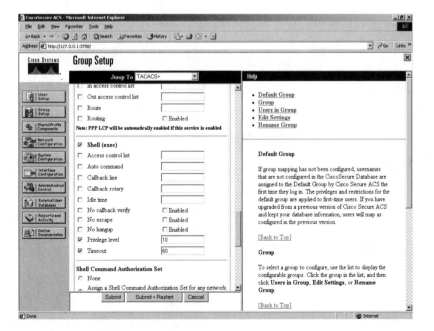

Figure 13-4 demonstrates a total of three AV pairs. The first AV is the **service=shell** AV pair. This is configured by placing a check mark in the box next to **Shell (exec)**. The second AV that is seen here is the **priv-lvl=10** AV pair. This sets the privilege level for the users of this group to 10. Finally, the third AV pair is the timeout value for the shell. This sets the timeout value to 60 minutes. This is the **timeout=60** AV pair.

AV Pair Discussion #3

Examine Figure 13-5.

Figure 13-5 *AV Pair Discussion #3*

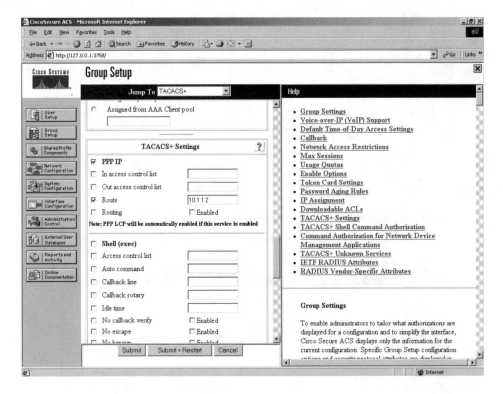

Figure 13-5 has the PPP AV pair selected. This is the equivalent to the **service=ppp** AV pair. The **route** AV pair is also selected. This is the same as configuring the **route="10.1.1.254 255.255.255.255 10.1.1.2"** AV pair. The route AV uses the PPP service. Without the PPP service, the route cannot be distributed.

AV Pair Discussion #4

Examine Figure 13-6.

Figure 13-6 *AV Pair Discussion #4*

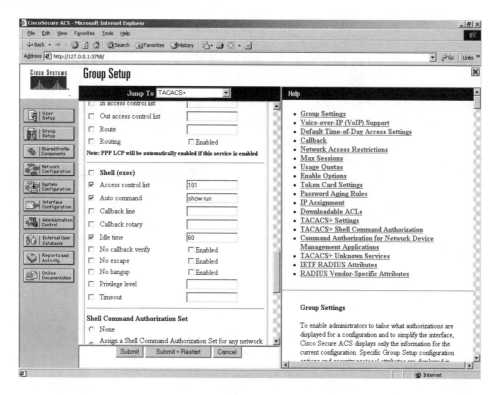

In Figure 13-6, you can see that there are three AV pairs configured. The first is the access control list that has a value of **101**. This is equivalent to the AV pair **acl=101**. This applies the access list 101 that is configured on the AAA client to the line that this user accesses the shell EXEC from.

The second AV pair configured in this example is the autocommand attribute with a value of **show run**. This executes the **show run** IOS command when the user authenticates and is authorized access to the command line. Once this command is issued, the connection is terminated.

The third AV pair configured is the idle time, and it is set to idle for 60 minutes before disconnect. This is the equivalent to the AV pair **idletime=60**.

This configuration is not valid and will not work because the **service=shell** AV is not selected in the ACS HTML interface.

AV Pair Discussion #5

To facilitate this example, an additional configuration was enabled. Figure 13-7 shows the time-of-day access grid configuration being enabled in interface configuration.

Figure 13-7 *Enabling Time-of-Day Access Grid for TACACS+*

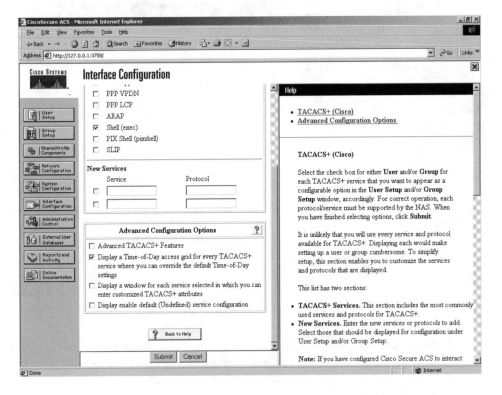

Once this option is selected, you can now see the time-of-day access grid. In Figure 13-8, you can see the selection of this grid.

Figure 13-8 *AV Pair Discussion #5*

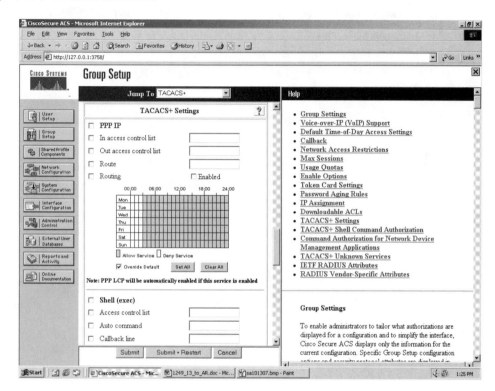

The answer here is LCP. By overriding the default time-of-day restrictions, you automatically override the LCP service. This configuration, however, will not work because of the fact that the **service=ppp** is not enabled.

Summary

As you can see, you can enable and manipulate many options that can be enabled using AV pairs. At this point, you should be comfortable with identifying and configuring these AV pairs. To help in your configurations, Cisco has many sample configurations that include the IOS configurations at the following URL:

http://www.cisco.com/pcgi-bin/Support/browse/psp_view.pl?p=Software:Cisco_Secure_ACS_NT&s=Implementation_and_Configuration#Samples_and_Tips

A valid Cisco login is required.

As always, it is recommended that you test your configurations prior to implementation. Much of what was done in this chapter can be tested with a router and an ACS.

As you proceed into Chapter 14, "Service Provider AAA and the Cisco CNS Access Registrar," you will now take a look at AAA security from a service provider prospective. This will give you the opportunity to work with the Cisco Access Registrar.

Service Provider AAA and the Cisco Access Registrar

In this chapter, you learn the following topics:

- The service provider (SP) model
- The service provider challenge
- Value added services
- Options of the Cisco CNS Access Registrar
- Installation requirements for AR
- Installing AR
- AR subdirectories
- Configuring Cisco CNS AR

## CHAPTER 14

Service Provider AAA and the Cisco CNS Access Registrar

In many cases, a service provider's role is to provide network access to a customer. To provide this type of service, a provider must have the ability to add, delete, and manipulate its infrastructure as customers are added and removed. This chapter looks at the role of authentication, authorization, and accounting (AAA) in a service provider environment and some of the benefits provided by AAA in this environment.

Service Provider (SP) Model

Not all service providers have the same business models. Some service providers build their infrastructure, and some don't. The ones that don't build their infrastructure typically purchase from those that do. For this reason, the AAA configurations might tend to be slightly different. In the end, AAA still serves the same purpose you saw in an enterprise environment. The difference here is that the server used for AAA might need to handle thousands of requests for service authorization per second. The Cisco CNS Access Registrar (AR) is a carrier class RADIUS server designed to specifically meet the needs of today's service providers.

Service Provider Challenge

The service providers of today are faced with many new challenges. The way a user is configured or provisioned for dialup access is most likely different than the way a user would be configured or provisioned for Digital Subscriber Line (DSL). AAA can support these differences using the Remote Authentication Dial-In User Service (RADIUS) protocol.

A popular service today that you see frequently is the wireless "hot spot." Many companies place a wireless hot spot in places of business, airports, hotels, and coffee houses. Agreements are made between service providers, and as a benefit to their subscribers, you can use a hot spot in an airport.

Take a look at an example. If you, as a subscriber to Verizon DSL service, for example, were to try to use a hot spot that was owned by another service provider, you would need some way to identify to the owner of the hot spot that you are part of an agreement that allows you to use it. When you connect, you are asked to provide your authentication credentials. You enter your trusty username preceded by some characters that Verizon has instructed you to enter. The authentication is successful, and you are surfing the Net. What happened behind the scenes is a mystery, but as long as you can get online, who really cares, right? The truth is that the service providers care.

When you entered your username that was provided by Verizon, preceded by those characters, you started an authentication request. That authentication request eventually makes it to a server at Verizon that said you were allowed to be online. The preceding characters are possibly defined as a realm in the hot spot owner's AAA server. If your username was VZW/username@verizon.net, VZW could indicate to the hot spot owner that you are a Verizon customer. This would cause the hot spot owner's AAA server to forward you to a Verizon AAA server where the rest of your username would indicate who you are.

This would make the hot spot owner a broker of sorts. In fact, the person sitting next to you might be a user of SBC services (as opposed to Verizon) and has provided information that forwards their credentials to an SBC AAA server.

Value Added Services

AAA in a service-provider environment can also be critical in the delivery of value added services. These services might include quality of service, tunnels, and other services out of the scope of a simple authorization. Service providers can also provide assistance with billing and accounting for usage. Many of these functions require an authorization by an AAA server.

The days of only supporting dialup are a thing of the past. Service providers now require newer access methods that, in turn, require different authentication methods such as EAP-TLS, EAP-MD5, and EAP-Cisco Wireless (LEAP) to meet customer needs.

Cisco CNS Access Registrar

Cisco Networking Services Access Registrar (CNS AR) is a RADIUS server developed by Cisco that answers the call to service provider AAA. AR is used as an access policy server and is designed to support the delivery of dial, Integrated Services Digital Network (ISDN), and new services including DSL, cable with telco-return, wireless, and Voice over IP.

Much of the design of AR provides ease of deployment and administration for service providers. This chapter focuses on the installation and deployment of version 3.5. AR provides many benefits including support for the latest wireless authentication protocols including EAP-SIM used in Global System for Mobile Communications (GSM) networks. AR also has the capability to make real-time AAA requests to billing systems that support the growing prepaid applications market such as cellular phone service.

AR is built on a multithreaded architecture to take advantage of multiprocessor systems and provide the highest AAA performance.

Options of AR

As each version of AR provides more functionality, the most current version of AR supports many of the functions of the previous versions including some new ones. The new features complement the most current technologies employed by service providers today. These features include, but are not limited to, the following:

- **Linux support**—In addition to running on Solaris Systems, AR now runs on Linux.

- **Prepaid billing**—A new generic prepaid billing application programming interface (API) allows a real-time interface to billing and rating systems.

- **Authentication protocol additions**—AR has added authentication protocol support including

  — HTTP Digest Authentication for Session Initiation Protocol (SIP) environments

  — EAP-PEAP v.0, inner methods: EAP-MSCHAP v2, EAP-SIM

  — EAP-PEAP v1, inner methods: EAP-GTC, EAP-SIM

  — EAP-TLS

  — EAP-MSCHAP v2

  — EAP-GTC

- **Enhanced configuration interface**—The product's configuration utility known as **aregcmd** has been enhanced for even faster and easier provisioning by providing the following:

  — Automatic command completion

  — Context-sensitive list of options

  — Recall of values for speedy editing

  — Faster and easier user return-attribute configuration

  — Faster and easier check-items configuration

  — Detailed configuration-error messages

- **Authentication database support**—AR includes database support for MySQL and Oracle 9.

- **View only**—AR now has the capability to create a view-only administrator that only allows the viewing of configurations.

Although these are features that are new to AR, the features from previous versions of AR can be obtained on the Cisco website at Cisco.com.

AR's Architecture

AR is built on a multithreaded architecture so that it can take advantage of multiprocessor systems and provide high AAA performance. This architecture is seen in Figure 14-1.

Figure 14-1 *AR's Architecture*

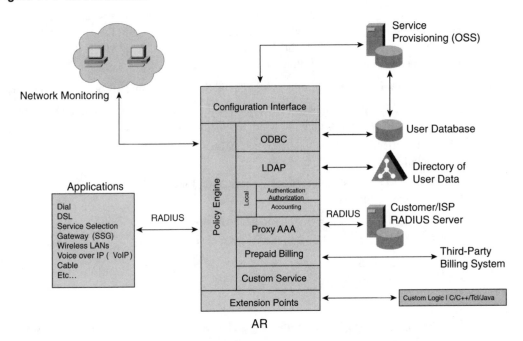

The following sections discuss specific components of AR's architecture further.

Policy Engine

The core of AR is its Policy Engine. This is indicated in Figure 14-2 with the number 1.

The Policy Engine provides the decision and policy enforcement for AR based on the contents of a RADIUS request packet. Within AR, multiple extension points provide customization using custom code. Although these extensions can be used for a number of purposes, one of them is the capability to influence how a request is processed and the capability to modify the incoming and outgoing packets to meet the special request.

Figure 14-2 *Policy Engine*

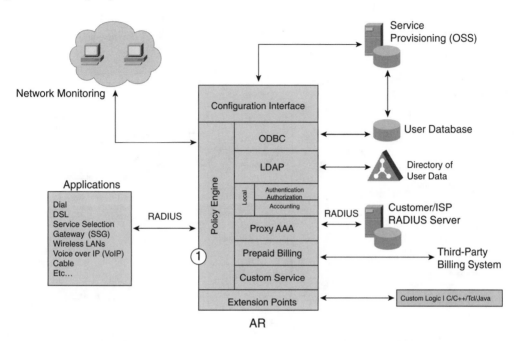

The processing methods that are available in AR include local, LDAP, ODBC, proxy, and prepaid (specifically AR Prepaid version). AR also allows custom service code to be inserted into its architecture to allow a service provider to accommodate special request processing and integration.

The AR Policy Engine can make the following decisions:

- Whether authentication against an LDAP directory or Oracle database is required
- Whether a request should be forwarded to an external RADIUS server
- What type of accounting is required
- Whether session limits apply
- Whether an IP address pool has been assigned

Extension Points

The extension points, indicated by the number 2 in Figure 14-3, are where the customization and integration can occur.

Figure 14-3 *Extension Points*

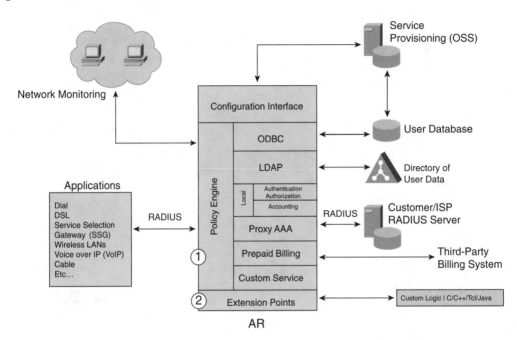

These custom calls and service use custom logic and are written by programming languages such as C, C+, Tcl, and Java. At certain times during a request-response program flow, a script written by the provider can be used to customize the process.

The extension points include the following:

- **Server incoming/outgoing**—These scripts run for every request packet coming into or leaving AR.

- **Vendor incoming/outgoing**—These scripts run only for requests from the specified client vendor.

- **Client incoming/outgoing**—These scripts run only for requests from the specified client (router, network access server [NAS], and so on).

- **Service incoming/outgoing**—These scripts run before/after a service.

- **Remote server incoming/outgoing**—These scripts run for requests using a Cisco CNS AR remote server.

- **Group authentication/authorization**—These scripts run for access requests for a user belonging to a group.

- **User authentication/authorization**—These scripts run for access requests for a particular user.

AR can use Extension Point Scripting (EPS) to request targeting. This means that a script that is applied to the server incoming extension point is used for all requests that arrive at AR. Requests can be either access requests or accounting requests. If you look at the different types of extension points, it is easy to understand when they will be invoked. Beginning with the first bulleted EPS, server incoming/outgoing scripts would indicate that all requests that arrive or leave AR would invoke this script. If you were to use the second bulleted EPS, vendor incoming/outgoing scripts, these would apply only to incoming or outgoing requests from a specific vendor. The same flow works for the rest.

When a RADIUS packet comes into AR, it goes through five general steps. These steps are done in the following order:

Step 1   Validate the AAA client.

Step 2   Invoke the Policy Engine if it is configured.

Step 3   Perform the required AAA service.

Step 4   Perform session management if it is needed.

Step 5   Create the response and send it to the AAA client.

When you use EPS, it allows you to manipulate the request and response attributes using AR's application programming interface (API) functions. This does not really change the steps that occur when a RADIUS packet comes in; it just adds a bit more to the process. Figure 14-4 shows the process.

Figure 14-4 *EPS Processing Order*

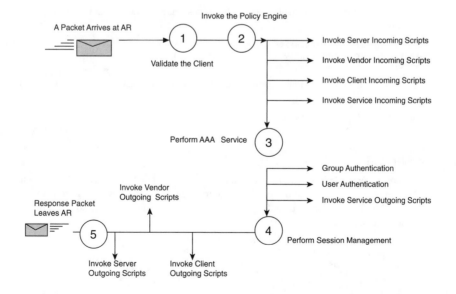

Manipulating environment variables also allows EPS to communicate with AR as well as with other scripts. These values are grouped into request attributes (which deal with requests), response attributes (which deal with responses), and environment variables. [1]Cisco AR supports many variables that scripts use to communicate with—or change the behavior of—the Cisco AR server, or to communicate with other scripts. For example, if the "Accounting-Service" environment variable is set, the server directs the request to the specified accounting service for processing. Likewise, you can set the "Authentication-Service" and "Authorization-Service" environment variables to direct requests to the appropriate authentication/authorization service.

Extension Point Scripting Examples

The EPS examples shown here are written in Toolkit Command Language (TCL) for the purpose of clarity.[2] All examples can be written in C or C++, and they all use the same APIs.

Basic Examples

The four examples shown in this section illustrate basic API commands as **put**, **get**, and **remove**.

The following request attribute example adds the attribute **Service-Type** to a request with its value set to **Outbound**:

```
$request put Service-Type Outbound
```

This response attribute example removes the **State** attribute from the Cisco AR response (some noncompliant RADIUS clients behave unpredictably when they receive this attribute):

```
$response remove State
```

The following environment variable example illustrates communicating with Cisco AR to set AAA services:

```
$environ put Authentication-Service auth-service
$environ put Authorization-Service auth-service
$environ put Accounting-Service acc-service
```

The following environment variable example returns the type of request received by Cisco AR, for example, Access-Request:

```
$environ get Request-Type
```

Selecting the Service

The following example illustrates how an extension point script looks at the DNS domain in the username and sets the AAA services. It also overrides the username in the request by setting the **User-Name** environment variable. The script can be run from the server incoming extension point so that it runs for every request that Cisco Access Registrar processes.

```
proc RealmServiceSelection {request response environ} {
    set userName [ $request get User-Name ]
    if { [ regexp {(([^@]+)@([^@]+)} $userName dummy newUserName realm ] } {
        $environ put User-Name $newUserName
```

```
                 $environ put Authentication-Service $realm
                 $environ put Authorization-Service $realm
                 $environ put Accounting-Service $realm
          }
     }
```

Handling Accounting Requests

The following example shows how an extension point script diverts accounting requests to a file.

To find all the accounting requests, the script must process every request. Hence, the script runs from the server incoming extension point. The script identifies accounting requests by examining the **Request-Type** environment variable. All accounting requests with the attribute **Acct-Status-Type** set to **Accounting-On** or **Accounting-Off** are then written to the local file accounting service named **SysAcc-file**:

```
proc divert-AccOnOff { request response environ } {
     set request-type [$environ get Request-Type]
     if { [string equal ${request-type} "Accounting-Request" ] } {
          set AST [ $request get Acct-Status-Type ]
          if { ( [string equal $AST "Accounting-On"] ||
          [string equal $AST "Accounting-Off"]) } {
          $environ put Accounting-Service SysAcc-file
          }
     }
}
```

Ignoring Accounting Signatures

This example script checks the **Request-Type** environment variable. If the packet is an accounting request packet, the script sets the **Ignore-Accounting-Signature** environment variable to **TRUE**. This script is useful in situations where a service provider has NASs that do not sign the accounting requests properly. This script allows the service provider to tell Cisco Access Registrar to ignore the accounting signature.

Because these NASs can be grouped under a vendor, this script can be run from the vendor incoming extension point:

```
proc ig-acc-sig { request response environ } {
     set request-type [ $environ get Request-Type ]
     if { [string equal ${request-type} "Accounting-Request"] } {
          $environ put Ignore-Accounting-Signature TRUE
     }
}
```

Controlling Debugging

In service provider environments with large volumes of production traffic, it is not feasible to turn on debugging (tracing) for long periods of time because debugging is resource intensive. Specifically, in attempting to analyze data, debugging overhead slows request processing and uses large amounts of disk space. EPS offers an easy and elegant way to turn debugging on and off selectively.

In the following example, EPS turns debugging on only for requests with username **bob@cisco.com**. The environment variable **Trace-Level** sets the trace level, and **Retrace-Packet** makes Cisco Access Registrar display the full contents of the request received. This script could be set at the server incoming extension point:

```
proc debug { request response environ } {
      set user [ $request get User-Name ]
      if { [ string equal $user "bob@cisco.com" ] } {
            $environ put Trace-Level 5
            $environ put Retrace-Packet TRUE
      }
}
```

Filtering Attributes

The following example illustrates how to use EPS to validate a response from a RADIUS server. In this example, the remote RADIUS server is not in your administrative control, so you need to validate its responses. Here, the script looks in the response for the **Framed-IP-Addr ess** attribute value of 255.255.255.255. If the script finds this value, it removes the attribute.

To target a specific RADIUS server, use the remote server incoming extension point to target the response from that server:

```
proc remove-bad-IP {request response environ} {
      if { [ $request containsKey Framed-IP-Address ] &&
      [ string equal [ $request get Framed-IP-Address ]
      "255.255.255.255" ] } {
            $request remove Framed-IP-Address
      }
}
```

To configure this example, create a file containing the TCL code. Name the file **remove-bad-IP.tcl**. Then, in **aregcmd** enter:

```
cd /Radius/Scripts
add remove-bad-IP
cd remove-bad-IP
set Language tcl
set Filename <yourscripts dir>/remove-bad-IP.tcl

cd /Radius/RemoteServers
cd myRemoteServer
set IncomingScript remove-bad-IP

save
reload
```

For more information on EPS scripting examples, refer to the samples that are part of your Cisco Access Registrar installation as follows:

For EPS examples in C:

```
<CAR DIR>/examples/rexscript/rexscript.c
```

For EPS examples in TCL:

```
<CAR DIR>/scripts/radius/tcl/tclscript.tcl
```

Proxy AAA

Proxy AAA is indicated in Figure 14-5 by the number 3. Proxy AAA enables the AR to proxy authentication requests to someone else's AAA server. This is done based on attributes it finds in the request. Providers can use filters that instruct AR to look at the dialed number (DNIS) or realm contained in the request packet.

Figure 14-5 *Proxy AAA*

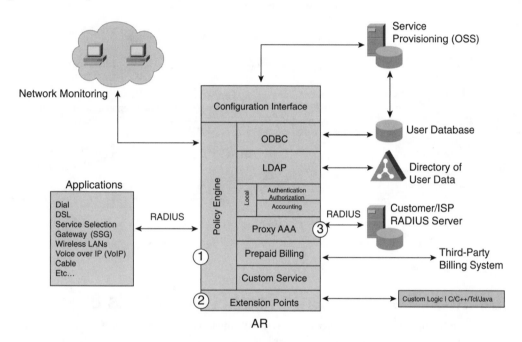

An example of a realm might be the cisco.com in userbob@cisco.com. The filters include User-name suffix and prefix, DNIS, and NAS-IP-Address. The extension points that were discussed in the previous section can also be used to define other information in the request that you want to match.

AAA

AAA is indicated in Figure 14-6 by the number 4. This is simply the module that manages the AAA process locally in the AR.

Figure 14-6 *AAA in AR*

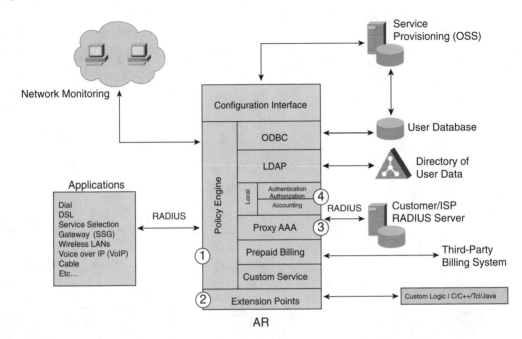

Installation Requirements for AR on Solaris 8

To begin the installation process of AR, you must meet the minimum requirements based on the type of install you are performing. You can perform three types of installs. You can perform a full install, which installs AR as well as the command-line interface (CLI) that is used to configure AR. You can do a server-only install, and this would indicate that you want to manage AR from another machine. The other machine that you want to access AR from would then require a CLI-only install. This would place the CLI known as **aregcmd** on the machine, and not the server components.

For a full install, you must meet the requirements in Table 14-1:

Table 14-1 *Full Install Requirements*

Component	Requirement
CPU Architecture	SPARC
OS Version	Solaris 8
Minimum RAM	64 MB

Table 14-1 *Full Install Requirements (Continued)*

Component	Requirement
Recommended RAM	128 MB
Recommended Disk Space	175 MB

For the installation of the AR server only, you must meet the system requirements in Table 14-2:

Table 14-2 *AR Server-Only Requirements*

Component	Requirement
CPU Architecture	SPARC
OS Version	Solaris 8
Minimum RAM	64 MB
Recommended RAM	128 MB
Recommended Disk Space	130 MB

For the AR CLI-only installation, you must meet the requirements in Table 14-3:

Table 14-3 *CLI-Only Requirements*

Component	Requirement
CPU Architecture	SPARC
OS Version	Solaris 8
Minimum RAM	32 MB
Recommended RAM	64 MB
Recommended Disk Space	50 MB

Of these requirements, the recommended disk space does not take into consideration the accounting records. You should provide enough disk space to adequately provide for this. To determine the amount of disk space needed, you should determine the size of each accounting file that will be stored locally on AR and multiply that figure by the number of accounting records you plan to keep. This will give you a ballpark estimate.

It is also recommended that AR be the only server service provided by this machine. You might choose to run collaborative servers such as an Oracle or SQL database system, an LDAP server, or another Solaris application. No known conflicts with any other Solaris applications exist.

You can also configure AR to avoid User Datagram Protocol (UDP) port conflicts with other network management applications. AR listens on UDP ports 1645 and 1646 for RADIUS request and TCP ports 2785 and 2786 for the CLI **aregcmd**. If you are using the CLI on another machine to configure your server, these TCP ports should not be used. You can configure AR to use non-default ports for RADIUS by performing the following configuration:

Step 1 Once logged into **aregcmd**, change the directory to /Radius/Advanced/ Ports.

Step 2 Use the **add** command (twice) to add ports in pairs.

Step 3 After modifying AR's default ports setting, you must add ports 1645 and 1646 to the list of ports to continue using them.

Step 4 Enter the **save** and **reload** commands to affect, validate, and save your modifications to the AR server configuration.

You can refer to the Cisco Documentation online for more information.

NOTE Also, Cisco provides the Sun Cisco Optimized Platform Recommended Part Numbers to help find the right hardware to install AR on. Refer to the Cisco website for more information.

Installing AR

Typically AR is installed from a downloaded file. To install AR from this file, perform the following tasks as the **root** user:

Step 1 Create a temporary directory, such as **/tmp-ar**, to hold the downloaded software package.

Step 2 Change to the directory where the downloaded file exists, as follows:

```
#cd /tmp-ar
```

Step 3 Uncompress the tar files and extract the installation files, as follows:

```
./gunzip -c ar-3.0r5-sunos58.tar.gz
```

After the preceding preparations have been made, you can proceed with the following steps. If you do not plan on using AR's Simple Network Management Protocol (SNMP) features, skip Steps 1 and 2 in the following step sequence:

Step 1 If you plan to use Cisco CNS AR's SNMP features, disable the Sun SNMP daemon by entering the following:

```
/etc/rc3.d/S76snmpdx stop
/etc/rc3.d/S77dmi stop
```

Step 2   If you plan to use Cisco CNS AR's SNMP features, prevent the Sun
SNMP daemon from restarting after a reboot by entering the following:

```
mkdir /etc/rc3.d/.disabled
mv /etc/rc3.d/S76snmpdx /etc/rc3.d/.disabled
mv /etc/rc3.d/S77dmi /etc/rc3.d/.disabled
```

Step 3   Add the AR package using the **pkgadd** command. Replace the following
directory in the example with the path where you have decompressed the
Cisco CNS AR files:

```
Pkgadd -d /tmp-ar CSCOar
```

Step 4   At this point, the installation script prompts you with a number of
questions. For some of these, you have the option of taking a default
value; for others, you must provide an answer. Example 14-1 is an install
of Cisco CNS AR on a SPARCstation. In the example, explanation has
been given for major configuration information.

Example 14-1 *Installing Cisco CNS Access Registrar*

```
!The following command initiates the installation if CISCO CNS ACCESS REGISTRAR.
#pkgadd -d /export/home/tmp-ar CSCOar

Processing package instance <CSCOar> from </export/home/tmp-ar>

Cisco CNS Access Registrar 3.0R1 [SunOS-5.8, official]
(sparc) 3.0R1
Copyright (C) 1998-2002 by Cisco Systems, Inc.
This program contains proprietary and confidential information.
All rights reserved except as may be permitted by prior written consent.
!The following is the default location of the install. You can hit !enter and accept
the default or you may choose to change the path of !the install.
Where do you want to install <CSCOar>? [/opt/CSCOar] [?,q]

Cisco AR provides extensions that can be written in Java.
If you intend to write Java extensions, the Java Runtime
Environment (JRE) is required.

Do you require the Cisco AR Java extension? [No]: [?,q]
!At this point you can choose what type of install you wish to perform.
This package contains the  Access Registrar Server and the Access
Registrar Configuration Utility.  You can choose to perform a Full
installation, just install the Server, or just install the
Configuration Utility.

What type of installation: Full, Server only, Config only [Full] [?,q]

!It is a good idea to install the sample configurations. Enter the letter "y" at
the prompt to install the sample configurations.
```

continues

Example 14-1 *Installing Cisco CNS Access Registrar (Continued)*

```
If you want to learn about Cisco CNS Access Registrar by following the examples
in the Installation and Configuration Guide, you need to populate the
database with the example configuration.

Do you want to install the example configuration now [y,n,?,q] y

You can delete the example configuration at any time by running the
command:

/opt/CSCOar/bin/aregcmd -f /opt/CSCOar/examples/cli/delete-example-
  configuration.rc

If you are not using ODBC, press Enter/Return to skip this step.
ORACLE installation directory is required for ODBC configuration.
ORACLE_HOME variable will be set in /etc/init.d/arserver script

Where is ORACLE installed ? [] [?,q] ←Here you need to hit Enter.
## Executing checkinstall script.
Using </opt/CSCOar> as the package base directory.
## Processing package information.
## Processing system information.
## Verifying package dependencies.
## Verifying disk space requirements.
## Checking for conflicts with packages already installed.
## Checking for setuid/setgid programs.

The following files are being installed with setuid and/or setgid
permissions:
   /opt/CSCOar/.system/screen <setuid root> ←This is set to root for Cisco TAC to
perform diagnostics.
   /opt/CSCOar/bin/aregcmd <setgid staff> ←This gives AR the permissions necessary
to write to this log file.

Do you want to install these as setuid/setgid files [y,n,?,q] y
This package contains scripts that will be executed with super-user
permission during the process of installing this package.

Do you want to continue with the installation of <CSCOar> [y,n,?] y

Installing Cisco CNS Access Registrar 3.0R1 [SunOS-5.8, official] as <CSCOar>
!At this point the installation begins and the files used in CISCO CNS ACCESS
REGISTRAR are !installed.

## Installing part 1 of 1.
/opt/CSCOar/.system/screen
/opt/CSCOar/README
/opt/CSCOar/bin/arbug

<text omitted>

/opt/CSCOar/ucd-snmp/share/snmp/snmpd.conf
[ verifying class <snmp> ]
```

Example 14-1 *Installing Cisco CNS Access Registrar (Continued)*

```
## Executing postinstall script.
# setting up product configuration file /opt/CSCOar/conf/Cisco CNS Access
  Registrar.conf
# linking /etc/init.d/arserver to /etc/rc.d files
# setting ORACLE_HOME variable in arserver
# removing old session information
# flushing old replication archive
# creating initial configuration database
Rollforward recovery using "/opt/CSCOar/data/db/vista.tjf" started Mon May 26
  15:35:59 2003
Rollforward recovery using "/opt/CSCOar/data/db/vista.tjf" finished Mon May 26
  15:35:59 2003

# installing example configuration
Starting Cisco CNS Access Registrar Server Agent..completed.

The Radius server is now running.

If SNMP needs to be reconfigured please follow the following
procedure:

(1) stop AR: /opt/CSCOar/bin/arserver stop
(2) edit: /cisco-ar/ucd-snmp/share/snmp/snmpd.conf
(3) restart AR: /opt/CSCOar/bin/arserver start

# done with postinstall.

Installation of <CSCOar> was successful.
```

At this point, the installation process is completed, and you can begin configuration of AR. However, first you should become familiar with AR's subdirectories.

AR's Subdirectories

AR installs numerous subdirectories. These subdirectories are seen in Example 14-2 by issuing the **ls** command.

Example 14-2 *AR's Subdirectories*

```
# cd /opt/CSCOar
# ls
README    conf      examples  logs      scripts   ucd-snmp
bin       data      lib       odbc      temp      usrbin
#
```

Table 14-4 lists these directories as well as a description of them.

Table 14-4 *ARs Subdirectories*

Directory	Description
.system	This is a hidden directory that contains executables that should not be run directly.
bin	This subdirectory contains the program executables.
usrbin	This contains a symbolic link that points to the bin directory.
data	The data subdirectory contains the RADIUS directory that contains session backing files, the db directory that contains configuration database files, the db.bak directory that contains backup files, and the archive directory that contains the replication archive.
logs	This contains system logs and is the default directory for RADIUS accounting information.
scripts	This contains sample scripts that you can use to customize your RADIUS server.
examples	This contains documentation, sample configuration scripts, and shared library scripts.
lib	This contains Cisco CNS AR software library files.
ucd-snmp	This contains the UCD-SNMP software Cisco CNS AR uses.
temp	This is used for temporary storage.
conf	This contains configuration files.

Configuring Cisco CNS AR

The configuration of AR is dependent on the product licensing. Every copy of AR requires a license. When you begin configuring AR, you create a cluster. You must enter your license the first time you configure each cluster. A cluster is nothing more than the AR server. The following bullet points highlight important information as to the licensing of AR:

- If you have a permanent license, you will not see the license prompt again unless you reinstall and overwrite the database.

- If you have a time-limited license that you are using to access AR, you have a license that will expire. When the license key expires, you will not be able to configure or manage AR. The server itself, however, will continue to function normally. To obtain a time-limited license, email car-license@cisco.com.

- If you have an invalid or missing licensing key, you will not be able to configure or manage AR.

You can follow these steps to log in to AR and enter a valid license:

Step 1   To begin configuring AR, you need to issue the **aregcmd** command in Solaris. This invokes the CLI used to configure AR.

Step 2   You need to log in to the cluster. The only case in which you would enter a cluster name is if you are accessing an AR server that is not on the same device as the CLI. If you leave the cluster blank, you log in to the local AR server.

Step 3   Enter the username. The default username is **admin**.

Step 4   Enter the password. The default password is **aicuser**.

Step 5   Next, you are prompted for your activation key. Enter the valid activation key. This completes your login to AR. This is seen in Example 14-3.

Example 14-3 *Entering a Valid License*

```
# ./aregcmd
Cisco CNS Access Registrar 3.0R5 Configuration Utility
Copyright (C) 1995-2002 by Cisco Systems, Inc.  All rights reserved.
Cluster:
User: admin
Password:aicuser
Logging in to localhost
Your current license key is invalid.
Please enter a valid license key: 6N16-SJIT-61RI-VU1A
```

Step 6   This completes the basic setup of AR. You can verify the status of AR by issuing the **arstatus** command. This is seen in Example 14-4.

Example 14-4 *Checking the Status of AR*

```
# ./arstatus
AR MCD lock manager running (pid: 178)
AR Server Agent running     (pid: 171)
AR MCD server running       (pid: 175)
AR RADIUS server running    (pid: 183)
```

Summary

In this chapter, you learned how AR is used in a service provider environment to facilitate AAA functionality. You have now performed a successful install and have verified the status of AR. In the configuration of this chapter, the installation performed was a full install because you accessed the CLI and the server on the same machine.

You can now proceed with the next chapter and configure a basic site. It would be wise to have some understanding of the Solaris operating system before attempting the install of AR; however, it is not necessary. In fact, because AR provides its own CLI you do not need to have much experience with Solaris to configure the AR server. The following chapter will focus on the configuration of AR in a basic site environment. There is no discussion of ODBC databases of Proxy AAA; however, there is a wealth of information in the form of white papers on the Cisco website. For more information, refer to these white papers.

End Notes

[1] http://www.cisco.com/warp/public/cc/pd/nemnsw/accreg/prodlit/carcs_wp.htm

[2] http://www.cisco.com/warp/public/cc/pd/nemnsw/accreg/prodlit/carcs_wp.htm

In this chapter, you learn the following topics:

- Using **aregcmd** to configure AR
- AR's server object hierarchy
- Configuring the ACE ISP as a basic site
- Configuring AR's administrators
- Configuring the RADIUS server
- Validating and saving your changes to AR
- Testing your configuration
- Troubleshooting your configuration with **trace**

## CHAPTER 15

Configuring the Cisco Access Registrar

In this chapter, you are taken through the process of creating a basic site configuration. If you want to configure a basic site, it is beneficial to learn the structure of the Access Registrar (AR) command-line interface called **aregcmd**. With a little practice, you will find it very easy to maneuver through the AR hierarchy. This allows you to configure the parameters that you require in your network deployment. The goal here is to make some of the basic configuration tasks a little simpler to understand.

NOTE   If you are not familiar with a Solaris operating system, some of the issues you might face involve getting used to command syntax and operating system behavior.

Using aregcmd to Configure AR

To configure AR, you use the **aregcmd** command-line interface (CLI). Accessing this CLI allows you to enter commands directly into AR. When using **aregcmd**, you need to know a few important commands. First off, you can think of **aregcmd** as a modified UNIX command line. You can use the UNIX command **cd** to change directories, or in the case of AR, configuration objects. You can use the UNIX command **ls** to list the elements in your current location of AR. To back out of a configuration object, use **"cd .."**. You'll find that maneuvering through the hierarchy is not that difficult. The following section discusses commands that are more specific to AR.

aregcmd Syntax

We said that the **aregcmd** command when invoked from the Solaris command line accesses the CLI that AR commands are entered into. The commands entered into **aregcmd** are not case sensitive and just like the Cisco IOS provide some context-sensitive help and command completion using the Tab key. If the command element that you are requesting is unique, you have to enter only a portion of the command for it to execute. Also, the **aregcmd** commands are command-line order dependent. This means the arguments are interpreted based on their position on the command line. Also, when **aregcmd** is invoked without the –**f** option or arguments, it starts in interactive mode and provides a prompt after logging in.

Some commands require you to enter data such as a description or some type of similar value. If you want to leave this option blank, you can do so by placing two single quotes. If an entry has spaces in the value you are entering you must quote the value.

[1]The **aregcmd** command syntax is

```
aregcmd [-C <clustername>] [-N <adminname>] [-P <adminpassword>]
[-f <scriptfile>] [-v] [-q] [-p] [-n] [<command> [<args>]]
```

-**C**—specifies the name of the cluster to log into by default

-**N**—specifies the name of the administrator

-**P**—specifies the password

-**f**—specifies a file that can contain a series of commands

-**v**—specifies verbose mode

-**q**—turns off verbose mode

-**p**—specifies prefix mode

-**n**—turns off prefix mode

Note, the verbose (-**v**) and prefix (-**p**) modes are on by default when you run **aregcmd** interactively (not running a command from the command line or not running commands from a script file). Verbose and prefix modes are off otherwise.

When you include a command (with the appropriate arguments) on the command line, **aregcmd** runs only that one command and saves any changes.

Categories of aregcmd Commands

The **aregcmd** CLI commands are entered after you are logged onto the AR cluster. To log in to the cluster, you actually invoke the **aregcmd** CLI. The commands can be grouped into the categories discussed in the following sections.

Navigation Commands

These commands navigate within the Cisco AR hierarchy; commands include **cd**, **ls**, **pwd**, **next**, **prev**, **filter**, and **find**. We discuss the first three in detail.

The **cd** and **ls** commands were already discussed; however, let's recap. The **cd** command simply allows you to move through the configuration hierarchy. The structure of AR is similar to a directory tree. You would use the **cd** command to move from one configuration object in the hierarchy to another.

When you move through the configuration hierarchy, you can use the **ls** command to list the contents of the current level. It is very similar to the UNIX command. If you enter the command followed by a path, it lists elements in the path you specify. No path lists the current locations objects. Optionally, you can add **–R** to the **ls** command to list all the objects in the current location in the hierarchy, as well as all those below it. This can be handy when you need to gather more information.

The **pwd** command works just like the UNIX **pwd** command. This prints the working directory or the absolute path that you are in within the configuration hierarchy.

Object Commands

These commands add or delete objects; commands include **add** and **delete**. These commands are pretty simple really. If you wanted to add an administrator to AR, you would simply navigate to the correct configuration object, in this case **Administrators**. In the Administrators level, you simply use the **add** command to add the administrator. You can see this in Example 15-1:

Example 15-1 *Using the* **add** *Command*

```
[ //localhost ]
    LicenseKey = 6N16-SJIV-61RI-VU1G (expires in 65 days)
    Radius/
    Administrators/

→ cd Administrators/ ←Change to the Administrators level.

[ //localhost/Administrators ]
    Entries 1 to 1 from 1 total entries
    Current filter: <all>

    admin/  ←Note there is only one Admin

→ add bcarroll ADMIN cisco  ←Using add to create the new user.

Added bcarroll  ←AR confirms that the admin was added.

→ ls  ←Use the ls command to view the Administrators level and see the new admin.
[ //localhost/Administrators ]
    Entries 1 to 2 from 2 total entries
    Current filter: <all>

    admin/
    bcarroll/  ←the new admin is present in the Administrator level.
```

Property Commands

These commands change the value of properties; commands include **set**, **unset**, and **insert**. Property commands are also pretty straightforward. You would use the **set** command to set parameters such as the default session manager.

Server Commands

These commands manage the server itself; commands include **save**, **validate**, **start**, **stop**, **reload**, **status**, **stats**, and **trace**. The **save** command commits the changes you have made to the configuration database of AR. It does not, however, update the running server so you use the **reload** command to do that. The **validate** command validates the configuration of AR. If AR finds an inconsistency, it displays it. The **start**, **stop**, and **status** commands deal with the RADIUS service. The **stats** command gives global statistics for RADIUS.

You can see an example of the **stats** command in Example 15-2.

Example 15-2 *Using the* **stats** *Command*

```
→ stats

Global Statistics for Radius:
serverStartTime = Thu Feb 19 22:34:24 2004
serverResetTime = Thu Feb 19 22:34:25 2004
serverState = Running
totalPacketsInPool = 1024
totalPacketsReceived = 0
totalPacketsSent = 0
totalRequests = 0
totalResponses = 0
totalAccessRequests = 0
totalAccessAccepts = 0
totalAccessChallenges = 0
totalAccessRejects = 0
totalAccessResponses = 0
totalAccountingRequests = 0
totalAccountingResponses = 0
totalStatusServerRequests = 0
totalAscendIPAAllocateRequests = 0
totalAscendIPAAllocateResponses = 0
totalAscendIPAReleaseRequests = 0
totalAscendIPAReleaseResponses = 0
totalUSRNASRebootRequests = 0
totalUSRNASRebootResponses = 0
totalUSRResourceFreeRequests = 0
totalUSRResourceFreeResponses = 0
totalUSRQueryResourceRequests = 0
totalUSRQueryResourceResponses = 0
totalUSRQueryReclaimRequests = 0
totalUSRQueryReclaimResponses = 0
totalPacketsInUse = 0
```

Example 15-2 *Using the* **stats** *Command (Continued)*

```
totalPacketsDrained = 0
totalPacketsDropped = 0
totalPayloadDecryptionFailures = 0


→
```

Application Commands

These commands allow user access to the application; commands include **login**, **logout**, **exit**, **quit**, and **help**. These commands are pretty much self explanatory. If you recall, during the installation you could install the AR server only, and the CLI could be installed on a separate machine. You can be logged in to one AR and use the **login** command to access another AR cluster. Remember that a cluster is nothing more than a way to specify an AR server.

Session Management Commands

These commands query the server about currently active user sessions or release active sessions; commands include **query-sessions** and **release-sessions**.

AR's Server Object Hierarchy

Now that you know a bit more about the AR commands, where do you use them? Well, the answer to that question is simple. It depends. Since AR's command line is built in a pretty structured fashion, you use certain commands based on your location in the server's objects. Let's look at how AR is built.

At the top of the Server Objects tree are two objects, Administrators and Radius. This is displayed to you when you log in to an AR cluster. This is very similar to a UNIX file system in that the object is sort of a directory. You can use the **cd** command to enter into either of the objects. Once in an object, there might be sub-objects. You can also **cd** into a sub-object. Some of AR's objects might contain a list, in which case you modify parameters in the list.

In Example 15-3, you can see that we have changed directories to the Radius object.

Example 15-3 *The Radius Object*

```
→ cd Radius/

[ //localhost/Radius ]
    Name = Radius
    Description =
    Version = 3.5.0.7
```

continues

Example 15-3 *The Radius Object (Continued)*

```
        IncomingScript~ =
        OutgoingScript~ =
        DefaultAuthenticationService~ = local-users
        DefaultAuthorizationService~ = local-users
        DefaultAccountingService~ = local-file
        DefaultSessionService~ =
        DefaultSessionManager~ = session-mgr-1
        UserLists/
        UserGroups/
        Policies/
        Clients/
        Vendors/
        Scripts/
        Services/
        SessionManagers/
        ResourceManagers/
        Profiles/
        Rules/
        Translations/
        TranslationGroups/
        RemoteServers/
        Advanced/
        Replication/
```

If you look at Example 15-3, you can see the sub-objects of the Radius object. These include the following:

- UserLists/
- UserGroups/
- Policies/
- Clients/
- Vendors/
- Scripts/
- Services/
- SessionManagers/
- ResourceManagers/
- Profiles/
- Rules/
- Translations/
- TranslationGroups/

- RemoteServers/
- Advanced/
- Replication/

You can tell that these are sub-objects because they have a **/** at the end of them. The other items in the Radius object include parameters that you can set, such as **IncomingScript**, **OutgoingScript**, and **DefaultAuthenticationService**. It is at this level that you could use the **set** command to manipulate one of these values.

Configuring the ACE ISP as a Basic Site

The simplest site configuration is one that uses a single user list for all its users, writes its accounting information to a local file, and does not use session management to allocate dynamic resources. For example purposes, we use a fictitious Internet service provider (ISP) named ACE. We assume that ACE ISP meets this criterion for a basic site.

To configure the ACE ISP, you need to perform the following tasks:

Step 1   Run **aregcmd** and log in to AR. You can find **aregcmd** in the default directory of **/opt/CSCOar/usrbin**. You can see this in Example 15-4.

Example 15-4 *Log In to AR*

```
# ./aregcmd
Cisco Access Registrar 3.5.0.7 Configuration Utility
Copyright (C) 1995-2004 by Cisco Systems, Inc.  All rights reserved.
Cluster:
User: admin
Password:
Logging in to localhost

[ //localhost ]
    LicenseKey = 6N16-SJIV-61RI-VU1G (expires in 65 days)
    Radius/
    Administrators/

Server 'Radius' is Running, its health is 10 out of 10

→
```

Step 2   Configure the AR server settings.

Step 3   Add users by copying the sample users.

Step 4   Configure the clients, that is, the network access servers (NASs) and proxies that communicate with Cisco AR.

Step 5   Change profile attributes as needed.

Step 6   Save your changes and reload AR.

Configuring AR's Administrators

In the previous section, you logged in to AR using the default username and password. You most likely want to change these. To do so, follow these steps:

Step 1   Change to the **Administrators** object, as follows:

```
→ cd ad  --This changes to the Administrator object
[ //localhost/Administrators ]
    Entries 1 to 1 from 1 total entries
    Current filter: <all>
    admin/
```

Step 2   Change to the **admin** object, as follows:

```
→cd admin -This changes to the admin user profile-
[ //localhost/Administrators/admin ]
    Name = admin
    Description =
    Password = <encrypted>
```

Step 3   Use the **set** command to set the password for admin.

```
→ set password cisco -Set is a Property command used to configure a
value, in this case the password.-
Retype password to confirm:cisco
Set Password <encrypted>
→
```

Step 4   Optionally, you can use the **set** command to change the description of admin.

```
→ set description "This is my Admin of AR" -Without the quotes, the
description ends at the first space.-
Set Description "This is my Admin of AR"
→ ls  -Use the ls navigation command to view the profile.-
[ //localhost/Administrators/admin ]
    Name = admin
    Description = This is my Admin of AR
    Password = <encrypted>
```

Step 5   Additionally, you can add another administrator by changing directories back a level to the **Administrators** object.

```
→ cd .. -This commands moves you back one level in the object tree.-
[ //localhost/Administrators ]
    Entries 1 to 1 from 1 total entries
    Current filter: <all>
    admin/
```

Step 6   Use the **add** command to add a new administrator.

> → **add bcarroll NewAdmin cisco2** -**Add** is the **Object** command that adds
> the user **bcarroll** which is considered to be an Object to AR.-

> Added bcarroll

Step 7   Check your work.

> → **ls**

> [//localhost/Administrators]
>   Entries 1 to 2 from 2 total entries
>   Current filter: <all>
>
>   admin/   Here you now see that there are two
>   bcarroll/   Administrators added

> →

Step 8   Return to the top level of the object tree.

> → **cd /**

> [//localhost]
>   LicenseKey = 72GA-756L-BESQ-4W9G (expires in 31 days)
>   Radius/
>   Administrators/

> →

Configuring the RADIUS Server

At the top level of AR is the Administrator object that you just configured and the Radius object. The Radius object specifies the name of the server and other parameters that are related to the way AR handles user requests. In configuring this site, you need to change only a few of these properties. This section of the chapter shows you how to configure some basic RADIUS parameters for AR.

Start with this step:

Step 1   Change to the Radius object, as seen in Example 15-5.

Example 15-5 *The Radius Object*

```
→ cd Radius/

[ //localhost/Radius ]
    Name = Radius
    Description =
    Version = 3.0R1
    IncomingScript~ =
    OutgoingScript~ =
    DefaultAuthenticationService~ = local-users
    DefaultAuthorizationService~ = local-users
    DefaultAccountingService~ = local-file
    DefaultSessionService~ =
    DefaultSessionManager~ = session-mgr-1
    UserLists/
    UserGroups/
    Policies/
    Clients/
    Vendors/
    Scripts/
    Services/
    SessionManagers/
    ResourceManagers/
    Profiles/
    Rules/
    Translations/
    TranslationGroups/
    RemoteServers/
    Advanced/
    Replication/

→
```

Earlier in this chapter, you saw the sub-objects of the Radius object. Your next step is to configure some basic parameters here. The next subsections take a look at these configurations in more detail.

Checking the System-Level Defaults

When you change to the Radius object, you see the Name, Description, and Version of AR. You might want to give the server a description. If so, use the following steps:

Step 1 You can edit the description by using the **set** command. When you enter the command, it echoes back on the screen to you, like so:

```
set Description "ACE ISP ACCESS REGISTRAR."
```

Step 2   To verify your work, simply type the **ls** command.

Other configurations that you can perform are the application of incoming and outgoing scripts. Because this site does not use incoming or outgoing scripts at this time, you do not need to change the scripts' properties (**IncomingScript** and **OutgoingScript**). These configurations can be left with the blank default values.

```
IncomingScript~ =
OutgoingScript~ =
```

Moving on to the authentication, authorization, and accounting (AAA) properties, you can point each service to different lists.

Step 3   Because the default authentication and authorization properties specify a single user list, you can leave these unchanged as well (**DefaultAuthenticationService** and **DefaultAuthorizationService**).

```
DefaultAuthenticationService~ = local-users
DefaultAuthorizationService~ = local-users
```

Step 4   Because this is a basic site, all accounting can be sent to a file as well. You can leave the default value here as well using **DefaultAccountingService**:

```
DefaultAccountingService~ = local-file
```

Step 5   Session management is something that is on by default. For a basic site, you might not want to use session management, so it needs to be disabled. To disable session management, use the **set** command:

```
→ set DefaultSessionManager ""

Set DefaultSessionManager ""
```

By using a set of double quotes, you essentially set the value to null, in this case disabling session management. For a small site, session management might be disabled because it has an effect on the performance of AR. Other actions that can affect the health of AR include the following:

- The rejection of an Access-Request
- Configuration errors
- Running out of memory
- Errors reading from the network
- Dropping packets that cannot be read (because the server ran out of memory)
- Errors writing to the network

When you log into **aregcmd**, you are informed of the health of AR. You can retrieve this information at any time in the command line. To do so, do the following:

Step 1   From the CLI enter the **status** command.

```
→ status

Server 'Radius' is Running, its health is 10 out of 10


→
```

Step 2   Another default value that you might need to change is the RADIUS ports. By default, AR listens on ports 1645 and 1646. Because these are not the new RADIUS port assignments, you might want to add 1812 and 1813. This needs to be done in the **Advanced** sub-object of **Radius** under the **Ports** sub-object. To do so, change to the proper object using the **cd** command, as seen in Example 15-6.

Example 15-6 *The* **Ports** *Object*

```
cd Advanced/Ports/
[ //localhost/Radius/Advanced/Ports ]
    <no ports specified, will be using the well-known ports, 1645, 1646>
```

Step 3   Use the **add** command to add the new ports:

```
→ add 1812

Added 1812

→ add 1813

Added 1813
```

Step 4   Check your work using the **ls** command:

```
→ ls

[ //localhost/Radius/Advanced/Ports ]
    Entries 1 to 2 from 2 total entries
    Current filter: <all>

    1812/
    1813/


→
```

You now have AR configured to perform authentication to a local list and listen on ports 1812 and 1813, and you have disabled session management to conserve the resources of AR. The next step is to add users to the local list that AR compares authentication requests against.

Displaying the UserLists

The **UserLists** object contains all the individual UserLists, which in turn contain the specific users.

When AR receives an Access-Request, it directs it to an authentication and/or authorization service based on what you have specified in the **DefaultAuthenticationService** parameter at the **Radius** level. If the service has its type set to **local-users**, the service looks up the user's entry in the specific **UserList** and authenticates and/or authorizes the user.

Earlier you saw that AR, by default, specifies a **DefaultAuthenticationService** called **local-users** that has the type local and uses the default UserList. You can now display the default UserList by following these simple steps:

Step 1   Use the **cd** command to change to **UserLists/Default**:

    --> cd /Radius/UserLists/Default

Step 2   Use the **ls -R** command to display the properties of the three users that are placed there by default, as seen in Example 15-7:

Example 15-7 *Viewing the Properties of the Added Users*

```
→ ls -R

[ //localhost/Radius/UserLists/Default ]
    Entries 1 to 3 from 3 total entries
    Current filter: <all>

    Name = Default
    Description =
    bob/
        Name = bob
        Description =
        Password = <encrypted>
        AllowNullPassword = FALSE
        Enabled = TRUE
        Group~ = PPP-users
        BaseProfile~ =
        AuthenticationScript~ =
        AuthorizationScript~ =
        UserDefined1 =
        Attributes/
        CheckItems/
```

continues

Example 15-7 *Viewing the Properties of the Added Users (Continued)*

```
jane/
    Name = jane
    Description =
    Password = <encrypted>
    AllowNullPassword = FALSE
    Enabled = TRUE
    Group~ = Telnet-users
    BaseProfile~ =
    AuthenticationScript~ =
    AuthorizationScript~ =
    UserDefined1 =
    Attributes/
    CheckItems/
joe/
    Name = joe
    Description =
    Password = <encrypted>
    AllowNullPassword = FALSE
    Enabled = TRUE
    Group~ = Default
    BaseProfile~ =
    AuthenticationScript~ =
    AuthorizationScript~ =
    UserDefined1 =
    Attributes/
    CheckItems/

→
```

As a result of executing the previous step sequence, you see that Cisco AR displays these three sample users:

- **bob** who is configured as a PPP user
- **jane** who is configured as a Telnet user
- **joe** who is configured as either a PPP or Telnet user depending on how he logs in

Working with Users

The previous section demonstrated the sample users that were already in AR as models. In this section, configure a few new users for ACE ISP. To do this, you need to access the default User List, and then use the add command to add the users. Follow these steps to add users to the ACE ISP server:

Step 1   Use the **cd** command to change to the default UserList.

Step 2 Use the **add** command to add a user. You must supply the name, an optional description, a password, whether the user is enabled (that is, is allowed access), and an optional group. The following example adds the user **beth** with the description **Marketing**, the password **123**, enabled set to **TRUE**, and specifying the **PPP-users** group. The options must be entered in the correct order.

> → **add beth Marketing 123 TRUE PPP-users**

Step 3 Repeat for the other users you want to add.

Step 4 Use the **ls** command to check your additions:

> → **ls**

Step 5 To delete the sample users, or to remove a user from the ACE ISP AR server from the appropriate UserList, use the **delete** command and specify the name of the user you want to delete. For example, to delete user **beth** from the default UserList, type the following:

> → **cd /Radius/UserLists/Default**
> → **delete beth**

This completely removes **beth**'s profile in AR.

Displaying and Configuring UserGroups

The **UserGroups** object contains the specific user groups. By default, the three group are **Default**, **PPP-users**, and **Telnet-users**. The **Default** group uses the script **AuthorizeService** to determine the type of service to provide the user. This group is intended for users that can use PPP and Telnet. If the user can use both, this is where you should place them. The **PPP-users** group uses the **BaseProfile** called **default-PPP-users** to specify the attributes of PPP service to provide the user. The **Telnet-users** group uses the **BaseProfile** called **default-Telnet-users** to specify the attributes of Telnet service to provide the user.

Specific **UserGroups** allow you to maintain common authentication and authorization attributes in one location. These groups are referenced in a user profile.

For the ACE ISP, you do not need to change these **UserGroups**, since we are configuring a basic site. To view the default user groups, follow these steps:

Step 1 Change to the **UserGroups** object using the **cd** command, as seen in Example 15-8.

Example 15-8 *Changing to the* **UserGroups** *Object*

```
→ cd usergroups/

[ //localhost/Radius/UserGroups ]
    Entries 1 to 3 from 3 total entries
    Current filter: <all>

    Default/
    PPP-users/
    Telnet-users/

→
```

Step 2 Later on, you might want to add or delete groups. You can use the **add** or **delete** commands to do so:

```
→ add Sample-User-Group
```

```
Added Sample-User-Group
```

Step 3 Check your work with the **ls** command, as seen in Example 15-9:

Example 15-9 *Using* **ls** *to Verify the Addition*

```
→ ls

[ //localhost/Radius/UserGroups ]
    Entries 1 to 4 from 4 total entries
    Current filter: <all>

    Default/
    PPP-users/
    Sample-User-Group/
    Telnet-users/

→
```

Configuring AAA Clients in AR

The **Clients** object contains all AAA clients and proxies that communicate with AR. Each client must be identified in AR and have the same secret key configured on both ends. This means that AR must be identified in the AAA client as well.

To add an AAA client to AR, perform the following steps:

Step 1   Use the **cd** command to change to the **Clients** object level, as seen in Example 15-10:

Example 15-10 *Changing to the* **Clients** *Object*

```
→ cd /radius/clients/

[ //localhost/Radius/Clients ]
    Entries 1 to 1 from 1 total entries
    Current filter: <all>

    localhost/
```

Step 2   Use the **add** command to add the NAS **Airport-AP1:**

```
→ add Airport-AP1

Added Airport-AP1
```

Step 3   Use the **ls** command to check your work, as seen in Example 15-11:

Example 15-11 *Verify the Addition of an AAA Client*

```
→ ls

[ //localhost/Radius/Clients ]
    Entries 1 to 2 from 2 total entries
    Current filter: <all>

    Airport-AP1/
    localhost/
```

Step 4   Use the **cd** command to change directory to the **Airport-AP1** object, as seen in Example 15-12:

Example 15-12 *Changing to the New Object*

```
→ cd airport-AP1/

[ //localhost/Radius/Clients/Airport-AP1 ]
    Name = Airport-AP1
    Description =
    IPAddress =
    SharedSecret =
    Type = NAS
```

continues

Example 15-12 *Changing to the New Object (Continued)*

```
        Vendor =
        IncomingScript~ =
        OutgoingScript~ =
        EnablePOD = FALSE

    →
```

Step 5 Use the **set** command to specify the description **WestTerminalAP**, the IP
address **196.168.198.100**, the shared secret key of **secretapkey**. You
could also configure incoming scripts that would be applied to this AAA
client, as seen in Example 15-13.

Example 15-13 *Configuring an AAA Client*

```
[ //localhost/Radius/Clients/Airport-AP1 ]
    Name = Airport-AP1
    Description =
    IPAddress =
    SharedSecret =
    Type = NAS
    Vendor =
    IncomingScript~ =
    OutgoingScript~ =
    EnablePOD = FALSE
```

Step 6 Configure the description of the entry.

    → **set Description WestTerminalAP**

    Set Description WestTerminalAP

Step 7 Configure the IP address of the AAA client.

    → **set IPAddress 192.168.198.100**

    Set IPAddress 192.168.198.100

Step 8 Configure the shared secret key of the AAA client.

    → **set sharedSecret secretapkey**

    Set SharedSecret secretapkey

    →

Configuring Profiles

The **Profiles** object allows you to set specific Request For Comments (RFC)-defined attributes such as frame type, login service, and ports that AR returns in the Access-Accept response packet. You can use profiles to group attributes in one place that you want to apply to more than one user. This is also where you can set different Attribute-Value (AV) pairs. This method saves you from configuring parameters over and over again. The sample users that you looked at earlier in this chapter reference the following AR profiles:

- **default-PPP-users**—This profile specifies the appropriate attributes for Point-to-Point Protocol (PPP) service.

- **default-SLIP-users**—This profile specifies the appropriate attributes for Serial Line Internet Protocol (SLIP) service.

- **default-Telnet-users**—This profile specifies the appropriate attributes for Telnet service.

If you want to add an attribute or modify the attributes for Radius, you use a profile to do so. In the following steps, you modify a profile using the **set** command, as follows:

```
→ cd /Radius/Profiles/Default-Telnet-users/attributes
```

Step 1   From the main level in AR, **cd** into the **Radius/Profiles** sub-object.

Step 2   Use the **set** command to add the name=value attribute. The following example adds the attribute `Service-Type=Framed`:

```
set Service-Type Framed
```

Step 3   To add more than one value, simply place each parameter in double quotes. For example, if you wanted to set Cisco AV pair values and you entered line by line `"set Cisco-Avpair "value"`, you would keep overwriting the previously entered value. To enter multiple values, use the syntax `"set Cisco-Avpair "value1" "value2" "value3"`.

Validating and Saving Your Changes to AR

After you have finished configuring your RADIUS server, you must save your changes. Saving your changes causes AR not only to save the changes, but also to validate them. In fact, prior to saving, it validates, and if there are any errors in your configuration, you are notified.

Using the **save** command, however, does not automatically update your servers active configuration. If you recall, the server must be reloaded after saving for AR to re-read the configuration.

To save and validate your changes, follow these steps:

Step 1 Use the **save** command to save your changes:

> → `save`

Step 2 Use the **reload** command to reload your server and update the active configuration:

> → `reload`

Testing Your Configuration

Now that you have configured some users and a NAS, you are ready to test your configuration. The way to test AR locally without configuring an AAA client is to use a utility called **radclient**. The **radclient** utility uses the default **Clients** entry in AR of 127.0.0.1. The **radclient** utility simply creates and sends a RADIUS packet to AR.

The following step sequence creates an Access-Request packet for user **john** with password **john** and the packet identifier **p001**. It displays the packet before sending it. It uses the **send** command to send the packet, which displays the response packet object identifier **p002**. Then, the sequence shows how to display the contents of the response packet.

Step 1 Run the **radclient** command. It prompts you for the cluster name, username, and password.

```
# /opt/CSCOar/usrbin/radclient
Cisco Access Registrar 3.5.0.7 RADIUS Test Client
Copyright (C) 1995-2004 by Cisco Systems, Inc.  All rights reserved.
```

Step 2 Log in to the **radclient** utility as you would log in to **aregcmd.**

```
Cluster:
User: admin
Password:
Logging in to localhost...done
```

Step 3 Create a simple Access-Request packet for username **john** and password **john**. At the prompt, type

```
→ simple john john <cr>
p001  ←The packet identifier is echo'd back to you
```

The **radclient** command displays the ID of the packet **p001**.

Step 4   Type the packet identifier to have the packet information echoed back to you as seen in Example 15-14:

Example 15-14 *Creating a Request Packet*

```
p001 <cr>
Packet: code = Access-Request, id = 0, length = 0, attributes =
        User-Name = john
        User-Password = john
        NAS-Identifier = localhost
        NAS-Port = 1

→
```

Step 5   Simulate an AAA client sending the packet to AR by using the packet identifier and the **send** command.

→ **p001 send**
p002 ←The response packet is echo'd back to you.

Step 6   Type the response packet's identifier to display the contents of the Access-Accept packet, in this case, a denied access response as seen in Example 15-15:

Example 15-15 *A Denied Response*

```
p002 <cr>
→ p002
Packet: code = Access-Reject, id = 1, length = 35, attributes =
        Reply-Message = Access Denied

→
```

Troubleshooting Your Configuration with trace

If you are unable to receive an Access-Accept packet from the Cisco AR server, you can use the **aregcmd** command trace to troubleshoot your problem.

The **trace** command is sort of like configuring debugging. It allows you to set the trace level on your server. You can set the trace levels from zero to four, the higher number indicating that more information is logged. In AR, the default is zero. This would indicate that nothing is being logged. To configure the trace level in AR, perform the following steps:

Step 1   Run the **aregcmd** command and log into AR, as seen in Example 15-16.

Example 15-16 *Log In to AR*

```
# /opt/CSCOar/usrbin/aregcmd
Cisco Access Registrar 3.5.0.7 Configuration Utility
Copyright (C) 1995-2004 by Cisco Systems, Inc.  All rights reserved.
Cluster:
User: admin
Password:*****
Logging in to localhost

[ //localhost ]
    LicenseKey = 6N16-SJIV-61RI-VU1G (expires in 64 days)
    Radius/
    Administrators/

Server 'Radius' is Running, its health is 10 out of 10
```

Step 2   Use the **trace** command to set the trace level to a value between 1–4.

    → **trace 3**

    Traced "localhost: Trace level is set to 3"

Step 3   Exit from **aregcmd**.

    → **exit**

    Logging out of localhost...
    #

Step 4   Log in to **radclient**.

Step 5   Create another test packet. You did this in the previous section.

Step 6   Send the test packet.

Step 7   Exit **radclient**.

Step 8   Use the UNIX **tail** command to view the end of the **name_radius_1_ trace** log where the failed attempt was logged, as seen in Example 15-17.

Example 15-17 *Reading the* **name_radius_1_trace** *Log*

```
# tail -f /opt/CSCOar/logs/name_radius_1_trace
02/23/2004 16:12:29: P268: Authenticating and Authorizing with Service local-users
02/23/2004 16:12:29: P268: Getting User john's UserRecord from UserList Default
02/23/2004 16:12:29: P268: Failed to get User john's UserRecord from UserList
Default
02/23/2004 16:12:29: P268: Trace of Access-Reject packet
02/23/2004 16:12:29: P268:    identifier = 2
02/23/2004 16:12:29: P268:    length = 35
02/23/2004 16:12:29: P268:    reqauth =
11:11:d5:56:dc:c3:ec:1d:89:8c:fd:f4:19:9d:57:2a
02/23/2004 16:12:29: P268:    Reply-Message = Access Denied
02/23/2004 16:12:29: P268: Sending response to 127.0.0.1
02/23/2004 16:12:29: Log: Request from localhost (127.0.0.1): User john rejected
(UnknownUser)
```

Step 9 Read through the log to see where the request failed. In this case, the user **john** is unknown.

Summary

With this chapter, you should now be able to set up a basic site using **aregcmd**. You should now be pretty comfortable using the **cli** and navigating the objects of AR. However, you might need to perform more detailed and complex configurations. The Cisco website has an abundance of configuration examples that detail more advanced configuration such as scripting, pre-paid billing, and advanced protocol configurations.

Now that you are comfortable with the basics of AAA, AAA in the enterprise, and AAA at the service-provider level, you are now ready to begin the more difficult configuration tasks. Keep in mind the tools available and that trial and error and a little persistence will be the answer.

End Notes

Portions of this chapter were derived from the following:

Getting Started Guide, Larry Lininger http://cisco.com/en/US/products/sw/
netmgtsw/ps411/products_getting_started_guide_book09186a008007fdcf.html

Appendix

RADIUS Attribute Tables

This appendix lists the additional RADIUS attributes and vendor-specific attributes (VSAs) supported by Cisco Secure Access Control Server (CSACS) version 3.2.[1]

3000 Series Concentrator VSAs

The CSACS supports numerous VSAs for the 3000 series virtual private network (VPN) concentrators. Table A-1 lists the supported VSAs for the VPN 3000 series.

Table A-1 *Cisco VPN 3000 Concentrator RADIUS*

Attribute	Number	Type of Value	Inbound/ Outbound	Multiple
VPN3000-Access-Hours	1	string (maximum length 247 characters)	Outbound	No
CVPN3000-Simultaneous-Logins	2	integer (maximum length 10 characters)	Outbound	No
CVPN3000-Primary-DNS	5	ipaddr (maximum length 15 characters)	Outbound	No
CVPN3000-Secondary-DNS	6	ipaddr (maximum length 15 characters)	Outbound	No
CVPN3000-Primary-WINS	7	ipaddr (maximum length 15 characters)	Outbound	No
CVPN3000-Secondary-WINS	8	ipaddr (maximum length 15 characters)	Outbound	No
CVPN3000-SEP-Card-Assignment	9	integer	Outbound	No
CVPN3000-Tunneling-Protocols	11	integer	Outbound	No
CVPN3000-IPSec-Sec-Association	12	string (maximum length 247 characters)	Outbound	No

continues

---

1. Tables in this chapter are from *User Guide for Cisco Secure ACS Windows Server* , Appendix C, "Radius Attributes," by Mark Wilgus.

Table A-1 *Cisco VPN 3000 Concentrator RADIUS (Continued)*

Attribute	Number	Type of Value	Inbound/ Outbound	Multiple
CVPN3000-IPSec-Authentication	13	integer	Outbound	No
CVPN3000-IPSec-Banner1	15	string (maximum length 247 characters)	Outbound	No
CVPN3000-IPSec-Allow-Passwd-Store	16	integer	Outbound	No
CVPN3000-Use-Client-Address	17	integer	Outbound	No
CVPN3000-PPTP-Encryption	20	integer	Outbound	No
CVPN3000-L2TP-Encryption	21	integer	Outbound	No
CVPN3000-IPSec-Split-Tunnel-List	27	string (maximum length 247 characters)	Outbound	No
CVPN3000-IPSec-Default-Domain	28	string (maximum length 247 characters)	Outbound	No
CVPN3000-IPSec-Split-DNS-Names	29	string (maximum length 247 characters)	Outbound	No
CVPN3000-IPSec-Tunnel-Type	30	integer	Outbound	No
CVPN3000-IPSec-Mode-Config	31	integer	Outbound	No
CVPN3000-IPSec-User-Group-Lock	33	integer	Outbound	No
CVPN3000-IPSec-Over-UDP	34	integer	Outbound	No
CVPN3000-IPSec-Over-UDP-Port	35	integer (maximum length 10 characters)	Outbound	No
CVPN3000-IPSec-Banner2	36	string (maximum length 247 characters)	Outbound	No
CVPN3000-PPTP-MPPC-Compression	37	integer	Outbound	No
CVPN3000-L2TP-MPPC-Compression	38	integer	Outbound	No
CVPN3000-IPSec-IP-Compression	39	integer	Outbound	No
CVPN3000-IPSec-IKE-Peer-ID-Check	40	integer	Outbound	No
CVPN3000-IKE-Keep-Alives	41	integer	Outbound	No
CVPN3000-IPSec-Auth-On-Rekey	42	integer	Outbound	No
CVPN3000-Required-Client-Firewall-Vendor-Code	45	integer (maximum length 10 characters)	Outbound	No
CVPN3000-Required-Client-Firewall-Product-Code	46	integer (maximum length 10 characters)	Outbound	No

Table A-1   *Cisco VPN 3000 Concentrator RADIUS (Continued)*

Attribute	Number	Type of Value	Inbound/ Outbound	Multiple
CVPN3000-Required-Client-Firewall-Description	47	string (maximum length 247 characters)	Outbound	No
CVPN3000-Require-HW-Client-Auth	48	integer	Outbound	No
CVPN3000-Require-Individual-User-Auth	49	integer	Outbound	No
CVPN3000-Authenticated-User-Idle-Timeout	50	integer (maximum length 10 characters)	Outbound	No
CVPN3000-Cisco-IP-Phone-Bypass	51	integer	Outbound	No
CVPN3000-User-Auth-Server-Name	52	string (maximum length 247 characters)	Outbound	No
CVPN3000-User-Auth-Server-Port	53	integer (maximum length 10 characters)	Outbound	No
CVPN3000-User-Auth-Server-Secret	54	string (maximum length 247 characters)	Outbound	No
CVPN3000-IPSec-Split-Tunneling-Policy	55	integer	Outbound	No
CVPN3000-IPSec-Required-Client-Firewall-Capability	56	integer	Outbound	No
CVPN3000-IPSec-Client-Firewall-Filter-Name	57	string (maximum length 247 characters)	Outbound	No
CVPN3000-IPSec-Client-Firewall-Filter-Optional	58	integer	Outbound	No
CVPN3000-IPSec-Backup-Servers	59	integer	Outbound	No
CVPN3000-IPSec-Backup-Server-List	60	string (maximum length 247 characters)	Outbound	No
CVPN3000-MS-Client-Intercept-DHCP-Configure-Message	62	integer	Outbound	No
CVPN3000-MS-Client-Subnet-Mask	63	ipaddr (maximum length 15 characters)	Outbound	No
CVPN3000-Allow-Network-Extension-Mode	64	integer	Outbound	No
CVPN3000-Strip-Realm	135	integer	Outbound	No

Cisco VPN 5000 Concentrator RADIUS VSAs

CSACS also supports VSAs for the Cisco VPN 5000 concentrators. Table A-2 lists the supported VSAs in CSACS version 3.1.

Table A-2 *Cisco VPN 5000 Concentrator*

Attribute	Number	Type of Value	Inbound/ Outbound	Multiple
CVPN5000-Tunnel-Throughput	001	integer	Inbound	No
CVPN5000-Client-Assigned-IP	002	string	Inbound	No
CVPN5000-Client-Real-IP	003	string	Inbound	No
CVPN5000-VPN-GroupInfo	004	string (maximum length 247 characters)	Outbound	No
CVPN5000-VPN-Password	005	string (maximum length 247 characters)	Outbound	No
CVPN5000-Echo	006	integer	Inbound	No
CVPN5000-Client-Assigned-IPX	007	integer	Inbound	No

Cisco Building Broadband Service Manager Dictionary of RADIUS VSA

Cisco Secure ACS supports a Cisco Building Broadband Service Manager (BBSM) RADIUS VSA. The vendor ID for this Cisco RADIUS implementation is 5263. Table A-3 gives the VSA for BBSM.

Table A-3 *Cisco Building Broadband Service Manager RADIUS*

Attribute	Number	Type of Value	Inbound/Outbound	Multiple
CBBSM-Bandwidth	001	integer	Both	No

IETF Dictionary of RADIUS Attribute Value Pairs

Table A-4 lists the supported RADIUS (IETF) attributes. If the attribute has a security server-specific format, the format is specified.

Table A-4 *Internet Engineering Task Force (IETF) RADIUS*

Attribute	Number	Description	Type of Value	Inbound/ Outbound	Multiple
User-Name	1	Name of the user being authenticated.	string	Inbound	No
User-Password	2	User password or input following an access challenge. Passwords longer than 16 characters are encrypted using IETF Draft #2 or later specifications.	string	Outbound	No
CHAP-Password	3	Point-to-Point Protocol (PPP) Challenge Handshake Authentication Protocol (CHAP) response to an Access-Challenge.	string	Outbound	No
NAS-IP Address	4	IP address of the AAA client that is requesting authentication.	ipaddr	Inbound	No
NAS-Port	5	Physical port number of the AAA client that is authenticating the user. The AAA client port value (32 bits) consists of one or two 16-bit values, depending on the setting of the RADIUS server extended portnames command. Each 16-bit number is a 5-digit decimal integer interpreted as follows: For asynchronous terminal lines, async network interfaces, and virtual async interfaces, the value is 00*ttt*, where *ttt* is the line number or async interface unit number. For ordinary synchronous network interfaces, the value is *10xxx.* For channels on a primary-rate Integrated Services Digital Network (ISDN) interface, the value is *2ppcc*. For channels on a basic rate ISDN interface, the value is *3bb0c*. For other types of interfaces, the value is *6nnss*.	integer	Inbound	No

continues

Table A-4 *Internet Engineering Task Force (IETF) RADIUS (Continued)*

Attribute	Number	Description	Type of Value	Inbound/ Outbound	Multiple
Service-Type	6	Type of service requested or type of service to be provided: In a request: Framed—For known PPP or Serial Line Internet Protocol (SLIP) connection. Administrative user—For enable command. In a response: Login—Make a connection. Framed—Start SLIP or PPP. Administrative user—Start an EXEC or enable ok. Exec user—Start an EXEC session.	integer	Both	No
Framed-Protocol	7	Framing to be used for framed access.	integer	Both	No
Framed-IP-Address	8	Address to be configured for the user.	—	—	—
Framed-IP-Netmask	9	IP netmask to be configured for the user when the user is a router to a network. This AV results in a static route being added for Framed-IP-Address with the mask specified.	ipaddr (maximum length 15 characters)	Outbound	No
Framed-Routing	10	Routing method for the user when the user is a router to a network. Only None and Send and Listen values are supported for this attribute.	integer	Outbound	No

Table A-4 *Internet Engineering Task Force (IETF) RADIUS (Continued)*

Attribute	Number	Description	Type of Value	Inbound/ Outbound	Multiple
Filter-Id	11	Name of the filter list for the user, formatted as follows: %d, %d.in, or %d.out. This attribute is associated with the most recent service-type command. For login and EXEC, use %d or %d.out as the line access list value from 0 to 199. For framed service, use %d or %d.out as interface output access list and %d.in for input access list. The numbers are self-encoding to the protocol to which they refer.	string	Outbound	Yes
Framed-MTU	12	Indicates the maximum transmission unit (MTU) that can be configured for the user when the MTU is not negotiated by PPP or some other means.	integer (maximum length 10 characters)	Outbound	No
Framed-Compression	13	Compression protocol used for the link. This attribute results in **/compress** being added to the PPP or SLIP autocommand generated during EXEC authorization. Not currently implemented for non-EXEC authorization.	integer	Outbound	Yes
Login-IP-Host	14	Host to which the user connects when the Login-Service attribute is included.	ipaddr (maximum length 15 characters)	Both	Yes
Login-Service	15	Service that should be used to connect the user to the login host. Service is indicated by a numeric value: 0: Telnet 1: Rlogin 2: TCP-Clear 3: PortMaster 4: LAT	integer	Both	No

continues

Table A-4   *Internet Engineering Task Force (IETF) RADIUS (Continued)*

Attribute	Number	Description	Type of Value	Inbound/ Outbound	Multiple
Login-TCP-Port	16	Transmission Control Protocol (TCP) port with which the user is to be connected when the Login-Service attribute is also present.	integer (maximum length 10 characters)	Outbound	No
Reply-Message	18	Text to be displayed to the user.	string	Outbound	Yes
Callback-Number	19	—	string	Outbound	No
Callback-Id	20	—	string	Outbound	No
Framed-Route	22	Routing information to be configured for the user on this AAA client. The RADIUS Request For Comments (RFC) format (*net/bits* [*router* [*metric*]]) and the old style dotted mask (*netmask* [*router* [*metric*]]) are supported. If the router field is omitted or 0 (zero), the peer IP address is used. Metrics are ignored.	string	Outbound	Yes
Framed-IPX-Network	23	—	integer	Outbound	No
State	24	Allows state information to be maintained between the AAA client and the RADIUS server. This attribute is only applicable to CHAP challenges.	string (maximum length 253 characters)	Outbound	No
Class	25	Arbitrary value that the AAA client includes in all accounting packets for this user (if supplied by the RADIUS server).	string	Both	Yes

Table A-4   *Internet Engineering Task Force (IETF) RADIUS (Continued)*

Attribute	Number	Description	Type of Value	Inbound/ Outbound	Multiple
Vendor-Specific	26	Allows vendors to support their own extended attributes. The Cisco RADIUS implementation supports one vendor-specific option using the format recommended in the specification. The Cisco vendor-ID is 9, and the supported option is vendor-type 1, cisco-avpair. The value is a string of the format: *protocol*:attribute sep value *protocol* is a value of the Cisco protocol attribute for a particular type of authorization. Attribute and value are an appropriate AV pair defined in the Cisco TACACS+ specification, and **sep** is "=" for mandatory attributes and "*" for optional attributes. This allows the full set of TACACS+ authorization features to be used for RADIUS. The following is an example: cisco-avpair= "ip:addr-pool=first" cisco-avpair= "shell:priv-lvl=15" The first example causes the Cisco multiple named IP address pools feature to be activated during IP authorization (during PPP Internet Protocol Control Protocol [IPCP] address assignment). The second example causes a user of a device-hosted administrative session to have immediate access to EXEC commands.	string	Outbound	Yes
Session-Timeout	27	Maximum number of seconds of service to be provided to the user before the session terminates. This AV becomes the per-user absolute timeout. This attribute is not valid for PPP sessions.	integer (maximum length 10 characters)	Outbound	No

continues

Table A-4 *Internet Engineering Task Force (IETF) RADIUS (Continued)*

Attribute	Number	Description	Type of Value	Inbound/ Outbound	Multiple
Idle-Timeout	28	Maximum number of consecutive seconds of idle connection time allowed to the user before the session terminates. This AV becomes the per-user session timeout. This attribute is not valid for PPP sessions.	integer (maximum length 10 characters)	Outbound	No
Termination-Action	29	—	integer	Both	No
Called-Station-Id	30	Allows the AAA client to send the telephone number the call came from as part of the access-request packet using automatic number identification or similar technology. This attribute has the same value as remote-addr in TACACS+. This attribute is only supported on ISDN and for modem calls on the Cisco AS5200 if used with PRI.	string	Inbound	No
Calling-Station-Id	31	Allows the AAA client to send the telephone number the user called into as part of the access-request packet, using dialed number identification server (DNIS) or similar technology. This attribute is only supported on ISDN and for modem calls on the Cisco AS5200 if used with PRI.	string	Inbound	No
NAS-Identifier	32	—	string	Inbound	No
Proxy-State	33	Included in proxied RADIUS requests per RADIUS standards. The operation of Cisco Secure ACS does not depend on the contents of this attribute.	string (maximum length 253 characters)	Inbound	No
Login-LAT-Service	34	System with which the user is to be connected by local-area transport (LAT) protocol. This attribute is only available in EXEC mode.	string (maximum length 253 characters)	Inbound	No
Login-LAT-Node	35	—	string	Inbound	No

Table A-4   *Internet Engineering Task Force (IETF) RADIUS (Continued)*

Attribute	Number	Description	Type of Value	Inbound/ Outbound	Multiple
Login-LAT-Group	36	—	string	Inbound	No
Framed-AppleTalk-Link	37	—	integer	Outbound	No
Framed-AppleTalk-Network	38	—	integer	Outbound	Yes
Framed-AppleTalk-Zone	39	—	string	Outbound	No
Acct-Status-Type	40	Specifies whether this accounting request marks the beginning of the user service (start) or the end (stop).	integer	Inbound	No
Acct-Delay-Time	41	Number of seconds the client has been trying to send a particular record.	integer	Inbound	No
Acct-Input-Octets	42	Number of octets received from the port while this service is being provided.	integer	Inbound	No
Acct-Output-Octets	43	Number of octets sent to the port while this service is being delivered.	integer	Inbound	No
Acct-Session-Id	44	Unique accounting identifier that makes it easy to match start and stop records in a log file. The Acct-Session-Id restarts at 1 each time the router is power cycled or the software is reloaded. Contact Cisco support if this is unsuitable.	string	Inbound	No
Acct-Authentic	45	Way in which the user was authenticated—by RADIUS, by the AAA client itself, or by another remote authentication protocol. This attribute is set to **radius** for users authenticated by RADIUS; to **remote** for TACACS+ and Kerberos; or to **local** for local, enable, line, and if-needed methods. For all other methods, the attribute is omitted.	integer	Inbound	No

continues

Table A-4   *Internet Engineering Task Force (IETF) RADIUS (Continued)*

Attribute	Number	Description	Type of Value	Inbound/ Outbound	Multiple
Acct-Session-Time	46	Number of seconds the user has been receiving service.	integer	Inbound	No
Acct-Input-Packets	47	Number of packets received from the port while this service is being provided to a framed user.	integer	Inbound	No
Acct-Output-Packets	48	Number of packets sent to the port while this service is being delivered to a framed user.	integer	Inbound	No
Acct-Terminate-Cause	49	Reports details on why the connection was terminated. Termination causes are indicated by a numeric value: 1: User request 2: Lost carrier 3: Lost service 4: Idle timeout 5: Session-timeout 6: Admin reset 7: Admin reboot 8: Port error 9: AAA client error 10: AAA client request 11: AAA client reboot 12: Port unneeded 13: Port pre-empted 14: Port suspended 15: Service unavailable 16: Callback 17: User error 18: Host request	integer	Inbound	No
Acct-Multi-Session-Id	50	—	string	Inbound	No
Acct-Link-Count	51	—	integer	Inbound	No

Table A-4 *Internet Engineering Task Force (IETF) RADIUS (Continued)*

Attribute	Number	Description	Type of Value	Inbound/ Outbound	Multiple
Acct-Input-Gigawords	52	—	integer	Inbound	No
Acct-Output-Gigawords	53	—	integer	Inbound	No
Event-Timestamp	55	—	date	Inbound	No
CHAP-Challenge	60	—	string	Inbound	No
NAS-Port-Type	61	Indicates the type of physical port the AAA client is using to authenticate the user. Physical ports are indicated by a numeric value: 0: Asynchronous 1: Synchronous 2: ISDN-Synchronous 3: ISDN-Asynchronous (V.120) 4: ISDN-Asynchronous (V.110) 5: Virtual	integer	Inbound	No
Port-Limit	62	Sets the maximum number of ports to be provided to the user by the network access server.	integer (maximum length 10 characters)	Both	No
Login-LAT-Port	63	—	string	Both	No
Tunnel-Type	64	—	tagged integer	Both	Yes
Tunnel-Medium-Type	65	—	tagged integer	Both	Yes
Tunnel-Client-Endpoint	66	—	tagged string	Both	Yes
Tunnel-Server-Endpoint	67	—	tagged string	Both	Yes
Acct-Tunnel-Connection	68	—	string	Inbound	No
Tunnel-Password	69	—	tagged string	Both	Yes
ARAP-Password	70	—	string	Inbound	No
ARAP-Features	71	—	string	Outbound	No

continues

Table A-4 *Internet Engineering Task Force (IETF) RADIUS (Continued)*

Attribute	Number	Description	Type of Value	Inbound/ Outbound	Multiple
ARAP-Zone-Access	72	—	integer	Outbound	No
ARAP-Security	73	—	integer	Inbound	No
ARAP-Security-Data	74	—	string	Inbound	No
Password-Retry	75	—	integer	Internal use only	No
Prompt	76	—	integer	Internal use only	No
Connect-Info	77	—	string	Inbound	No
Configuration-Token	78	—	string	Internal use only	No
EAP-Message	79	—	string	Internal use only	No
Message-Authenticator	80	—	string	Outbound	No
Tunnel-Private-Group-ID	81	—	tagged string	Both	Yes
Tunnel-Assignment-ID	82	—	tagged string	Both	Yes
Tunnel-Preference	83	—	tagged integer	Both	No
Acct-Interim-Interval	85	—	integer	Outbound	No
NAS-Port-Id	87	—	string	Inbound	No
Framed-Pool	88	—	string	Internal use only	No
Tunnel-Client-Auth-ID	90	—	tagged string	Both	Yes
Tunnel-Server-Auth-ID	91	—	tagged string	Both	Yes

Table A-4   *Internet Engineering Task Force (IETF) RADIUS (Continued)*

Attribute	Number	Description	Type of Value	Inbound/ Outbound	Multiple
Primary-DNS-Server	135	—	ipaddr	Both	No
Secondary-DNS-Server	136	—	ipaddr	Both	No
Multilink-ID	187	—	integer	Inbound	No
Num-In-Multilink	188	—	integer	Inbound	No
Pre-Input-Octets	190	—	integer	Inbound	No
Pre-Output-Octets	191	—	integer	Inbound	No
Pre-Input-Packets	192	—	integer	Inbound	No
Pre-Output-Packets	193	—	integer	Inbound	No
Maximum-Time	194	—	integer	Both	No
Disconnect-Cause	195	—	integer	Inbound	No
Data-Rate	197	—	integer	Inbound	No
PreSession-Time	198	—	integer	Inbound	No
PW-Lifetime	208	—	integer	Outbound	No
IP-Direct	209	—	ipaddr	Outbound	No
PPP-VJ-Slot-Comp	210	—	integer	Outbound	No
Assign-IP-Pool	218	—	integer	Outbound	No
Route-IP	228	—	integer	Outbound	No
Link-Compression	233	—	integer	Outbound	No
Target-Utils	234	—	integer	Outbound	No
Maximum-Channels	235	—	integer	Outbound	No
Data-Filter	242	—	Ascend filter	Outbound	Yes
Call-Filter	243	—	Ascend filter	Outbound	Yes
Idle-Limit	244	—	integer	Outbound	No

Microsoft Radius VSAs

Microsoft Point-to-Point Encryption (MPPE) is an encryption technology developed by Microsoft to encrypt point-to-point (PPP) links. These PPP connections can be via a dialup line or over a VPN tunnel such as PPTP. MPPE is supported by several RADIUS network-device vendors that Cisco Secure ACS supports. The following Cisco Secure ACS RADIUS protocols support the Microsoft RADIUS VSA:

- Cisco IOS
- Cisco VPN 3000
- Cisco VPN 5000
- Ascend

Note the information in Table A-5.

Table A-5 *Microsoft RADIUS*

Attribute	Value	Type of Value	Additional Description (If Necessary)
MS-CHAP-Response	1	string	
MS-CHAP-Error	2	string	
MS-MPPE-Encryption-Policy	7	integer	Signifies whether the use of encryption is allowed or required. If the Policy field is equal to 1 (Encryption-Allowed), any or none of the encryption types specified in the MS-MPPE-Encryption-Types attribute can be used. If the Policy field is equal to 2 (Encryption-Required), any of the encryption types specified in the MS-MPPE-Encryption-Types attribute can be used, but at least one must be used.
MS-MPPE-Encryption-Types	8	integer	Signifies the types of encryption available for use with MPPE. A 4-octet integer is interpreted as a string of bits.
MS-CHAP-Domain	10	string	
MS-CHAP-Challenge	11	string	
MS-CHAP-MPPE-Keys	12	string	Contains two session keys for use by MPPE. This attribute is included only in Access-Accept packets. Note that the MS-CHAP-MPPE-Keys attribute value is autogenerated by Cisco Secure ACS; there is no value to set in the HTML interface.

Table A-5   *Microsoft RADIUS (Continued)*

Attribute	Value	Type of Value	Additional Description (If Necessary)
MS-MPPE-Send-Key	16	string	Contains a session key for use by MPPE. As the name implies, this key is intended for encrypting packets sent from the NAS to the remote host. This attribute is only included in Access-Accept packets.
MS-MPPE-Recv-Key	17	string	Contains a session key for use by MPPE. As the name implies, this key is intended for encrypting packets received by the NAS from the remote host. This attribute is only included in Access-Accept packets.

Ascend RADIUS

Table A-6 includes Ascend RADIUS dictionary translations for parsing requests and generating responses. All the transactions are composed of AV pairs. The value of each attribute is specified as one of the following valid data types:

- **string**—0–253 octets.

- **abinary**—0–254 octets.

- **ipaddr**—4 octets in network byte order.

- **integer**—32-bit value in big endian order (high byte first).

- **call filter**—Defines a call filter for the profile.

- **date**—32-bit value in big-endian order. For example, seconds since 00:00:00 universal time (UT), January 1, 1970.

- **enum**—Enumerated values are stored in the user file with dictionary value translations for easy administration.

Of the call filters, these RADIUS filters are retrieved only when a call is placed using a RADIUS outgoing profile or answered using a RADIUS incoming profile. Therefore, filter entries are applied in the order in which they are entered. When changes are made to a filter in an Ascend RADIUS profile, the changes do not take effect until a call uses that profile. It is then that they are applied.

Table A-6 *Ascend RADIUS*

Attribute	Number	Type of Value	Inbound/ Outbound	Multiple
Dictionary of Ascend Attributes				
User-Name	1	string	Inbound	No
User-Password	2	string	Outbound	No
CHAP-Password	3	string	Outbound	No
NAS-IP-Address	4	ipaddr	Inbound	No
NAS-Port	5	integer	Inbound	No
Service-Type	6	integer	Both	No
Framed-Protocol	7	integer	Both	No
Framed-IP-Address	8	ipaddr	Both	No
Framed-IP-Netmask	9	ipaddr	Outbound	No
Framed-Routing	10	integer	Outbound	No
Framed-Filter	11	string	Outbound	Yes
Framed-MTU	12	integer	Outbound	No
Framed-Compression	13	integer	Outbound	Yes
Login-IP-Host	14	ipaddr	Both	Yes
Login-Service	15	integer	Both	No
Login-TCP-Port	16	integer	Outbound	No
Change-Password	17	string	—	—
Reply-Message	18	string	Outbound	Yes
Callback-ID	19	string	Outbound	No
Callback-Name	20	string	Outbound	No
Framed-Route	22	string	Outbound	Yes
Framed-IPX-Network	23	integer	Outbound	No
State	24	string	Outbound	No
Class	25	string	Outbound	Yes
Vendor-Specific	26	string	Outbound	Yes
Call-Station-ID	30	string	Inbound	No
Calling-Station-ID	31	string	Inbound	No
Acct-Status-Type	40	integer	Inbound	No
Acct-Delay-Time	41	integer	Inbound	No

Table A-6   *Ascend RADIUS (Continued)*

Attribute	Number	Type of Value	Inbound/ Outbound	Multiple
Dictionary of Ascend Attributes (Continued)				
Acct-Input-Octets	42	integer	Inbound	No
Acct-Output-Octets	43	integer	Inbound	No
Acct-Session-Id	44	integer	Inbound	No
Acct-Authentic	45	integer	Inbound	No
Acct-Session-Time	46	integer	Inbound	No
Acct-Input-Packets	47	integer	Inbound	No
Acct-Output-Packets	48	integer	Inbound	No
Tunnel-Type	64	string	Both	Yes
Tunnel-Medium-Type	65	string	Both	Yes
Tunnel-Client-Endpoint	66	string (maximum length 250 characters)	Both	Yes
Tunnel-Server-Endpoint	67	string (maximum length 250 characters)	Both	Yes
Acct-Tunnel-Connection	68	integer (maximum length 253 characters)	Inbound	No
Ascend-Private-Route	104	string (maximum length 253 characters)	Both	No
Ascend-Numbering-Plan-ID	105	integer (maximum length 10 characters)	Both	No
Ascend-FR-Link-Status-Dlci	106	integer (maximum length 10 characters)	Both	No
Ascend-Calling-Subaddress	107	string (maximum length 253 characters)	Both	No
Ascend-Callback-Delay	108	string (maximum length 10 characters)	Both	No
Ascend-Endpoint-Disc	109	string (maximum length 253 characters)	Both	No
Ascend-Remote-FW	110	string (maximum length 253 characters)	Both	No
Ascend-Multicast-GLeave-Delay	111	integer (maximum length 10 characters)	Both	No
Ascend-CBCP-Enable	112	string	Both	No

continues

Table A-6 *Ascend RADIUS (Continued)*

Attribute	Number	Type of Value	Inbound/ Outbound	Multiple
Dictionary of Ascend Attributes (Continued)				
Ascend-CBCP-Mode	113	string	Both	No
Ascend-CBCP-Delay	114	string (maximum length 10 characters)	Both	No
Ascend-CBCP-Trunk-Group	115	string (maximum length 10 characters)	Both	No
Ascend-AppleTalk-Route	116	string (maximum length 253 characters)	Both	No
Ascend-AppleTalk-Peer-Mode	117	string (maximum length 10 characters)	Both	No
Ascend-Route-AppleTalk	118	string (maximum length 10 characters)	Both	No
Ascend-FCP-Parameter	119	string (maximum length 253 characters)	Both	No
Ascend-Modem-PortNo	120	integer (maximum length 10 characters)	Inbound	No
Ascend-Modem-SlotNo	121	integer (maximum length 10 characters)	Inbound	No
Ascend-Modem-ShelfNo	122	integer (maximum length 10 characters)	Inbound	No
Ascend-Call-Attempt-Limit	123	integer (maximum length 10 characters)	Both	No
Ascend-Call-Block_Duration	124	integer (maximum length 10 characters)	Both	No
Ascend-Maximum-Call-Duration	125	integer (maximum length 10 characters)	Both	No
Ascend-Router-Preference	126	string (maximum length 10 characters)	Both	No
Ascend-Tunneling-Protocol	127	string (maximum length 10 characters)	Both	No
Ascend-Shared-Profile-Enable	128	integer	Both	No
Ascend-Primary-Home-Agent	129	string (maximum length 253 characters)	Both	No

Table A-6   *Ascend RADIUS (Continued)*

Attribute	Number	Type of Value	Inbound/ Outbound	Multiple
Dictionary of Ascend Attributes (Continued)				
Ascend-Secondary-Home-Agent	130	string (maximum length 253 characters)	Both	No
Ascend-Dialout-Allowed	131	integer	Both	No
Ascend-BACP-Enable	133	integer	Both	No
Ascend-DHCP-Maximum-Leases	134	integer (maximum length 10 characters)	Both	No
Ascend-Client-Primary-DNS	135	address (maximum length 15 characters)	Both	No
Ascend-Client-Secondary-DNS	136	address (maximum length 15 characters)	Both	No
Ascend-Client-Assign-DNS	137	enum	Both	No
Ascend-User-Acct-Type	138	enum	Both	No
Ascend-User-Acct-Host	139	address (maximum length 15 characters)	Both	No
Ascend-User-Acct-Port	140	integer (maximum length 10 characters)	Both	No
Ascend-User-Acct-Key	141	string (maximum length 253 characters)	Both	No
Ascend-User-Acct-Base	142	enum (maximum length 10 characters)	Both	No
Ascend-User-Acct-Time	143	integer (maximum length 10 characters)	Both	No
Support IP Address Allocation from Global Pools				
Ascend-Assign-IP-Client	144	ipaddr (maximum length 15 characters)	Outbound	No
Ascend-Assign-IP-Server	145	ipaddr (maximum length 15 characters)	Outbound	No
Ascend-Assign-IP-Global-Pool	146	string (maximum length 253 characters)	Outbound	No

continues

Table A-6   *Ascend RADIUS (Continued)*

Attribute	Number	Type of Value	Inbound/ Outbound	Multiple
DHCP Server Functions				
Ascend-DHCP-Reply	147	integer	Outbound	No
Ascend-DHCP-Pool-Number	148	integer (maximum length 10 characters)	Outbound	No
Connection Profile/Telco Option				
Ascend-Expect-Callback	149	integer	Outbound	No
Event Type for an Ascend-Event Packet				
Ascend-Event-Type	150	integer (maximum length 10 characters)	Inbound	No
RADIUS Server Session Key				
Ascend-Session-Svr-Key	151	string (maximum length 253 characters)	Outbound	No
Multicast Rate Limit Per Client				
Ascend-Multicast-Rate-Limit	152	integer (maximum length 10 characters)	Outbound	No
Connection Profile Fields to Support Interface-Based Routing				
Ascend-IF-Netmask	153	ipaddr (maximum length 15 characters)	Outbound	No
Ascend-Remote-Addr	154	ipaddr (maximum length 15 characters)	Outbound	No
Multicast Support				
Ascend-Multicast-Client	155	integer (maximum length 10 characters)	Outbound	No
Frame Datalink Profiles				
Ascend-FR-Circuit-Name	156	string (maximum length 253 characters)	Outbound	No
Ascend-FR-LinkUp	157	integer (maximum length 10 characters)	Outbound	No
Ascend-FR-Nailed-Group	158	integer (maximum length 10 characters)	Outbound	No
Ascend-FR-Type	159	integer (maximum length 10 characters)	Outbound	No

Table A-6   *Ascend RADIUS (Continued)*

Attribute	Number	Type of Value	Inbound/ Outbound	Multiple
Frame Datalink Profiles (Continued)				
Ascend-FR-Link-Mgt	160	integer (maximum length 10 characters)	Outbound	No
Ascend-FR-N391	161	integer (maximum length 10 characters)	Outbound	No
Ascend-FR-DCE-N392	162	integer (maximum length 10 characters)	Outbound	No
Ascend-FR-DTE-N392	163	integer (maximum length 10 characters)	Outbound	No
Ascend-FR-DCE-N393	164	integer (maximum length 10 characters)	Outbound	No
Ascend-FR-DTE-N393	165	integer (maximum length 10 characters)	Outbound	No
Ascend-FR-T391	166	integer (maximum length 10 characters)	Outbound	No
Ascend-FR-T392	167	integer (maximum length 10 characters)	Outbound	No
Ascend-Bridge-Address	168	string (maximum length 253 characters)	Outbound	No
Ascend-TS-Idle-Limit	169	integer (maximum length 10 characters)	Outbound	No
Ascend-TS-Idle-Mode	170	integer (maximum length 10 characters)	Outbound	No
Ascend-DBA-Monitor	171	integer (maximum length 10 characters)	Outbound	No
Ascend-Base-Channel-Count	172	integer (maximum length 10 characters)	Outbound	No
Ascend-Minimum-Channels	173	integer (maximum length 10 characters)	Outbound	No

continues

Table A-6   *Ascend RADIUS (Continued)*

Attribute	Number	Type of Value	Inbound/ Outbound	Multiple
IPX Static Routes				
Ascend-IPX-Route	174	string (maximum length 253 characters)	Inbound	No
Ascend-FT1-Caller	175	integer (maximum length 10 characters)	Inbound	No
Ascend-Backup	176	string (maximum length 253 characters)	Inbound	No
Ascend-Call-Type	177	integer	Inbound	No
Ascend-Group	178	string (maximum length 253 characters)	Inbound	No
Ascend-FR-DLCI	179	integer (maximum length 10 characters)	Inbound	No
Ascend-FR-Profile-Name	180	string (maximum length 253 characters)	Inbound	No
Ascend-Ara-PW	181	string (maximum length 253 characters)	Inbound	No
Ascend-IPX-Node-Addr	182	string (maximum length 253 characters)	Both	No
Ascend-Home-Agent-IP-Addr	183	ipaddr (maximum length 15 characters)	Outbound	No
Ascend-Home-Agent-Password	184	string (maximum length 253 characters)	Outbound	No
Ascend-Home-Network-Name	185	string (maximum length 253 characters)	Outbound	No
Ascend-Home-Agent-UDP-Port	186	integer (maximum length 10 characters)	Outbound	No
Ascend-Multilink-ID	187	integer	Inbound	No
Ascend-Num-In-Multilink	188	integer	Inbound	No
Ascend-First-Dest	189	ipaddr	Inbound	No
Ascend-Pre-Input-Octets	190	integer	Inbound	No
Ascend-Pre-Output-Octets	191	integer	Inbound	No
Ascend-Pre-Input-Packets	192	integer	Inbound	No
Ascend-Pre-Output-Packets	193	integer	Inbound	No

Table A-6   *Ascend RADIUS (Continued)*

Attribute	Number	Type of Value	Inbound/ Outbound	Multiple
IPX Static Routes (Continued)				
Ascend-Maximum-Time	194	integer (maximum length 10 characters)	Both	No
Ascend-Disconnect-Cause	195	integer	Inbound	No
Ascend-Connect-Progress	196	integer	Inbound	No
Ascend-Data-Rate	197	integer	Inbound	No
Ascend-PreSession-Time	198	integer	Inbound	No
Ascend-Token-Idle	199	integer (maximum length 10 characters)	Outbound	No
Ascend-Token-Immediate	200	integer	Outbound	No
Ascend-Require-Auth	201	integer (maximum length 10 characters)	Outbound	No
Ascend-Number-Sessions	202	string (maximum length 253 characters)	Outbound	No
Ascend-Authen-Alias	203	string (maximum length 253 characters)	Outbound	No
Ascend-Token-Expiry	204	integer (maximum length 10 characters)	Outbound	No
Ascend-Menu-Selector	205	string (maximum length 253 characters)	Outbound	No
Ascend-Menu-Item	206	string	Outbound	No
RADIUS Password Expiration Options				
Ascend-PW-Warntime	207	integer (maximum length 10 characters)	Outbound	No
Ascend-PW-Lifetime	208	integer (maximum length 10 characters)	Outbound	No
Ascend-IP-Direct	209	ipaddr (maximum length 15 characters)	Outbound	No
Ascend-PPP-VJ-Slot-Comp	210	integer (maximum length 10 characters)	Outbound	No
Ascend-PPP-VJ-1172	211	integer (maximum length 10 characters)	Outbound	No

continues

Table A-6 *Ascend RADIUS (Continued)*

Attribute	Number	Type of Value	Inbound/ Outbound	Multiple
RADIUS Password Expiration Options (Continued)				
Ascend-PPP-Async-Map	212	integer (maximum length 10 characters)	Outbound	No
Ascend-Third-Prompt	213	string (maximum length 253 characters)	Outbound	No
Ascend-Send-Secret	214	string (maximum length 253 characters)	Outbound	No
Ascend-Receive-Secret	215	string (maximum length 253 characters)	Outbound	No
Ascend-IPX-Peer-Mode	216	integer	Outbound	No
Ascend-IP-Pool-Definition	217	string (maximum length 253 characters)	Outbound	No
Ascend-Assign-IP-Pool	218	integer	Outbound	No
Ascend-FR-Direct	219	integer	Outbound	No
Ascend-FR-Direct-Profile	220	string (maximum length 253 characters)	Outbound	No
Ascend-FR-Direct-DLCI	221	integer (maximum length 10 characters)	Outbound	No
Ascend-Handle-IPX	222	integer	Outbound	No
Ascend-Netware-Timeout	223	integer (maximum length 10 characters)	Outbound	No
Ascend-IPX-Alias	224	string (maximum length 253 characters)	Outbound	No
Ascend-Metric	225	integer (maximum length 10 characters)	Outbound	No
Ascend-PRI-Number-Type	226	integer	Outbound	No
Ascend-Dial-Number	227	string (maximum length 253 characters)	Outbound	No
Connection Profile/PPP Options				
Ascend-Route-IP	228	integer	Outbound	No
Ascend-Route-IPX	229	integer	Outbound	No
Ascend-Bridge	230	integer	Outbound	No
Ascend-Send-Auth	231	integer	Outbound	No

Table A-6   *Ascend RADIUS (Continued)*

Attribute	Number	Type of Value	Inbound/ Outbound	Multiple
Connection Profile/PPP Options (Continued)				
Ascend-Send-Passwd	232	string (maximum length 253 characters)	Outbound	No
Ascend-Link-Compression	233	integer	Outbound	No
Ascend-Target-Util	234	integer (maximum length 10 characters)	Outbound	No
Ascend-Max-Channels	235	integer (maximum length 10 characters)	Outbound	No
Ascend-Inc-Channel-Count	236	integer (maximum length 10 characters)	Outbound	No
Ascend-Dec-Channel-Count	237	integer (maximum length 10 characters)	Outbound	No
Ascend-Seconds-Of-History	238	integer (maximum length 10 characters)	Outbound	No
Ascend-History-Weigh-Type	239	integer	Outbound	No
Ascend-Add-Seconds	240	integer (maximum length 10 characters)	Outbound	No
Ascend-Remove-Seconds	241	integer (maximum length 10 characters)	Outbound	No
Connection Profile/Session Options				
Ascend-Data-Filter	242	call filter	Outbound	Yes
Ascend-Call-Filter	243	call filter	Outbound	Yes
Ascend-Idle-Limit	244	integer (maximum length 10 characters)	Outbound	No
Ascend-Preempt-Limit	245	integer (maximum length 10 characters)	Outbound	No
Connection Profile/Telco Options				
Ascend-Callback	246	integer	Outbound	No
Ascend-Data-Svc	247	integer	Outbound	No
Ascend-Force-56	248	integer	Outbound	No

continues

Table A-6 *Ascend RADIUS (Continued)*

Attribute	Number	Type of Value	Inbound/ Outbound	Multiple
Connection Profile/Telco Options (Continued)				
Ascend-Billing-Number	249	string (maximum length 253 characters)	Outbound	No
Ascend-Call-By-Call	250	integer (maximum length 10 characters)	Outbound	No
Ascend-Transit-Number	251	string (maximum length 253 characters)	Outbound	No
Terminal Server Attributes				
Ascend-Host-Info	252	string (maximum length 253 characters)	Outbound	No
PPP Local Address Attribute				
Ascend-PPP-Address	253	ipaddr (maximum length 15 characters)	Outbound	No
MPP Percent Idle Attribute				
Ascend-MPP-Idle-Percent	254	integer (maximum length 10 characters)	Outbound	No
Ascend-Xmit-Rate	255	integer (maximum length 10 characters)	Outbound	No

Nortel RADIUS

Table A-7 lists the Nortel RADIUS VSAs supported by Cisco Secure ACS. The Nortel vendor ID number is 1584.

Table A-7 *Nortel RADIUS*

Attribute	Number	Type of Value	Inbound/ Outbound	Multiple
Bay-Local-IP-Address	035	ipaddr (maximum length 15 characters)	Outbound	No
Bay-Primary-DNS-Server	054	ipaddr (maximum length 15 characters)	Outbound	No
Bay-Secondary-DNS-Server	055	ipaddr (maximum length 15 characters)	Outbound	No
Bay-Primary-NBNS-Server	056	ipaddr (maximum length 15 characters)	Outbound	No
Bay-Secondary-NBNS-Server	057	ipaddr (maximum length 15 characters)	Outbound	No
Bay-User-Level	100	integer	Outbound	No
Bay-Audit-Level	101	integer	Outbound	No

Juniper RADIUS

Table A-8 lists the Juniper RADIUS VSAs supported by Cisco Secure ACS. The Juniper vendor ID number is 2636.

Table A-8   *Juniper RADIUS*

Attribute	Number	Type of Value	Inbound/ Outbound	Multiple
Juniper-Local-User-Name	001	string (maximum length 247 characters)	Outbound	No
Juniper-Allow-Commands	002	string (maximum length 247 characters)	Outbound	No
Juniper-Deny-Commands	003	string (maximum length 247 characters)	Outbound	No

INDEX

Symbols & Numerics

* (asterisk), optional attribute values, 317
= (equal sign), mandatory attribute values, 317

3000 series concentrator VSAs, 389–391
802.1x Switchport Authentication, ACS
   configuration, 138

A

AAA (authentication, authorization, and
   accounting), configuring method lists, 55–58
accountActions table, 278
accounting, 10
   ACS reports, 293
      RADIUS+, 294
      TACACS+, 293
      VoIP+, 294
   example of, 12
   RADIUS, 49
   remote accounting, configuring, 201
   TACACS+, 36
      AV pairs, 37–41
   types of, 10–11
acl= attribute, 318
ACLs (access control lists)
   creating, 219
   downloadable, 165–166, 169
      configuring, 218–220
      troubleshooting, 237–238
ACS (Access Control Server)
   802.1x Switchport Authentication,
     configuring, 138
   accounting reports, 293
      RADIUS+, 294
      TACACS+, 293
      VoIP+, 294
   ActivCard Token Servers, configuring, 267
   adding new AAA clients, 121, 208–209
   adding users to database, 114–116

address assignment, 163–165
administrative policies, switch configuration,
   142–143
Admission Control menu, 102
advanced configurations, 138
CRYPTOCard Token Servers, configuring,
   268–269
database backups, performing, 275–276
database group mappings, configuring, 271
device synchronization, 277–280
downloadable IP ACLs, 165–166, 169
EAP support, configuring, 138
external databases, configuring, 244–262
External User Database menu, 104
features, 75
for Windows Server Version 2.0, 66
for Windows Server Version 2.1, 67
for Windows Server Version 2.3, 67–68
for Windows Server Version 2.6, 68–69
for Windows Server Version 3.0, 69
for Windows Server Version 3.1, 69–71
for Windows Server Version 3.2, 71
Group Setup menu, 92
interface configuration, 111
   TACACS+ settings, 112
Interface Configuration menu, 100–102
local AAA pools, configuring, 134–136
NARs
   applying to user gruops, 158–159
   configuring, 155–157
   matching conditions, 155
   shared NARs, 159
Network Configuration menu, 95–97
obtaining, 76
Online Documentation menu, 107
PassGo Defender Token Servers,
   configuring, 267–268
positioning on network
   dialup access, 82
   VPNs, 83–84
   wireless deployment, 85

B-C

F-G

H-I

J-K-L

S

T

V

W-X-Y-Z

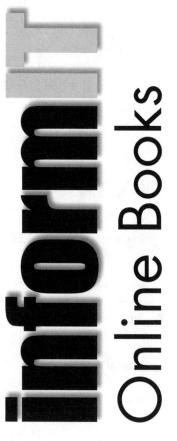

DISCUSS
NETWORKING PRODUCTS AND TECHNOLOGIES WITH CISCO EXPERTS AND NETWORKING PROFESSIONALS WORLDWIDE

VISIT NETWORKING PROFESSIONALS
A CISCO ONLINE COMMUNITY
WWW.CISCO.COM/GO/DISCUSS

THIS IS THE POWER OF THE NETWORK. now.

CISCO SYSTEMS

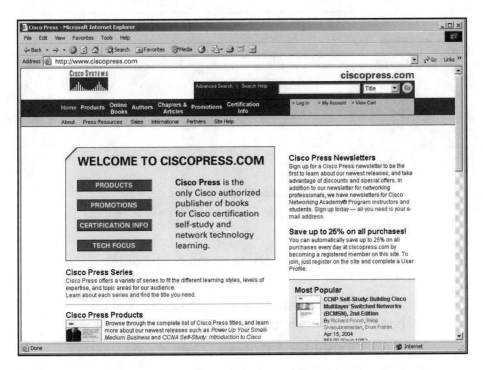
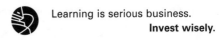

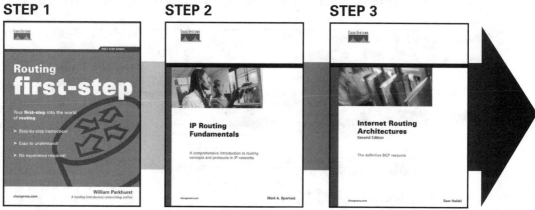